12/02

The Author and his wife in their art gallery in Milan.

Giacomo Wannenes

EIGHTEENTH CENTURY
FRENCH FURNITURE

Editions Vausor

Contents

An open letter to the reader

In writing the history of French and Italian furniture over several hundred years, from its beginnings to the 20th century, we have retraced the development of an aspect of the decorative arts which is linked to styles, fashion and taste. These evolved very gradually over time before finally reaching the era of modern industrialisation, a period that seems to us to have been characterised by the almost total disappearance of imagination and fantasy in favour of productivity and consumption.

This journey through history is also a journey through my life: from my adolescence to my activities as an expert and connoisseur who has accumulated a modest amount of experience and knowledge. This I now affectionately dedicate and bequeath to all whose sensibility draws them to the history of human creation, from its most sublime to its most humble aspects.

I have written, or tried to write, an analysis of the historical personality of furniture, in relation to its period and to its aesthetic qualities. But I wonder, is what I am seeking to do, what I am writing here the work of a historian? The answer is almost certainly yes. Have I written a work of aesthetic analysis? Again, almost certainly yes. I have tried to do my best. It is clear that in the material world of today value must instantly be echoed in the metallic sound of figures. Yet the attribution of value is an act of the imagination alone, which the intrinsic worth of an item makes palpable and obvious. For this reason I have tried to approach my valuations of the 18th-century pieces that we shall encounter together here in the most balanced way, without forgetting that beauty and rarity can provoke real passions which drive connoisseurs or simple admirers to pay a 'collector's price'.

On the other hand there is no reason not to give free rein to one's imagination, while keeping one's feet firmly on the ground.

These considerations are of a familiar, practical nature. But I want to reveal to you now something I most certainly believe to be true. All these pieces of furniture have a soul; this soul is your soul, it is the soul of your parents, your grand-parents, of all your ancestors who have passed through this life, experiencing their joys, hopes and dreams in the decorative setting formed by the sum of all the objects created for the family.

These mute spectators are custodians of past feelings, bearing witness to terrible conflicts between love and death, such as those so sublimely recounted in The Leopard *by Tomasi de Lampedusa or* La Comédie Humaine *and* Le Cabinet des Antiques *by Balzac. In times gone by, as in every time in the history of the decorative arts, it is women who have provided the most important inspiration to creativity.*

A complete, in-depth study of a society during a given period – or indeed that of a single personality – is impossible if one does not take account of the setting in which the principle participants in our human comedy live, hope, develop, reproduce and die. Let us not forget that each piece of furniture has witnessed the unfolding of real lives, either as servant or spectator.

The factors that lead us to love the furniture of the past stem from their power of radiation, the phantoms they invoke, the feelings they inspire, the hopes they foster, the desires they heighten. We love the things that belong to us. The things that belong to us are the things we love.

This is almost certainly the real secret that draws us to objects from the past with genuine passion, no matter what value may be attributed to them. For, all figures aside, what matters is our love of our own culture, history and roots, which we joyfully rediscover every time that we become the owners of one of these witnesses to days gone by. For, worn by the centuries though they are, in their silence these pieces still have many things to tell us, bringing the past to life.

Notice to beginners preparing to buy antiques

Given the breadth and multi-faceted nature of this discussion, we do not claim to provide people who are preparing to buy period furniture for the first time with an infallible method which will enable them to build up a large or small collection of classic or fine pieces while avoiding fakes, pieces entirely covered in modern ormolu, or those items known as 'late' pieces.

However, we do feel able to give novice collectors some information in the form of a series of explanations and suggestions. These may be useful to them when the time comes to buy and will prevent them falling prey to swindlers.

In France the purchase and sale of period furniture and antiques in general necessarily takes place through the intermediary of either public auction houses or antiques dealers. Many of the latter have set up restoration workshops employing a dozen or more craftsmen (carpenters, cabinet-makers, *marqueteurs-cireurs*, chasers, bronze and wood gilders, etc.) working under the supervision of a foreman who is accredited by the Court of Cassation.

If a close friend, or someone who has read a few books on the topic, claims to be an illustrious art connoisseur and pronounces that the table or chair you have just bought does not have the requisite charisma so that you find yourself in doubt, we would advise you to ask an expert from one of the auction houses and an expert from the tribunal. This will cost you very little compared to the price of a work of art. In such cases you should proceed as follows:

1. In the interests of collectors and antiques dealers it is imperative that you avoid selecting a workshop foreman as the expert to whom you address your queries, no matter who recommended him to you. You may later be concerned about the possibility of complicity between the experts and their backers, not simply with regard to the objectivity of the advice in general, but primarily because of the lack of importance they may accord to any modifications made to pieces of furniture. In the long run any adverse comments or mere doubts themselves may do irreparable damage to the image of antique dealers and experts throughout Europe as well as deterring existing and potential collectors.

2. Contact several experts, without telling them who else you may be speaking to.

3. If you are asked for the source of the piece under examination, it is imperative that you state that it has been in the possession of your family for some time and has recently been restored, or is about to be restored.

4. Only trust experts who are prepared to give you a clear, written verdict on the authenticity of the piece. Writing endures long after spoken words are gone with the wind and can no longer be quantified in either financial or legal terms should you be obliged to go to law.

In conclusion, after fifty years of experience in the international art markets, we would respectfully offer you the following words of advice: before you embark on collecting antiques, read up on the subject carefully and compare what you have learned with what is on display in the antiques dealers' windows. If you still have doubts, dispel them by asking advice from people involved in the field that interests you. You will discover a fascinating world and the answers you obtain will also enable you to distinguish those people who know what they are talking about from those who do not. Above all you will gain that sense of satisfaction one gets from reaching a new level of knowledge and gradually reaching the point where one can talk to antiques dealers as an equal. If you are short of time, avoid the large firms that deal in art on an industrial scale. Their overheads oblige them to raise their prices to exorbitant levels which cannot easily be recovered in the course of a generation.

It is better to go to a good dealer who has a gallery he runs himself, or which is run by members of his family. Ask him to buy for you, on condition that you can exchange items he sells or procures for you for other pieces from his gallery.

If he accepts, you have found your antiques dealer. Over time this arrangement will enable you to acquire a small or large collection to suit your financial means.

Why is fine furniture so expensive?

Human beings have always been preoccupied with the idea of leaving behind them some visible, tangible trace of their thoughts, skills, tastes, life-styles, dreams and intelligence. To this end they have created great works of art synthesising all these elements, not just to give themselves and their descendants pleasure, but more importantly to prolong their own existence and to escape from the oblivion that comes with the passing of time. From the earliest times to the present day, our ancestors have been handing down masterpieces large and small from one generation to the next, particularly in the fields of painting, sculpture and architecture.

Unlike commodes or chairs, which are intended to serve precise domestic functions, paintings have never established a close relationship with people; instead they have always represented something less tangible. This is because, in physical terms, they are made using more insubstantial, fragile materials. Painting lacks the materiality of furniture, and it is precisely this quality that enables it to convey scenes from life, or simply the image of the beloved, through the use of colour. It contains something magical which has the power to stimulate the imagination and to arouse the interest and intense feelings of later generations in a way that furniture cannot do. The history of painting has given rise to great quantities of writing and it goes without saying that this production has stimulated the understanding and development of the art in all its different forms, and indeed the attribution of value to them. Even writing that is mere intellectual titillation or hysterical emoting never fails to draw the attention of the whole world to the subject or subjects under discussion. The same can be said of sculpture. Whether the material used is stone, marble or wood and the scenes depicted are from the pages of the Bible, mythology or real life, this art carries within it something mysterious and spiritual since it immortalises actions, images, emotional states, history and legends that are an integral part of human life. If we also bear in mind that sacred painting and sculpture were the first media used for publicity purposes by political and religious powers seeking to conquer, seduce or convert the masses, we can easily understand why the arts of the brush and chisel have always attracted the attention of the intellectuals of every period, independently of their cultural and spiritual importance. It is due to the respect and faith that they inspired as cult objects that a great number of masterpieces were kept safe and have come down to us perfectly preserved.

If we now consider architecture, leaving aside any discussion of its historical or artistic merit or value in relation to the fabric of our towns and cities, we need only remember how the romantic charm of ruins has set succeeding generations talking, dreaming and writing in prose and poetry. There is therefore no doubt that each of these arts has a capital A and can be considered as a major Art. However, while these three domains held centre stage, the role assigned to furniture, even in its most elevated manifestations, was always far more humble. Constant contact with people reduced the status of any piece to that of a familiar object, indispensable to a house's practical existence and lacking in the respect and consideration reserved for a 'sacred' object that must be handed down intact from father to son. Furniture was far more likely than pictures, stone or marble to become worn as a result of its function and the passage of time. Pieces would gradually deteriorate, unrecognised and forgotten, not least because they did not carry any political or religious 'message'. Who knows how many masterpieces, half-destroyed by lack of care and the passage of time, have been used as firewood to warm human ignorance? It was not until the early 18th century, when cabinet-making had acquired some importance, that pieces of furniture began to be regarded as objects of study. At first this was confined to research and analysis by competent specialists in the sector and was carried out without any great fuss throughout the century. In the 19th century, however, the new bourgeoisie took a great interest in all the styles of the past, and this led to the rediscovery of old furniture. Around 1830 this rediscovery found concrete expression in the more or less faithful recreation of pieces of very fine cabinetwork. Unlike some sterile whim that vanishes once it has been satisfied, the study, recreation and imitation of these bygone glories played a major part in attracting the attention of 20th century intellectuals to the art of antique furniture, which had hitherto gone almost entirely unrecognised and been relegated to a dark corner in museums, for the sole pleasure of a few connoisseurs and interested antiques dealers. Yet, although specialist publications in the general field of furniture made their appearance, until the end of the Second World War antique pieces were not to be found outside the secret circles of the old nobility, the new bourgeoisie and the dealers. The nobility used the most prestigious examples of cabinet-work (chairs, armchairs, commodes, desks, etc.) to enhance their social status or to lend added magnificence to their family crest, but were careful not to foster a knowledge of fine furniture beyond the confines of their own world. The bourgeoisie, who generally moved in the same social circles, were obliged to bow to the rule of silence imposed upon them. Meanwhile, up until the end of the Second World War, antiques dealers conducted their business in murmurs and whispers worthy of the confession-box and prospered only by following the rule of silence. How, in such conditions, could a knowledge of antique furniture be more widely valued and encouraged?

Fortunately, the period since the end of the Second World War has seen a proliferation of specialist books discussing the furniture of the different regions in Italy and in many other countries. These have gradually brought furniture, one of the most expressive elements in the everyday life of every period, centre stage. All across Italy and in other countries, the many public exhibitions of antiques and auction houses of greater or lesser commercial importance have spread and developed a wider knowledge of every aspect of the sector.

In France exhaustive monographs on the most remarkable cabinet-makers are now being published. These include a discussion of the life and works of Adam Weisweiler, who had previously gone almost unrecognised and to whom is attributed a piece that has beaten every price record for furniture sold at auction.

In Italy monographs have been written on Piffetti and Maggiolini, to name but two; however in our opinion knowledge of the field has hitherto been superficial and the process of increasing understanding is only just beginning. Yet, although knowledge of the antique furniture sector may be patchy, that which has now been acquired allows us to state, without the shadow of a doubt, that pieces of furniture can no longer be regarded as less important creations, to be relegated to the category of the minor arts. Such artistic racism is unworthy of the modern world. Items costing hundreds of thousands of pounds cannot be dismissed as bagatelles for the rich; on the contrary, what we are seeing here are examples of the proper valuation of works of art.

If a painting can be a masterpiece, so can a piece of furniture with inlaid decoration of remarkable delicacy. Just like a painting, such a work can be considered and assessed without prior constraint or prejudice. The same can be said of Chinese or Coromandel lacquer, chased ormolu mounts and silver of great artistic merit. However, to avoid any ambiguity, we should state that, while we wish to do justice to furniture and to correct a definition which could be justified in the 15th century – before the advent of the baroque, Barocchetto and neoclassicism – we do not subscribe to the current trend in which all human creations, no matter how insignificant, are termed works of art. Since it has taken almost fifty years of study and research for the world to notice the skill and art of cabinet-makers, we should allow more time to pass before attempting to make a truly objective judgement.

What is meant by a 'collector's price'?

Many writers have described the feelings of desire and pleasure that can be aroused by the possibility of possessing a fine antique, whatever financial sacrifice may be involved, and the more or less self-interested motives that drive individuals to acquire collections of all kinds of art. Much less has been said, however, about the antiques market, with all its secret laws, contexts and exceptions, its many different manifestations and concomitant variations.

At the dawn of the twenty-first century it cannot be denied that there is a vast market in antique art, dealing in a very wide range of items of different types that vary greatly in both quality and price. To be more explicit, today one can sell everything from great-grandmother's old oil lamp to a museum piece, from worthless daubs to masterpieces, old copper pans to valuable bronzes, ordinary period rugs which deceive the untrained eye to antique carpets whose pedigree is beyond reproach; dealers trade in 'rustic' ivory statuettes as well as in pieces carved with all the refinement of art, silverware worked by beginners as well as items chased to perfection, while alongside majolica fired in the kilns of the gods one can buy other far less immortal but still useful pieces.

With analysis and study the most secret details will reveal every aspect of every piece, from the greatest artistic refinement to the most mundane craftsmanship. They will also indicate its value, whether it be among the most costly or of little financial worth.

The difference between the ugly and the sublime is to be found at numerous levels, which cannot be quantified solely in terms of their artistic qualities; practically speaking they must also be considered in relation to different commercial values. For a long time the uninitiated imagined that any antique must be exorbitantly valuable and regarded art with a kind of mystical respect, due in part to a limited understanding of the sector, which prevented them from recognising a humbler item or distinguishing it from a masterpiece.

Due to the enormous growth of the institutions that manage the trade in antique art (antiques dealers, clandestine dealers, impromptu intermediaries, cheats, wheeler-dealers and auction houses, with all their different ways of proceeding) and for other motives mentioned above, we have chosen to give a precise assessment of the quality of each piece of furniture presented in this book – which will be either classic, fine, modest, good, excellent or exceptional – and a basic valuation reflecting current market prices.

In principle, since the Second World War, prices for furniture of every period and style have increased markedly every four or five years. At the moment this upward trend seems to apply over shorter periods, especially where pieces of particular artistic worth are concerned. Pieces of a more average nature take longer to increase in value.

Everyone knows that in order to place a value on a piece of antique art it is necessary to consider all pieces of a similar type but of different quality and appearance. The comparative analysis of their various characteristics makes it possible to determine their value. For example, if an expert is valuing three classic commodes from the Empire period, all in mahogany veneer with foliate inlays and almost identical structures, he bases his different valuations on the greater or lesser quantity and quality of the chased and mercury-gilt ormolu mounts and the state of preservation of the pieces, according to comparative criteria and the commercial values of the moment. Generally speaking, his valuations will prove to be accurate, if approximately so, since his expertise will be derived from several years experience and close observation of the great many Empire commodes that he has seen, bought or sold over that time. In other words, an expert must have an in-depth knowledge of the market, with all its variations. This market is and always has been based on the quantity of pieces available and those sought by the clientele – the eternal law of supply and demand. If this same expert is asked to value a masterpiece for which there are no analogies with other similar pieces, it is clear that the real, effective value of the piece can be determined only by the will of the collectors, who generally determine its worth through successive sales at auction.

Over almost forty years of activity we have noted that experts throughout Europe tend to value masterpieces at prices far lower than the amounts they actually reach in salesrooms of international repute. Let us briefly consider the reasons for this.

Antiques dealers and experts tend to value works of art in the light of their professional experience. This tells them that when a masterpiece of any kind, be it furniture, painting, majolica or silverware, is sold through private negotiation, in their own shop for example, the whole process takes a very long time and the price is always negotiated downwards. On the other hand if the same masterpiece is sold by an auction house, the sale takes place in a few seconds to the highest bidder. The ultimate price almost always depends on the whim of a collector, who has none of the constraints that the dealer applies to himself. Collectors do not buy a piece in order to increase their stock but for the pleasure of possessing a particular masterpiece and they are prepared to pay a great deal for it – a 'collector's price' in fact.

Another reason why the experts are very conservative in their judgements lies in the fact that when the item is passed to the auction house, whatever its degree of importance and whether it is being sold by a private individual or a dealer, there will be no dispute over the price it reaches at auction as long as this is higher than the expert valuation.

In the case of exceptional pieces we have preferred to indicate a 'collector's price' rather than supplying a valuation that will automatically be disproved by the sale price at auction. Such prices are more often due to the desires and financial might of buyers than to the extensive knowledge of experts and antiques dealers. Let us now look a little more closely at the consequences of this singular aspect of the market in antique art. For about ten years almost all masterpieces have been sold at auction; the few pieces sold by antiques dealers always go for less than the asking price, after lengthy private negotiations. At auction the expert valuations of masterpieces are always half or a quarter of the actual price the piece reaches in the sale.

A question may spring to mind: so are all these experts just incompetent? Who is right? If we want to establish the real value of a masterpiece in the salesroom, should we trust the expert valuation or that of the collector? At the risk of seeming surprising or illogical, we can only answer that both are right.

Let us take an example: in Venice in 1983 a commode of excellent quality from the Roman Barocchetto period was given an expert valuation of nearly 200 million lira. At auction, following a struggle between battle-hardened collectors, it was sold to one of these individuals for no less than 517 million lira, including the auction fee. Soon afterwards a kind of legend grew up around this commode: every antiques dealer had an opinion; the press enhanced its glory by mentioning the price in their news reports; art books and specialist magazines printed photographs of it and discussed its provenance, possible attributions and important qualities. If this commode were to reappear in a salesroom today, when the market is still just as hungry for exceptional pieces of furniture, its price would undoubtedly be confirmed and indeed increased, remembering that, generally speaking, with inflation as it now is in our economic system, it takes at least ten years to recover the capital invested in any kind of antique. The publicity that this commode automatically received confirmed and validated both the very high price it had reached at auction and its intrinsic importance as a piece of very fine quality, two values which mutually and naturally affect each other. In this case the collector was right to buy at a high price, thereby removing from the market a very fine, unique and irreplaceable piece. So was the expert who had valued it at 200 million lira wrong? Absolutely not ! For were it not for the competition between two collectors with practically limitless financial means that took place at the auction, the commode might have been bought by some antiques dealer (or by a collector) for a little above 250 million lira and would have then been sold more discreetly for an appropriate profit. In practice the expert and the antiques dealer cannot take collectors' whims into account; however these whims often do manifest themselves during auctions, creating particular circumstances that defy the predictions of the experts and the laws of the market.

Lastly, the 'collector's price' refers to pieces of furniture of exceptional quality. Readers should not however imagine every time they see the words 'collector's price' that this automatically translates as an amount corresponding to several hundred thousand dollars. What it does mean is that the piece in question is rare and important, of very fine quality, and that it is therefore hard to estimate its value in relation to the valuations given to other similar pieces available on the market.

Note

In valuing these pieces the author has taken account of fluctuations in the value of the pound and dollar in relation to the other European currencies over the last twenty years and of fluctuating prices.
In view of fluctuations in the relative values of sterling and the dollar we have calculated current valuations on the following basis:
£ 1 = Lit. 3.000, $ 1 = Lit. 2.000.

Eighteenth-century furniture

After many centuries of Italian domination, in the 18th century it was once again in France that new styles in art and furniture were developed. As always, there was a search for new models of elegance, while those that had gone before were rejected. The pupil had now become the teacher, with a great many lessons to impart. It was in Paris, France's greatest centre of culture, that the door was closed on the great periods in furniture and the way opened to a series of styles of brief, yet intense existence, which were copied throughout Europe. For this reason we should not speak of eighteenth-century furniture, but more precisely of eighteenth-century styles, which gradually give the century its profile. France created five styles in furniture, naming them after either the reigning monarch or the form of government. These are the Régence and Louis XV styles, the Louis XV–Louis XVI transitional style, the Louis XVI style and the Directoire style.

To understand this artistic ferment a little better, we shall briefly consider the historical, social and cultural conditions that prevailed in France at the time.

Louis XIV died early in the century (1715), having made France one of the richest and most powerful nations in Europe and having fostered a style in the art of furniture-making that was both national and international.

Life at court under the regency of the Duc D'Orléans (1715–1723), during Louis XV's minority, contrasted with the severe manners that had been imposed by the dead king. A new note of frivolity crept in and was echoed in the society and art of the time.

On coming to power, Louis XV the Well-Beloved (1710–1774) at once showed himself to be a monarch more inclined to combat in the field of love than in battle. Guided by the most intelligent of his mistresses, Madame de Pompadour, he revealed a bent for encouraging and patronising the arts, which were carried to greater heights than ever before. Two major events in his reign, the Austrian war of succession (1740–1748) and the Seven Years War (1756–1763), during which France lost its colonies in India and Canada, seem to have left not a single trace on the character of this king, who lacked the skills necessary to guide his country's political life.

On his death, France faced a serious political, economic and social crisis. Furthermore, new revolutionary ideas espoused by the intellectual elite were spreading among the common people. As a sovereign Louis XVI was neither energetic nor able enough to stem the flood with appropriate, far-sighted reforms.

We now come to the French Revolution which, with the symbolic taking of the Bastille prison (1789), put an end to the monarchy and ushered in the mythical figure of General Napoleon Bonaparte.

If the 18th century first exalted the political power of the monarchs before presiding over their subsequent fall, the same can be said, with a few decades difference, of the art of furniture-making. Never did political and artistic development follow each other so closely as in this period.

The first reaction against the imposing baroque of the Louis XIV style was the *Régence* style, which lightened all the materials used in furniture, restructured designs and introduced curving lines. It was in the Louis XV style however that curves became dominant. This style took the female body as its symbol and model. Furthermore, and uniquely in the history of art, Louis XV furniture asserted its total independence from the architectural structures of its time and, where it does retain a link to architecture, the relationship between the two is very subtle, notably in the abundant use of decorative elements such as rocailles and cartouches. A style that was so independent of and complementary to architecture was bound to elicit a reaction from the traditionalists, who tried to bring furniture back to its traditional parallelepiped forms.

At this point we see the emergence of the furniture of the Louis XV–Louis XVI transitional style, in which feet and curved legs (in other words the Louis XV style) support straight carcases, heralding the arrival of the Louis XVI style. This latter style is more commonly known as the neo-classical style, since it reinterpreted the art of Ancient Greece, Rome and Egypt in a different manner from that of the Renaissance. Speaking of the neoclassical style in literature the poet André Chénier, a contemporary of the last king of France, said, 'With new ideas we write old verse'. These words could be paraphrased to apply to Louis XVI furniture: 'With old models we make new furniture'. However the pitiless 'red widow', the guillotine, was to fall on the neck of Louis XVI. A century of history died with him, the furniture that bore his name died out soon afterwards and the last style of the 18th century was born to its short life. This was the *Directoire* style, which takes its name from the French government of the period (1793–1799).

Pieces in this style retain the straight lines of the preceding style (Louis XVI) but the decorative motifs are influenced by Egyptian art and revolutionary symbols (cockades, pikes, arrows). It is a style that can be described as vaguely military, acting as a conduit between Louis XVI designs and those of the later Empire style.

The Directoire saw the arrival of Napoleon as a presence and, in furniture, a shift away from allusions to woman and towards the epic of the Napoleonic wars. These were to be illustrated in Empire style furniture with a richness of colour and a clever, refined interplay of contrasts between the darkness of mahogany and the brilliance of ormolu, which also heralded the start of the period of creative decadence. However, before the advent of the *Directoire*, this century so rich in styles drawing on feminine grace and nostalgia for the past had seen the creation of an infinite variety in furniture design. Things could not have been otherwise. The tendrils of the fading baroque period had stretched into the emerging 18th century, laying the foundations for all later styles in furniture.

The creative drive of the 18th century found expression by developing, perfecting and diversifying the inheritance of the past. The great coffer with drawers and legs became the commode, and the commode became a small commode. Then we see the emergence of many types of commode and small commodes with two, three or four drawers, with or without a traverse between them. *The fauteuil* or armchair becomes a *fauteuil bergère* or a *fauteuil cabriolet*. Two *bergeres* and a *pouffe* together form a *chaise longue* or a *duchesse brisèe*. Chairs diversify, taking on forms and names appropriate to the use they receive (*chaise à fumer* or 'smoking chair', *chaise à nourrice* or 'nursing chair', *chaise prie-Dieu* or 'praying chair') and so on.

The bureau becomes a *bureau à dos d'âne* ('donkey's back bureau'), a *bureau plat* ('flat bureau') or a bureau à *cylindre* ('cylinder bureau'). The sofa becomes a *canapé corbeille* ('basket settee') or a *canapé à oreilles* ('winged settee'). Small salon tables take on a rich variety of shapes and sizes. In the 18th century dressing tables for men and women, which had been very unusual in the 17th century, found the perfect context in which to evolve for daily use.

The most characteristic inventions of the French 18th century were:
- *encoignures* or corner cabinets
- the *secretaire en pente* or 'sloping writing desk'
- the *chiffonier* (a tall, narrow cabinet with five or six drawers used to contain trinkets and

small fabric items: ribbons, belts and so on),
- the bureau *à cylindre*
- the *bonheur du jour* (a small table)
- the *servante* or 'dumb waiter'
- the dressing-table
- the *athénienne*
- the psyché.

The period saw a kind of pre-industrialisation of the art of cabinet-making, giving the society of the time access to creative skills that expressed themselves through changes of style and fashion and in variations on a single theme.

This phenomenon is easily explained if we remember that 18th-century furniture had a social function and was the reflection of the intense cultural life of the period, which was a very different time from that of the baroque.

Fashion was no longer dictated by the sovereign and an aristocracy ignorant of the past; instead an elite of intellectuals and artists guided tastes from generation to generation, leaving to their kings and governments the prerogative and honour of giving their names to the styles which emerged. Furthermore, the aristocracy and the wealthy bourgeoisie, who had formerly been suspicious of culture, caring only for titles and wealth, now loved to surround themselves with famous writers such as Voltaire, Rousseau, Diderot, or Chateaubriand and talented painters such as Watteau, Fragonard, Greuze, Bouchet or Chardin. These men undoubtedly contributed to the flowering of French art and thought.

During this period, due to the influence of the intellectuals and a group of highly talented cabinet-makers, France set the fashion and was studied by all the other countries of Europe. Of these, Italy in particular fell under the French spell.

Acknowledgements

The author would like to thank his French colleagues, Sotheby's, Christie's and all the Parisian auctioneers who have kindly contributed to the illustrations for this book. He is particularly grateful to Jacques Tajan, who was kind enough to make his archives available. Without these collaborators, this book could neither have been produced nor published.

The *Régence* style

Furniture in the *Régence* style first appeared in Paris and took its name from the regency of the Duc d'Orléans during the minority of the future king Louis XV. However the spirit it manifests covers a longer time than this brief historical period. The new style was born with the century and lasted until around 1730.

This style, like all those of a distinctly French character, could have originated only in the French capital. Paris was the place where all the new social, political and, therefore, artistic trends met, interacted and evolved.

The death of king Louis XIV, a ruler with the highest possible estimation of his own reign and of his nation, as well as an excessive pride that earned him the name of the 'Sun King', rang out like a liberation hymn for the French nobility, who were weary of the formality and strict etiquette of life at court. When we remember that the simple fact of sitting down in the king's presence was considered one of the greatest honours, giving rise to jealousy and gossip among the courtiers, this gives us only the slightest idea of the hierarchy of importance in which individuals were given different positions according to their titles.

The first reaction to the king's death was precisely to liberalise etiquette. This initially led the high society of the time to tolerate the presence of people of inferior rank and intellectuals who lacked illustrious ancestry but were rich in wit and imagination; subsequently they would invite to their homes any individual, of no matter what origins, who could bring a touch of anti-conformism and brio to a society desperate for frivolity and seeking a completely new, more private lifestyle.

At first the nobility avoided Versailles, with its tiresome ceremonies, to gather in the Paris salons that had been established by free-thinking princesses and grand ladies of refined taste. The key to success, which opened all doors – including those in Paris – was, and still is, *savoir-faire* or 'know-how'.

These receptions were not like those of the preceding period, which had been designed to astound and dazzle. During the Sun King's reign the crowds had gathered in palaces and vast apartments of somewhat theatrical magnificence, full of immense armoires and sculptural consoles gleaming with gold. The guests who met at such gatherings would sometimes argue or avoid each other but only rarely tried to enjoy each other's company.

Under the regency, on the other hand, class barriers were brought down, opening the way to a dialogue between all those who knew how to talk and had something interesting to say. A desire for intimacy and a willingness to meet with others in places adapted to suit the new tastes and requirements spread rapidly. This time saw the emergence of the apartment, in the modern sense of the term.

In the gothic period a house was essentially either a fortress or a cathedral; in the Renaissance it was a compromise between a dwelling and a fortress and during the baroque period it was a stage. In the 18th century it finally became a true dwelling on a human scale, inhabited by human beings. A respectable house would have several salons, many bedrooms, a games room, a library and a small private salon or 'boudoir'.

The commodes, beds, mirrors, settees and bergeres that decorated these rooms had to be proportioned to suit the space. Thus furniture had to abandon the excessively large, stiff forms of the Louis XIV style.

In addition, it was now women who began to dictate the new fashion. Women had attained a maturity that enabled them to dominate the future of furniture, bringing to it a note of pretty, refined sensuality. Commodes began to reflect the female form. Their rounded fronts echoed the rounded breast of a young woman.

Commodes were drawing on the female body, but they did not yet dare take it as sole model. At the same time all the other types of furniture tended to adopt curving lines in one or more parts of their structure. In the interests of comfort chairs and bergeres were given curved legs, rounded backs and less rigid, functional structures, so that sitting would be pleasurable rather than tiring, as conversation in the salon required.

While women were behind the new fashion and turned it into reality, we must also acknowledge the contribution of a great many skilled cabinet-makers. Of these we should particularly mention Charles Cressent, who is rightly regarded as the father of the *Régence* style. However it was the new lifestyle that determined the development of furniture in general and chairs in particular.

The *Régence* style interpreted the caprices of the period until a particular date, and then disappeared. It can therefore be regarded as the most varied of the transitional styles. It is also the historical link in the chain, marking the passage from the pomposity of Louis XIV style furniture to what was to become, a few years later, the refined sensuality of the Louis XV style.

We shall now concentrate on those specific designs that were most deeply marked by the *Régence* style, starting with commodes, seating, bureaux, bibliothèques or bookcases, consoles and, lastly, the very rare small tables.

However, before launching into detailed technical descriptions, it is as well to pause for an instant to consider the materials and decorations used most frequently in the making of furniture in the *Régence* style. It must be said at the outset that the new style rejected the ebony and metal inlays that had been favoured by the Louis XIV style. The *Régence* had a predilection for simple veneers or veneers with geometrical designs (divisions into squares or diamonds) in amaranth, kingwood or rosewood.

The decorative mercury-gilt ormolu mounts and carvings in the wood of consoles and chairs took the form of five-ribbed scallop shells, female heads with diadems, fauns' heads, dragons and asymmetrical acanthus leaves. Monkeys, pagodas, exotic flowers and human faces were used for Asiatic themes.

High-quality, in other words Parisian, seating was made in natural beechwood and finely carved with the motifs described above, or gilt. Such seats were also very occasionally made in walnut.

Typical furniture

Let us now consider in detail some of the most typical designs of furniture in this style.

Commodes

Commode carcases would be made in oak or soft wood, generally with oak drawers. Two principal types of commode are known. The first, very frequently-found type is known as the *commode en tombeau* or 'tomb commode' because its form is reminiscent of a sarcophagus. It has three rows of drawers, the lower two each consisting of a single drawer stretching across the width of the commode, the third, beneath the marble top, generally having two drawers.

This commode stands on short legs, is veneered in precious wood and decorated with ormolu mounts typical of the *Régence* style.

The second type of commode is also veneered and mounted with ormolu, but has only two rows of drawers, with or without a visible traverse. The side supports of this commode, each comprising the angle and leg, are curved in the shape of a double 's'. This is the rarest and most carefully detailed piece from the *Régence* period.

Its profile is *arbalète* shaped, taking its name from the French word for a crossbow. This shape is indicative of the *Régence* style. The front is slightly rounded and seldom narrower than the back. Commodes with broader backs are extremely rare and of very high quality, much sought-after by collectors. The piece is completed by extensive ormolu mounting.

The tops of commodes of both types are made of fine marble (Spanish brocatelle, *brèche d'Alep*, brown breccia, etc.).

Bureaux plats

There are two types of very large bureau plat. The first is in blackened pear-wood with the body framed by four legs with double 's' curves and five drawers. It has one large drawer in the centre of the table and the four others arranged vertically in pairs on either side. The leatherbound top always has a rectilinear shape, edged with ormolu. The same type of bureau can also be found with three drawers in a row beneath the top. Extensive ormolu mounting illustrating typical themes of the *Régence* style complete the whole.

The second type of bureau has only three drawers in a row beneath the writing surface, which is again rectilinear in shape. It is veneered in amaranth, kingwood or rosewood and the whole is mounted with ormolu.

Encoignures

Encoignures are veneered and have two doors. They are extensively mounted with ormolu and have marble tops. They almost always have *arbalète* shaped fronts.

Bibliotheques

In form the bibliotheque is like an armoire with two doors, standing on a light, straight base with sharp or rounded corners. Generally speaking there are two types of bibliotheque, the first with a serpentine pediment that protrudes in the centre, the second with a pediment *à doucine* (curving inwards).

Both types are veneered and can be distinguished from armoires by their doors, which consist of a veneered frame into which the metal grill or glass is set.

Consoles

Régence consoles are very rare in comparison with Louis XV consoles and are made in finely-carved natural oak or giltwood. The most typical console has four legs with double 's' curves, which may or may not be linked by a stretcher, supporting a rectangular frame and a marble top. The deep front frieze may be *arbalète* shaped and its centre is almost always decorated with the five-ribbed scallop shell typical of the *Régence* style. The curved legs may be decorated with dragons, female heads or mascarons.

There is also a rarer type of console, smaller than the version with four legs. This type has two legs with double 's' curves linked by a stretcher and supporting the console's rectangular frieze on which the marble top rests.

Mirrors

Mirrors are generally gilt with a curved pediment. They are chased and carved with decorations representing dragons, scallop shells, acanthus leaves, flowers and female heads. But the movement of these mirror is restricted at the feet and pediment and it is the decoration rather than the form that distinguishes them from those of the Louis XIV style.

Bronze and gilt-lead mirrors are very rare.

Small tables

There are two types of very small, practical tables. The first, in natural carved wood with decorative elements in the *Régence* style, has curved legs without a stretcher and the frieze, in which the drawers are set, usually has an *arbalète* shaped profile. The second, very rare type is veneered on all sides and known as the *'table à toutes faces'* ('table with all sides') to distinguish it from the bedside table, which is veneered only on the front and sides.

Seats

The way in which seating developed out of the Louis XIV style was quite remarkable, particularly where designs from the late *Régence* period are concerned. There are two types of chairs and fauteuils: those intended for summer use, which have caned seats and backs, and those for winter, with padded seats and backs.

The most frequently-used woods are beech and walnut, but different woods may sometimes be used in the same seat, particularly in small chairs that were later gilt.

The armrests of the armchairs are no longer aligned with the front legs, as they were in the Louis XIV style, but are set back to allow ladies to sit comfortably and gracefully to spread the large skirts which were in fashion at the time. The legs are curved and even the geometry of the backs and seats has begun to adopt a curve, while, in many cases, the upper part of the seat has been given an *arbalète* shaped profile. The stretchers linking chair legs tend to disappear or to take on a curving 'x' shape, an English design that is lighter and flatter than the Louis XIV style.

The canape

There are two types of canape. The first, with armrests, is generally a three-seater, either caned or with non-detachable padding on the seat and back and covered in fabric or tapestry. The second type, known as a *canapé à oreilles* is a three-seater and is padded. It has a higher back than the first type, with large, padded wings at the sides.

The bergere

This is a creation of the *Régence* period which seems to have developed out of the confessional armchair in the Louis XIV style. The difference between an ordinary armchair and a bergere lies in the absence of a space between the armrests and seat. The seat itself is entirely padded and the sides of the armrest are made in such a way as to enable fabric to be nailed or otherwise attached to them.

Bergeres are extremely rare and generally winged. The shape is that of a *Régence* fauteuil but perceptibly larger, with or without stretchers, with a higher back and wings at the side to act as a headrest. The bergere can be regarded as the ancestor of the 'comfy' chairs of today.

The *voyeuse*

This is a padded or caned chair whose seat is wider at the front and much narrower where it meets the back, to enable the sitter to bestride it comfortably. There is a strip of padding across the toprail on which one can rest one's arms to listen to the conversation or watch a game of cards, hence the name, which means something like 'the watcher's chair'.

It was in the *Régence* period that desks and secretaires *à dos d'âne* ('shaped like a donkey's back') first made the occasional appearance.

They were to be found in their greatest number during the period of the Louis XV style.

After this brief account we should stress that while the pieces identified are certainly those whose characteristics most typify the *Régence* style, there are others in which the artist has interpreted the style a manner so original that he has created a masterpiece beyond the confines of all established rules, even though it may bear the typical signs of the period.

A closer examination of the Régence style

The *Régence* style, like all transitional styles, produced furniture of a hybrid nature. Things could not have been otherwise. As the connecting link between the Louis XIV style and the Louis XV style, it both drew on the past and foreshadowed the future, without managing to express the present and create its own personality. It could be said that the *Régence* style lacks an intermediate period of maturation and stagnation, which would have allowed the production of furniture with a well-defined character.

In fact, the works of the *Régence* demonstrate that the style never settled down. As we move gradually towards the Louis XV style, *Régence* commodes, secretaires and chairs acquire an ever-greater richness of structural and decorative elements, reflecting the style's evolution and the aspiration to go beyond its limitations. In this it illustrates an essential characteristic of transitional styles, which are very alive to foretastes of the fashion to come. We might therefore ask why this was the first transitional style to generate so much interest. The answers are clear.

In earlier times the great eras of furniture had been long periods of gestation and flowering. As they unfolded so the components of their evolution gradually faded, becoming almost intangible. Furthermore these elements touched only the few indispensable items of furniture made by human beings. It is however indisputably the case that, however slow their evolution, all periods and styles eventually disappear.

When we pass from the gothic to the Renaissance and from the Renaissance to the baroque, this evolution seems less clear, principally because of the very small number of items that have survived. On the other hand things become far more interesting with the *Régence* style which, unlike previous periods, has left us a generous bequest of materials, permitting a more precise and deeper analysis.

One of the most characteristic and least fortunate creations of the *Régence* is the commode tombeau *toute ventrue* ('entirely rounded tomb commode'). Its body curves both horizontally and vertically, heralding one of the rules of shape on which the Louis XV style is based, but its appearance lacks the latter style's grace and lightness. This signifies that the *Régence* had identified one of the principles of the future style, but not how to use it to harmonious effect.

The commode's resemblance to a sarcophagus and the heavy architecture that binds it to the past mean that this piece can unequivocally be identified as belonging to the *Régence*. This style seems to have chosen a tomb-like form to characterise itself, bestriding as it did the two very different worlds of what had gone before and what was yet to come.

It is certainly impossible to use the word beautiful to describe this massive, squat piece on its short legs, covered in ormolu mounts which, in most cases, have not been chased but simply cast and gilt. Yet we should acknowledge that the commode tombeau has two great merits: it demonstrated the use of this type of furniture, which was still very rare in its Louis XIV version and, where the influence of the Italian baroque had partly failed, it succeeded in liberating the commode from the taste for symmetry and balanced shapes. Like one of those ugly but lovable actors whom the crowds adore, this inelegant piece of furniture was produced in vast numbers and long outlasted the decline of its own period.

In contrast the commodes with two rows of drawers and an *arbalète* profile, sometimes made by famous cabinet-makers such as Charles Cressent, whom we have already mentioned, are too rare to allow us to identify in them some new stylistic feature of general significance, or to regard them as the masterpiece of a new art that was looking towards the future. These pieces are far removed from the traditions of the past, yet

still lack some small element that would make them Louis XV.

The same feeling is generated by the armoires and bibliotheques. This is because no transitional work can do anything other than remind us of what has been created before or what will come after. One obvious example of this phenomenon is provided by two types of bureau plat. The first of these, in blackened pearwood with five drawers, looks a little like an eight-legged Mazarin bureau, from which the *Régence* has removed four legs and curved the four remaining, also removing one row of side drawers. The second, which has a single row of drawers beneath the desk top, is very similar in shape and interpretation to the future Louis XV style.

But the workmanship, new ideas and most profound transformations are to be found in seating, which had evolved very slowly in preceding periods. Essentially or, more precisely, architecturally, chairs had not changed; only their settings had changed, which made their style appear to change as well.

The high gothic backs had noticeably shortened with the Renaissance and decorative elements were now of human rather than divine inspiration. With the arrival of the baroque, seats tended to be padded, legs were twisted or transformed into elegant little pilasters, while backs leaned slightly backwards. Yet in reality chairs had not abandoned their severe structure, which could be contained within an imaginary cube. Until the *Régence* no artistic development had managed to bring about a harmonious reconciliation of aesthetics with convenience and practicality. Comfort had always been sacrificed to appearance.

Suddenly the *Régence* revolutionised traditional forms and decorations to offer something truly new which broke violently with all the examples from the past. Responding to the needs of a society that wanted to sit comfortably, yet did not want to abandon beauty, the craftsmen and artists worked a miracle: they shattered the cube and replaced it with a circle, thereby reconciling function with beauty. And if the harmony that would be attained in the future Louis XV style is still lacking in the alternating 's' shaped curves of the *Régence*, this style must nevertheless be credited with having solved a problem which had until that time seemed insoluble.

Curves reveal the human figure, bringing the study of anatomy into the art of chair design. Before the *Régence* a chair was a thing in itself, and the same was true of the body that sat on it. After the *Régence* new efforts were made to adapt different types of chair to the human body. From this point of view the bergere and *voyeuse* are creative masterpieces of a transitional style which, during its brief existence, revolutionised taste, technique, shapes and traditions with regard to all types of furniture, opening the way to one of the most brilliant, refined centuries in the history of cabinet-making. The *Régence* did this through three important metamorphoses which synthesised its evolutionary process and value in relation to the past and future.

The first metamorphosis consisted, on the one hand, in the gradual liberation of shapes from architecturally-inspired structural motifs and, on the other, in the almost total transformation of the concept of decoration in relation to the Louis XIV style. The latter was rich in sculptural elements and favoured inlays of semiprecious stones and metal, its finest exponent being Boulle. In the *Régence* lion's heads, the Sun King's favourite motif, tended to disappear, as did the symbols of war (shields, helmets, arrows).

The second metamorphosis involved the adoption of curves, not in the restricted, timid manner of the Louis XIV style, where curves were limited to legs or to the rounded angles of commodes, but allowing them gradually to invade the entire structure. If, generally speaking, the style did not achieve the flow that was to characterise the Louis XV style – a failure evident in the commode tombeau for example – the *Régence* nevertheless has the distinction of having opened the way to a new aesthetics in furniture design.

The third and final metamorphosis, a logical consequence of the other two, was to bring the shapes of pieces into harmony with their decoration, without either element becoming dominant.

In practice the *Régence* was only just successful in highlighting the new shapes with its decorations, but the message would be received by the Louis XV style, which succeeded where its predecessor partially failed.

In conclusion, we should not forget that this style also marks the passage from masculine to feminine in the character of furniture. This resulted in the creations of the 18th century being stripped of any connotations of a symbolic or religious (gothic) or humanist and cultural (Renaissance) or political (baroque - Louis XIV) nature. Instead there was a return to decorative elements old and new that owed their existence solely to a quest for the most perfect elegance, while stylistic change accelerated at a pace never seen before.

The French cabinet-makers

If we consider the short time in which it was developed – from about 1700 to about 1730 – our heritage of *Régence* furniture, carefully preserved and handed down from generation to generation, is truly remarkable.

The causes can be found in the refined, capricious manners of the time which demanded – resources permitting – two types of seating, one for winter and one for summer. At the same time variations of the same article of furniture were continually being brought on to the market with a view to increasing sales. Commodes, chairs and secretaires were regarded, particularly by the ladies, as ephemeral fashion items, like a dress or hairstyle.

When they had no social engagements the great ladies of the time would visit the furniture-sellers just as today people visit antiques dealers and painters' studios, to see what was new, or to catch the latest creation by the master then in vogue. In this way the quality furniture market was stimulated by continual demand and the 18th century proved to be one of the most prosperous periods in the history of the cabinet-makers' corporation.

We must therefore consider the customs and practices of this corporation. Each branch of French manufacturing and commercial activity was monopolised by a certain number of privileged specialists, whose work was given royal recognition. The same person could not belong to two different corporations; everyone had to do their own work and do it properly.

Cabinet-makers could not open a workshop without first obtaining their *maîtrise* or 'master's' qualification, a kind of commercial license recognising their skill in the art of making furniture.

It was possible for a candidate to be promoted to the position of master cabinet-maker directly by the king; otherwise he had to work a certain number of years as an apprentice in the workshop of a master and then present a 'masterpiece' to a special panel. These people would decide on his degree of artistic maturity and his right to belong to the corporation (which, in 1723 in Paris, had the considerable number of 895 members) and to sign his own work.

A newly-promoted master cabinet-maker could pass on his art to one employee, but there was no limit to the numbers of children and grandchildren who could inherit the workshop. This right of inheritance also extended to widows, which explains why marriages between a cabinet-maker's widow and the workshop's employee were quite common.

To prevent fraud and to restrict competition, the corporation created a stamp in the form of three letters joined to form the monogram JME (*juré maitre ébéniste*, meaning 'sworn master cabinet-maker'), which cabinet-makers were obliged to have stamped on all their furniture. Pieces were marked in a special office with a small tax being levied on the process; however, since tax-evasion is not a new phenomenon, most pieces of furniture were not stamped and did not bear the cabinet-maker's mark.

This is the reason why the stamp on furniture of all periods, and on *Régence* furniture in particular, is not necessarily of great importance. It is possible to find stamped pieces of *Régence* furniture in antique dealers' shops at lower prices than other *Régence* pieces that are not stamped.

Is this a mystery or a paradox? Not at all. Let us suppose that the master cabinet-maker had put his name to a secondary work, chosen or ordered by a client who wanted a modest piece for his country house, and that on the other hand he had not signed his most important creation, which he was to deliver to a place a few hundred yards from his workshop. The risk of being caught delivering an unstamped piece was far greater for furniture that had to travel from one city to another than for something to be delivered round the corner.

We must stress that the value of a bergere, secretaire or commode has nothing at all to do with the stamp. In fact, when antiques dealers are examining a piece they are mainly concerned with three very important factors: 1) the period when it was made; 2) the state of preservation; 3) the quality of the workmanship. We could add the stamp as a fourth factor, but it would have only a purely relative value.

To confirm what has been said above we should add that many more or less famous cabinet-makers did not like to stamp their furniture. Of these we need only mention Charles Boulle and Charles Cressent, who very rarely signed his pieces because he had so personal a style that the stamp was unnecessary.

Sometimes pieces were stamped at the request of foreign clients, who wanted to display the furniture they had bought in Paris on their return home.

Lastly, in some rare cases, a piece of furniture will bear the mark of two master cabinet-makers. The first, generally known for his skill in giving his creations a perfect shape, would have made the carcase. The second would have been known for the quality of his veneers or inlays and would have carried out the decoration. These rare artistic marriages gave birth to little masterpieces and in such cases the stamps acquire a chronological and historical value.

Apart from the master cabinet-makers, the market was also supplied by 'workers of the crown', who worked for the court and could therefore sell their products without having to have them stamped. In addition, the asylum offered by churches and universities made them patrons of a great many craftsmen, particularly foreigners, who introduced quality furniture on to the market at competitive prices in comparison to those of the corporation.

These factors meant that only some of the furniture was stamped, irrespective of the quality or rarity of pieces. This tends to lessen the value of the stamp itself. On the other hand, and contrary to the above, the stamp becomes very important and crucial to the evaluation of a work if it is that of one of the famous cabinet-makers who stand out among their many hundred colleagues working in the 18th century. The signatures of Cressent, Boulle, Heurtaut, Jacob, Riesener, Roentgen, Weisweiler, Tilliard and the initials BVRB meaning Bernard de Van Risen Burgh, to mention only the best-known, are in themselves enough to raise valuations considerably, often independently of the aesthetic aspects of the piece or any particularly unusual qualities it may have.

We should also mention those pieces bearing the mark of a famous chateau. This signifies that one or several cabinet-makers provided furniture for the interior. The household records often reveal the names of the suppliers.

The main centre of production for *Régence* furniture was Paris, which set an example to the rest of France and Europe as a whole with the quantity and variety of its furniture. The French provinces did not have the capital's wealthy and demanding clientele and so, while Parisian cabinet-makers were very careful in their selection of wood, in other places rustic pieces were produced. These copied Régence forms in their overall lines, but used regional woods to make the prices more accessible to a clientele of more limited means.

This does not mean that the provinces lacked talented artists who could make quality furniture. We need only mention the Hache family, whose ancestor was working in Toulouse around 1650 and whose most prestigious son, Pierre Hache, became famous in Grenoble, where he died in 1776.

But the quality of provincial creations is generally determined by the materials used and, a few exceptions aside, these pieces do not attain the technical and selective perfection of Parisian furniture. We shall now try to establish the basic differences between Parisian and provincial furniture.

In Paris in the *Régence* period the carcase of a piece, including the drawers, would generally be made entirely of oak, or possibly of oak with walnut drawers, or the body might be made in soft wood and the drawers in oak. As we have seen

the carcase would then be veneered in precious wood and decorated with ormolu mounts.

The carcases of provincial furniture, including the drawers, would be made in softwood or fruitwood. Very occasionally the drawers were made in walnut.

Even provincial furniture could be of high quality, particularly if it was veneered in precious wood. In such cases the cabinet-maker would not veneer those parts that were not visible, which meant that the piece would have the outer appearance of a Parisian piece. As a consequence of these differences a piece of Parisian furniture was and still is more expensive than a provincial piece.

Lastly we have furniture of a rustic nature destined for the homes of the common people. The most sought-after pieces of this type were made in solid walnut or some other regional wood of lesser value.

These pieces adopt the shapes of the *Régence* style while its principal decorations (scallop shells, acanthus leaves, female heads, etc.) are carved into the wood; the ormolu handles and all the other decorative ormolu mounts are for the most part simply cast and varnished rather than gilt.

In producing rustic seating the craftsmen confined themselves to creating *arbalète*-shaped profiles, which would be highlighted to a greater or lesser degree by scallop shells carved into centre fronts of chairs, bergeres and canapes.

Often however rustic furniture reflected the influence of the Louis XIV style and even the Louis XV style in its shapes. This was due to the fact that the precepts of the Paris fashion made very slow progress through the provinces, leading to an intermingling of different styles.

Fakes and copies

Let us now consider the main kinds of faking to which *Régence* furniture could and can be subjected by unscrupulous dealers.

Furniture that follows conventions, as French pieces do, is very easy to transform. Let us suppose that we own a provincial commode tombeau. To transform it into a Parisian commode tombeau we need only replace the soft-wood linings of the drawers with old oak or walnut; we should then have to chase and gild the ormolu mounts (if they had been simply cast and gilt with varnish) and lastly, if the marble top is of mediocre quality and poor colour, replace it with Spanish brocatelle or *brèche d'Alep* and the 'miracle' has occurred.

Only a canny antiques dealer would be able to identify the sections that had been reworked or embellished. Parisian furniture is less likely to have undergone such transformations and more likely to have been stamped posthumously with the names of famous cabinet-makers in order to facilitate a sale.

Let us return to the example of the commode en tombeau, one of the most commonly-found pieces from the first half of the century. The addition of a signature to this type of commode, which is very hard to sell due to its large size and squat form, may make it easier to attract a buyer. This is not the worst kind of swindle since signatures on period furniture have generally been added.

The authenticity of the signature is, moreover, easy to discern since, as we have seen, to be authentic, in other words from the period when the piece was made, the stamp must be either preceded or followed by the monogram JME. It is a well-known fact that the forgers' skills are based more on their abilities as craftsmen than on extensive cultural knowledge; the proof of this is that we can personally attest to having seen many pieces of furniture signed at a later date from which the monogram JME was absent. Such stratagems should be viewed with a degree of indulgence; they were employed, particularly in the past, by craftsmen, dealers and petty swindlers as a result of the excessive importance unconsciously given to signed pieces by buyers of period furniture.

On the contrary, when the stamp of a great cabinet-maker, such as Charles Boulle or Charles Cressent, is added to a copy of one of their most famous pieces made between 1840 and 1900, this is true fraud.

The ability to distinguish copies from originals is the mark of a knowledgeable dealer who, when confronted with an important signature of this kind, will recall that cabinet-makers rarely stamped their works. He will then carefully analyse the finish on the wood and the ormolu mounts, generally concluding that sadly this is not an original but a more or less well-made copy.

Where seating is concerned, one rarely comes across transformations that are even worthy of closer inspection. Leaving aside the fairly rare 19th century copies, which are transformed into original period seats by chemically enhancing the finish, we should say that the most frequent manipulations are carried out on provincial pieces.

While provincial armchairs, bergeres and canapes are made in beechwood or walnut, they may later have been enhanced with carvings to enrich the decoration and raise them to Parisian heights. However if the engraving was done at the distance of some hundreds of years, it will have encountered the irregular tunnels caused by woodworm, cutting into them in such a way as to give the impression that the worm has furrowed the surface. If there are a great many furrows on the surface of the marquetry, this is a sure sign that the piece has been embellished at a later date. The worm furrows are often plugged with plaster that has been tinted to match the colour of the wood. It takes sharp eyes to detect this kind of trick.

However – and this is an important factor – seating that has been enhanced at a later date with sculptures should not be confused with canapes, bergeres and chairs that were originally gilt and have been returned to the natural wood. Similar traces of worms are often visible on the surface of such pieces; however this is due not to any embellishment but to the fact that the worm has attacked the gilding or, more exactly, the layer of plaster underneath the gilding and, lacking the strength to penetrate this where it is thick, has dug into the surface between wood and plaster until it has reached an easier place to pierce. When the gilding is removed the sculpture appears to be eaten away in some places, in the same way as a seat that has been given later embellishments.

The difference between a chair that has been 'stripped' and one that has been embellished is to be found in the traces of gold or plaster that remain in the carving and which can be seen using a magnifying glass. If the stripping has been too well done for such traces to appear, the final judgement must rest with the antiques dealer, who will be able to identify the treatment undergone by the piece from the style and vigour of the carvings.

To conclude, furniture in the *Régence* style was reproduced from 1840 until the early 20th century. Copies were made of the commodes and bureaux enhanced with ormolu mounts originally created by Charles Cressent; these were faithfully reproduced in considerable quantities.

Many 19th-century works imitating pieces made by prestigious cabinet-makers have been reworked by skilful fakers to make them look like originals.

In the case of seats, which were reproduced in smaller numbers, it is mainly the gilt versions rather than those in natural wood that have been reworked.

However, in the final analysis, the quantity of *Régence* furniture reproduced in the 19th century was manifestly smaller than that of Louis XIV and Louis XV pieces and thus there are almost no reworked pieces on the market today.

Ormolu mounts

Ormolu was used rather timidly in the Renaissance and is more frequently found in the baroque style, which assimilated and adopted the former period's many decorative motifs in wood, such as balustrades, mascarons, columns, caryatids and statues. These were reproduced in much smaller sizes and elegantly arranged on cabinets inlaid with semiprecious stones.

The cabinet-maker who made the most and best use of ormolu mounts in the Louis XIV period was André-Charles Boulle. The mounts were either simply cast in bronze or chased and gilt. The most valuable were mercury-gilt and these constitute the great majority of 18th century mounts and a large proportion of those of the 19th century.

Opinions differ as to the origins of mercury gilding. Some date the first gilding to the Middle Ages and even to Roman antiquity, others to the

17th century, while yet others argue that this was an invention of the *Régence* period.

Based on our own experience and research, we believe that this technique became known in the 17th century. But, whatever its exact chronology, the technique of mercury-gilding spread in the late 17th century, was developed throughout the 18th century and continued to be used throughout a large part of the 19th century. Its use alternated with that of electrogilding and, thanks to a few workshops and craftsmen, it still survives today.

We know that gold is the most ductile of metals and that an almost transparent gold leaf can be obtained. The properties of gold require that it should be alloyed with other metals in order to obtain a consistency that can be worked. In mercury gilding it is first necessary to obtain an amalgam. To do this a certain quantity of gold is poured into heated mercury and the result is poured over the bronze; the whole item is then heated to a sufficiently high temperature to evaporate the mercury (about 430° C); the gold is thus fixed to the bronze, which may be burnished with semiprecious stones until it shines or left matt.

Mercury-gilding was not the only technique known, but it was by far the best and above all the most durable. This technique maintained the colour of the gold unchanged, since the metal penetrated into the fibres of the bronze (due to the heat) and was fixed there. This process did not have the disadvantages of varnish-gilding, which soon became opaque, thereby losing all its effect.

From an artistic point of view, gilding that enabled ormolu mounts to retain the colour of gold unchanged was fundamental for a type of furniture like the Louis XV style, whose beauty was often heightened by the contrasting colours of the different woods and mounts.

Before the use of ormolu mounts, some pieces of furniture (coffers, chairs and mirrors) were parcel-gilt or gilt overall. Over time however gold that has been applied to wood loses its shine, becoming opaque and dull; it does not have the same degree of resistance to tarnishing by atmospheric agents. In addition, the slightest shock would cause the gilt sections to flake, so that the owner would have to have the piece restored.

Such considerations probably fuelled the growth in the use of ormolu mounts, which could easily be regilt and which, when their gilding darkened with age, could be easily restored to their original splendour by plunging them into a bath of acid, which purified them of the ravages of time.

One can find ormolu mounts from the 18th and 19th centuries which have almost no gilding at all. There are various reasons for this: firstly too little gold used in the gilding; secondly wear brought about by cleaning (with certain chemical substances) and lastly, the destructive work of atmospheric agents.

Today we can state that very few 18th-century ormolu items – from decorative mounts for furniture to wall lights, fire irons, candelabra, etc. – have come down to us with their original mercury gilding. The exception to this are the few ormolu items made for the royal families, which had a layer of gold a millimetre thick, and a few others that were left abandoned in attics and found later under a thick layer of dirt, which had protected them from the ravages of cleaning and atmospheric agents. It is also the case that some mercury-gilding workshops survived through the 19th and 20th centuries by diversifying into electrogilding, a far less expensive process which expanded rapidly in the second half of the 19th century. As we have already noted, many pieces of furniture have been preserved with ormolu mounts that have almost no gilding. As we suggested earlier, the responsibility for this may lie with the craftsman, whose trade led him to economise on gold, a material that was already very expensive at the time; but it may also be due to the fact that many pieces of furniture were replaced by new pieces in later styles, so that the mounts on earlier pieces were not regilt, as was the regular practice throughout the whole of the 18th century, much of the 19th century and even in the 20th century. It therefore seems opportune to consider this question more closely to avoid drawing inappropriate conclusions. We should remember that there were about seven hundred and fifty certified mercury gilders (masters and apprentices) from 1696 to the early 18th century in the city of Paris alone. From chandeliers, ormolu mounts for furniture, clocks and fire-irons to humble uniform buttons, everywhere mercu-

ry-gilding reigned unchallenged. The silvering so favoured by the Louis XIV style did not survive beyond the collections of a few connoisseurs. In the 18th century France left its gilt fingerprint on the whole of Europe.

If we now consider the 19th century, the French Revolution had put an end to the regulations of the corporations and it is hard to make a trustworthy inventory of mercury-gilding workshops active in the first half of the century. But on the basis of tangible evidence (Empire furniture, objects, chandeliers, wall lights, table centrepieces, clocks, etc.) that have been preserved, we can conclude that mercury-gilding continued at full pace in France as in the rest of Europe. On this point we believe it is enough to cite the *Bottin Diderot* of 1863 which, alongside dozens of electrogilding workshops, gives the name and addresses of a dozen craftsmen who were gilding in the old style, in other words using mercury.

Today there are still mercury-gilding workshops working at full stretch in Paris. These include the Mahieu company, which has been gilding since 1880, and Schmidt. We should also mention the old Poggiali company in Florence and the Rossi workshop, which opened recently in central Rome, a stone's throw from the Piazza del Popolo. The windows of this establishment look on to the street, so that it is possible to watch the patient work of the chasers and gilders who are restoring ornamental bronzes and mercury-gilding them.

These days there is a group of workshops large and small working with ormolu; however there are not enough of them to meet the demand from antiques dealers, who often prefer to pay the heavy price of mercury-gilding in order to respect the tradition of restoring a period piece according to the rules of the art.

On this point we should not forget that there are some who economise by using electrogilding or mercury nitrate on 18th-century or Empire items, thereby betraying the unwritten rules of the antiques dealer's profession.

When many of our colleagues assert, in all good faith, that the ormolu mounts on their furniture have their original mercury-gilding, it always raises a smile. We are within our rights to ask whether they are referring to the first gilding, carried out in the reign of Louis XV (1743–1774) or to the penultimate gilding dating from the period of Napoleon III, in other words from the second half of the 19th century, or the gilding that has just been completed in the Paris workshop. For this reason regilding cannot diminish the value of an ormolu mount. For everyone knows that the beauty and value of an item in ormolu rest on the quality of execution (sculptural intensity, finesse of the chasing) and not on a few grams of gold to restore its original colour.

Naturally we are speaking here of chandeliers, wall lights, clocks, statues and above all of fire-irons, whose function subjected their gilding to greater wear and which have therefore undergone more regilding than any other ornamental ormolu items. Where the ormolu mounts on a piece of furniture (handles, sabots, escutcheons, chutes) have been replaced, or some items reworked, this does not in itself devalue the item as a whole. The value of a piece of furniture is determined by its shape, the quality of the execution of the marquetry and the precious woods of the veneer rather than the few ormolu mounts intended for practical use, in other words, when the aesthetic effect of the piece is not created by a large quantity of ornamental ormolu mounts. Of course everything changes completely when the piece is enhanced by extensive ormolu mounting which, in combination with the marquetry, veneer and shape, determine both its beauty and value. In such cases the ormolu mounts should be at least 90% original, irrespective of mercury-gilding. If the mounts were reworked in the 19th or 20th century, the value of the piece may be brought down by between 20 and 40%.

Having discussed mercury-gilding we must also mention the many *bronziers-ciseleurs* working in the field of the restoration and reworking of ornamental ormolu mounts for furniture, particularly in Paris.

From the great Renotte company, where any mount can be made using either house designs or those of the client, to Couste, Lavigne and Moreira, to mention only a few, it is clear that without such *bronziers-ciseleurs* the great French tradition of decorative ormolu mounts would not have survived.

The ormolu mounts on Empire furniture in particular are generally said to be by far the finest in the history of the decorative arts. Let us now discuss the reasons for this.

In the periods preceding the Empire ormolu mounts were generally given a single coating of an amalgam of mercury and gold. Once the mercury had evaporated at a high temperature, as we described above, any necessary retouching was carried out when a large amount of gilding was missing on parts of the mount. But, since the personality of Napoleon I required that the Empire style should gleam with gold, ormolu mounts on furniture were given up to three successive coatings. This procedure led to the accumulation of layers of gold to great effect, made even more apparent by the alternation of gilt and burnished sections or parts that were gilt but left matt. It is clear that some ormolu mounts were thus gilt two or three times.

Another reason why they gleam so much lies in their lesser degree of wear, since the gilding of the Empire period is far more recent than that of the 17th and 18th centuries. However those pieces described as 'classic' to distinguish them from more important, magnificent pieces, including the vast production made for the less wealthy strata of society, have shown us that mercury-gilding consisting of a single layer of mercury and gold does not survive a century of wear.

We ourselves bought a few hundred classic Empire secretaires for the CIGA chain of grand hotels. The original ormolu mounts on these pieces bore only a few traces of gilding. At the request of Orazio Bagnasco, who was head of the hotel chain at the time, these mounts were all regilt and can be seen in the rooms of CIGA hotels in Italy.

In addition, many of the most knowledgeable and honest experts in ormolu maintain that when mercury-gilding is replaced according to the correct process and patinated with particular ingredients and waxes that were already in use at the time when mounts were first made, it is almost impossible to date them precisely.

How to find *Régence* furniture

When discussing *Régence* furniture, we should not forget that pieces in this style continued to be produced beyond the brief duration of the government (1715–1723) whose name they bear. This explains the relative ease with which they can still be found on the market.

Of course this ease applies only to the international market and principally to its three main centres of Paris, London and New York. This is where it is possible to buy a *Régence* commode, bookcase, bureau plat, encoignure, chair or bergere, either from an antiques dealer or, from time to time, in an auction house.

However, if one is looking for a masterpiece, the situation is completely different. Pieces by the great master cabinet-makers such as Nicolas Pineau, Charles Cressent or Pierre Migeon, to mention only a few famous names, rarely appear on the art market. When they are put up for sale in internationally-known sales rooms (Sotheby's and Christie's in London, Hôtel Druot in Paris or Sotheby Park Bernet in New York), they send ripples of excitement through the world of the collectors, generating a level of interest similar to that of a film premiere. Of course enormous sums are wielded in the struggle for ownership, generally far greater than the more sensible valuations of the experts.

On the other hand, if a *Régence* masterpiece is put up for sale in an antiques dealer's shop, the transaction is made far more discreetly and on the basis of a more realistic valuation. This said, if another dealer or a collector mentions having seen or bought a piece of remarkable quality from an antiques dealer, the news quickly spreads and the art market becomes interested.

However the *Régence* period did not only produce masterpieces for an elite. One can also find commodes and bibliotheques of reduced size along with armchairs that can be easily integrated into an interior and are on sale at accessible prices.

Quality and valuation

If we consider the commodes made in the *Régence* period, the finest are certainly those created by Charles Cressent, who is rightly regarded as the inventor of the style. These are true masterpieces of cabinet-making with long legs, two

drawers and impressive chased ormolu mounts decorating the entire structure. In a Paris sale in 1969 a commode attributed to Charles Cressent was sold for the impressive sum of 700,000 FF. Commodes imitating designs by Charles Cressent are quoted at similar prices. The same is true of another type of very rare commode, also with two drawers, whose flared sides have two doors concealing shelves.

When valuing a *Régence* commode, or any other piece of period furniture, one should consider the quantity and quality of the ormolu mounts and the degree of wear to the mercury-gilding. A large piece whose extensive mounting has lost its gilding (which can be imputed to insufficient gilding, neglect and the ravages of time) should be avoided, since regilding is very expensive.

The rarest and most valuable mirrors are gilt-lead. The same advice applies to encoignures as to commodes. The finest pieces are those where the combination of the cabinet-work and ormolu mounts form a harmonious whole. Lacquered encoignures with oriental motifs are very rare.

On the other hand shallow bibliotheques that have two or four doors with glass or grills do not have large wooden surfaces on which to display the bronzier's skills and are not regarded as the most successful creations of the *Régence* style. Their rarity and more modest size in comparison to the bibliotheques of the Louis XIV period do however mean that they are sought-after by collectors.

So we should say that it is demand that causes pieces to reach high prices, irrespective of any objective analysis.

It may be helpful to remember that the value of any piece of furniture depends on two important elements: the quality of the piece, whatever type it is, and its rarity. These two elements are not always inseparable. It may be that two rare *Régence* pieces, for example bergeres or bureaux à *double dos d'âne* – also known as bureaux de notaire or 'lawyer's bureaux' – reach exorbitant prices in the salesroom, even though the quality of the workmanship is judged no more than adequate by the experts. This may be justified by their rarity.

But let us concentrate on cabinets. The finest of the bureaux plats are those that have four slender, curved or cabriole legs and a single row of drawers and whose structure is enhanced by re-fined, chased ormolu mounts, or the bureaux plats that resemble a bureau Mazarin in shape (with eight legs, one large central drawer and three rows of drawers on either side almost touching the ground), as long as the quality of the cabinet-work and mounts is enough to erase the memory of a shape that is too familiar and too often seen in Louis XIV furniture.

The bureau plat in blackened pearwood with ormolu mounts takes third place in the hierarchy of bureau furniture.

Valuations are based on the aesthetic and spec-ulative values of *Régence* furniture, or those of the furniture of any other period, and should be understood as an estimate of value only, since in the field of period furniture every general rule or truth always has an exception. It is quite possible to find a bureau plat in blackened pearwood with an exquisite shape and ormolu mounts of such quality that it may reach and indeed surpass the prices attained by bureaux veneered in precious wood.

Where seating is concerned, for both caned summer seats and their padded winter counter-parts, valuations are always very high due to their rarity.

But from the purely aesthetic point of view, the most interesting pieces are the chairs. Their per-fect contours, in which the characteristic ele-ments of the style (asymmetrical scallop shell, acanthus leaf, female head with headdress) are shown off to best effect by skilful carving, are combined with the value, colour and quality of the tapestries (Gobelins, Beauvais, Aubusson) covering the padded parts. Seats with oriental motifs are the rarest and thus the most expen-sive.

It is important to distinguish between gilt seats and seats in waxed natural wood: it is the latter that receive the highest valuations, given equal aesthetic values and quality of execution. A seat that has suffered too many depredations from worms should not be bought unless it is so rare a design that in itself it constitutes a particular vari-ation of the style. While the above is true for chairs, everything changes when we come to consider canapes and day-beds.

The famous canapes *à oreilles* or winged canapes and chaises longues, which are too large for the rooms of modern apartments, are not very popular with buyers; therefore, despite their aesthetic value, they do not reach noteworthy prices; these valuations are even lower in the case of gilt canapes and day beds.

Irrespective of needs and fashions, which seem to favour modern padded divans, it is right to ad-vise clients to purchase *Régence* period canapes, for fashions pass, but true art remains and today one can still buy pieces of this type at compara-tively reasonable prices.

Due to its typical characteristics, *Régence* style furniture is much sought-after both in France and throughout the world. Masterpieces in this style are generally more highly valued than Louis XIV and Louis XV pieces of the same quality.

In Italy, however, *Régence* style furniture is al-most unknown. The reasons for this lie in the fact that the transition of Italian furniture from the baroque to the Barocchetto, in other words what we might define as the Italian *Régence*, manifest-ed itself in a softening of the baroque forms: lean-er curves and lighter structures. Although some ideas crossed the Alps, Italian furniture contin-ued to lack the characteristics of uniformity and repetition of style.

In Italy it is possible to find furniture in the style known as early Barocchetto which has *ar-balète* shapes very similar to those found in French pieces (particularly in pieces from the Piedmont, Genoa, Naples and Sicily); however, with a few very rare exceptions, these pieces al-most never attain the level of the French produc-tion in quantity and vigour of style. A pronounced taste for *Régence* furniture, whether its French version or that of the vaguer early Barocchetto, has not developed in Italy, where this style is al-most unknown. We can conclude from this that there is no particular demand for French or Ital-ian *Régence* furniture among the collectors of the peninsula and that it is thus not highly valued. It is therefore possible to find such furniture in Italy at better prices than in its country of origin.

Important, fine commode attributed to Charles Cressent. The rosewood veneer shows geometric designs and the top is of purple breccia marble. In our opinion the exuberance, quality and creativity of the ormolu mounts can be attributed to the skill of the style's pioneer. Current valuation: collector's price.

Small commode, partly fine, partly classic in quality, with two rows of drawers surrounded by exuberant yet refined ormolu mounts with a top of pink breccia marble. Small pieces in the *Régence* style are quite rare.Sold in Paris in 1973: £ 10,000, $ 17,300. 1984 valuation: £ 8,600 $ 11,400. 1991 valuation: £ 9,880 $ 13,000. Current valuation: £ 8,600 $ 11,400, € 15,250.

Classic small commode in rosewood veneer, with two drawers and visible traverse. Although the legs are already very curved, the framework is still too solid, having not yet attained the lightness of Louis XV commodes. 1984 valuation: £ 8,600 $ 11,400. 1991 valuation: £13,570 $ 23,900. Current valuation: about £ 15,300, $ 25,400, € 22,880.

Classic commode with an *arbalète* profile and three rows of drawers. This is the most characteristic design of commode tombeau and the most frequently produced, with minor variations in the shape and the ormolu mounts. Sold in Paris in 1971: £ 970, $ 1,690. 1984 valuation: £ 8,600, $ 11,400. 1991 valuation: £ 13,300, $ 23,500. Current valuation: £ 18,400, $ 30,480, € 27,450.

Very good quality commode, with kingwood veneer and geometrical designs, representing a new variation on the classic commode tombeau. It is far more elegant than the example above. Sold in Paris in 1971: £ 6,200, $ 10,700. 1984 valuation: £ 12,900, $ 17,100. 1991 valuation: £ 17,000, $ 30,100. Current valuation: £ 20,400, $ 33,800, € 30,500.

Right: rare, fine commode attributed to Charles Cressent (elected to the Académie de Saint-Luc on 17 August 1714). Of particular note are the rosewood and kingwood veneer with geometric designs characteristic of the *Régence* style and the extensive ormolu mounting emphasising the curved shape of the piece. *Brèche d'Alep* marble top. Current valuation: collector's price.

Commode tombeau with classic *arbalète* profile, with rosewood and kingwood veneer. *Brèche d'Alep* marble top. Sold in Paris in 1972: £ 2,650, $ 4,600. 1984 valuation: £ 12,900, $ 17,100. 1991 valuation: £16,500, $ 29,260. Current valuation: £ 20,400, $ 33,800, € 30,500.

Fine commode in precious wood with doors in its concave sides, attributed to Gaudreaux. The combination of drawers and side doors is extremely rare and synonymous with quality. Noteworthy also for its ormolu mounts typical of the style, including a head of Diana and *arbalète* handles. Sold in Paris in 1970: £ 20,800, $ 36,000. 1984 valuation: £ 51,600, $ 68,400. Current valuation: collector's price.

Fine caned armchair in beautifully carved beechwood. The *arbalète* shape of the upper part of the back and the apron is a distinctive sign of the *Régence* style.
1984 valuation: £ 860, $ 1,140 each, £ 2,600, $ 3,400 the pair. 1991 valuation: £ 10,000 $ 17,700 the pair. 1998 valuation: £ 12,270, $ 20,300, € 18,300 the pair.

Below: finely carved caned canape with foliage motifs. Noteworthy for the triple *arbalète* of the seat and toprail.
1984 valuation: £ 1,400, $ 1,900. 1991 valuation: £ 7,500, $ 13,300 . Current valuation: £ 7,000, $ 12,400, € 10,670.

Fine gilt salon table, the marble top resting on four winged caryatids. The caryatid on a straight support was the preferred decorative and structural element of the Louis XIV style. However in the example pictured below, the supports are curved, as are the elements forming the stretcher, signalling the early *Régence* style.
Sold in Paris in 1973: £ 6190, $ 10,700.
1991 valuation: £ 10,000, $ 17,700. Current valuation: £ 15,300, $ 25,400. € 22,880

Rare and unusual dining-room buffet in kingwood veneer. Noteworthy for the geometric decoration on the doors. In contrast to the usual practice in Paris, the top is veneered rather than marble; this is extremely rare. 1984 valuation: £ 19,500, $ 25,880.
1991 valuation: £ 43,000, $ 76,100.
Current valuation: £ 38,800, $ 64,350. € 57,960.

Important bibliotheque with grills to the doors and rosewood veneer. Noteworthy for the classic *arbalète* profile of the traverses and the upper part of the doors. Sold in Paris in 1971: £ 860, $ 1400. 1984 valuation: £ 18,900, $ 25,000. 1991 valuation: £ 35,000, $ 62,000. Current valuation: £ 40,800, $ 67,600, € 61,000.

Fine encoignure, one of a pair, in kingwood and rosewood veneer, with *brèche d'Alep* marble top, attributed to Charles Cressent. The *arbalète* profile and veneer with geometric designs reflect the *Régence* style; the vigour, exuberance and imaginative design of the chased ormolu mounts reflect the skill of the great cabinet-maker, who himself cast, chased and gilded the ormolu mounts for his creations. Current valuation: collector's price.

Classic armoire with two doors and the base outlined with an ormolu mount. Of particular note are the butterfly kingwood veneer and classic geometric decoration on the door panels, characteristic of the *Régence* style. Sold in Paris in 1971: £ 5,750, $ 9,900. 1984 valuation: £ 10,750, $ 14,250. 1991 valuation: £ 20,000, $ 35,400. Current valuation: £ 25,500, $ 42,250, € 38,100.

Fine encoignure, one of a pair, attributed to Charles Cressent. The more refined, less vigorous ormolu mounts mark the transition from the *Régence* to the Louis XV style.
Current valuation: collector's price.

Fine console from the *Régence* period in carved giltwood. Noteworthy for the originality of the mascarons on the legs and the scallop shell at the front, characteristic of the style.

Sold by Sotheby's in New York in 1993: £ 90,540, $ 136,000. Current valuation: collector's price.

Fine canape and pair of armchairs in natural carved beechwood. Noteworthy for the arched toprails and aprons characteristic of the style and the rich carving that highlights the structures of both armchairs and canape.

Sold by Etude Tajan in Paris in 1996: £ 18,850, $ 29,300. Current valuation: £ 15,300, $ 25,350, € 22,880.

Fine salon furniture consisting of a suite of six armchairs in natural walnut with high padded backs and armrests carved with fleurons. The shaped apron is decorated with an asymmetrical cartouche, foliage and agrafe. Cabriole legs with sabots. The armchairs are covered in period tapestry in gros point and petit point with a design of musicians, animals, birds and mythological subjects surrounded by foliage on a black background.

Three-seater canape with winged back and serpentine apron standing on eight cabriole legs. Provenance: Bourg de Bozas collection (photo: Tajan, Paris). Sold in Paris in 1996: £ 77,900, $ 121,200. Current valuation: £ 102,000, $ 169,000, € 152,500.

Pair of important, fine armchairs, from a suite of four, with flat, serpentine backs in natural wood with mouldings and carvings showing scallop shells, small flowers, foliage and lambrequins. Standing on four cabriole legs linked by an x-shaped stretcher.

(Photo: Tajan, Paris).
Sold in Paris in 1994: £ 36,500, $ 55,900.
Current valuation: £ 40,800, $ 67,600, € 61,000.

Rare, fine small armoire *à hauteur d'appui* ('of a height to lean on'), veneered in amaranth, the doors with lacquered panels showing chinoiseries. (Photo: Tajan, Paris).

Sold in Paris in 1979: £ 1,950, $ 4,300. 1984 valuation £ 1,580, $ 2,100. Current valuation: collector's price.

Rare, fine small commode of exceptional quality, veneered in ama-
ranth and extensively mounted with ormolu, attributed to Charles
Cressent. Noteworthy for the mounts showing typical subjects of the
Régence style, including *arbalète* handles, mascarons and scallop
shell escutcheons.
Sold in Paris in 1983: £ 49,150, $ 74,400. 1984 valuation: £ 48,760,
$ 64,600. Current valuation: collector's price.

Opposite: rare, fine commode with two drawers and side doors, satinwood and amaranth veneer. The mercury-gilt mounts, including
arbalète handles, female heads and lion's paw sabots, are typical of
the *Régence* style. (Photo: Tajan, Paris).
Sold in Paris in 1979: £ 25,300, $ 56,000. 1984 valuation: £ 28,700,
$ 38,000. Current valuation: collector's price.

Fine commode in satinwood veneer, which can be attributed to
Charles Cressent. The extensive ormolu mounting brings out every
detail of the piece. Sold in London by Sotheby's in 1988: £ 93,200,
$ 123,570. Current valuation: collector's price.

Fine bibliotheque in kingwood veneer. The chased ormolu mounts
enhance the piece as a whole.
Current valuation: collector's price.

Fine salon table in minutely carved giltwood. The *arbalète* shape of the front is a very particular characteristic of the *Régence* style. (Photo: M. Meyer, Paris). Current valuation: collector's price.

Fine bureau plat in amaranth veneer, with fine ormolu mounts, attributed to Charles Cressent. Sold in Paris in 1981: £ 45,670, $ 91,900. 1984 valuation: £ 43,000, $ 57,000. Current valuation: collector's price.

Fine armchair, carved and gilt, one of a pair, late *Régence* style. (Photo: Tajan, Paris). Sold in Paris in 1990: £ 41,270 $ 73,450.
1991 valuation: £ 40,200, $ 70,800.
Current valuation: £ 51,000, $ 84,500, € 76,250.

Very rare, fine canape in giltwood, particularly noteworthy for the foliate carving covering the entire structure. (Photo: Tajan, Paris).
Sold in Paris in 1975: £ 590, $ 1,300.
1984 valuation: £ 8,600, $ 11,400.
Current valuation: collector's price.

Opposite: fine mirror in minutely carved giltwood.
(Photo: M. Meyer, Paris).
Current valuation: collector's price.

Bureau armchair of exceptional quality, finely carved and gilt. (Photo: Tajan, Paris). Sold in Paris in 1983: £ 22,540, $ 34,100.
1984 valuation: £ 22,360, $ 29,600.
Current valuation: collector's price.

Rare, fine salon table in carved giltwood with agate top. (Photo: Sotheby Parke Bernet).

Sold in Monte-Carlo in 1976: £ 8,100, $ 16,700. Current valuation: collector's price.

Large, fine bureau plat veneered in rosewood with brass inlay. Severe shape apart from the cabriole legs, with extensive ormolu mounting typical of the *Régence* style.
Sold in Paris in 1971: £ 8,670 $ 15,000. 1984 valuation: £ 59,340, $ 78,600. Current valuation: collector's price.

Rare pair of stools, partly classic, partly fine, in minutely carved natural beechwood. Tapestries showing Chinese figures surrounded by flowers and foliage. These seats have the typical shape of the *Régence* style. Sold in Paris in 1973: £ 480, $ 930.
1984 valuation: about £ 2,580, $ 3,400.
1991 valuation: £ 9,000, $ 16,000.
Current valuation: £ 8,160, $ 13,500, € 12,200.

Rare, fine, small lady's bureau veneered in rosewood with elegant ormolu mounts. The frieze has a clear *arbalète* profile and two drawers. 1984 valuation: £ 8,600, $ 11,400.
Current valuation: collector's price.

Fine console in carved giltwood with *brèche d'Alep* marble top. (Photo: M. Meyer, Paris).
Current valuation: collector's price.

Fine armchair, one of a pair, in minutely carved wood. Original Brussels tapestry. 1991 valuation: £ 22,100, $ 38,900.
Current valuation: £ 20,400, $ 33,800, € 30,500.

Rare, fine, small salon table, one of a pair, in minutely carved giltwood. The pronounced curve of the cabriole legs reflects the style of the end of the *Régence* period. The beautiful shape and delicate carving are reminiscent of a design by Daniel Marot. (Photo: M. Meyer, Paris). Current valuation: collector's price.

Fine bibliotheque in kingwood veneer and rosewood contours. Extensive chased ormolu mounts depicting foliage and female heads provide the finishing touch to this quality piece, which has two doors, glazed in the upper part.

Sold in Paris in 1972: £ 870, $ 1,500. 1984 valuation: £ 21,500, $ 28,500. 1991 valuation: £ 45,240, $ 79,650. Current valuation: £ 51,000, $ 84,500, € 76,250.

Pair of classic encoignures with *arbalète* profile, veneered in rosewood with *brèche d'Alep* marble top. Sold in Paris in 1972: £ 8,900, $ 16,200. 1984 valuation: £ 8,600, $ 11,400. 1991 valuation: £ 18,100, $ 31,860. Current valuation: £ 15,300, $ 25,350, € 22,880.

Below: rare, fine chaise longue in natural beechwood, with carving depicting foliage and pomegranates. The earliest examples are rarer and more valuable. The piece shown here, made in two parts, is called a d*uchesse brisée*. Today this piece is not much in demand and its comparatively low price does not reflect its true value as a fine piece. 1984 valuation: £ 1,720, $ 2 280. 1991 valuation: £ 3,650, $ 6,460. Current valuation: £ 5,100, $ 8,450, € 7,600.

Rare, fine, small table in natural oak with Chinese lacquered top. The slender structure identifies this piece as belonging to a period close to the end of the *Régence* and the period of transition to the Louis XV style. 1984 valuation: £ 8,600, $ 11,400. 1991 valuation: £ 13,700, $ 24,250. Current valuation: £ 13,260, $ 21,970, € 19,800.

Pair of classic small canapes known as marquises in natural beechwood with cabriole legs. Marquises from the *Régence* period are very rare. Sold in Paris in 1970: £ 350, $ 600. 1984 valuation: £ 3,000, $ 4,000. 1991 valuation: £ 10,000, $ 17,700.
Current valuation: £ 10,200, $ 16,900, € 15,250.

The Louis XV style

The Louis XV style is also known as the Pompadour style, after one of the king's most famous mistresses, and the rocaille style, after one of its most frequently-used decorative elements, imitation rock. In Italy it is called Barochetto or Rococo. Emerging around 1730 in Paris, the undisputed European capital of 18th-century fashion, this style developed and perfected the innovations of *Régence* furniture. The Louis XV style is characterised by asymmetry of both structure and decoration, and by a more generalised use of curves, which now tend to invade the overall shape of pieces, breaking with the traditions of the past.

Taking the historical development of cabinetmaking as a whole, in other words from the high Middle Ages to the 18th century, we can say that, with the precepts of the Louis XV style, furniture freed itself from all structural and architectural influences. In so doing it reached its peak of technical and artistic maturity.

Throughout its slow evolution, furniture had always been dependent on architecture for its shapes, adopting pillars, columns, balustrades, caryatids and consoles. The wooden structures of furniture had always revealed their formal and decorative dependency on the architecture of their period. But with the Louis XV style (1720–1770) furniture set out on its own solitary path. The commodes, bureaux, bibliotheques, bergeres and armchairs have no models in the buildings of the period, being convex or serpentine both vertically and horizontally. Indeed, given the limitations of building materials, architecture could only ever give its constructions a serpentine shape on the horizontal plane; if it had adopted curves and convex shapes on the vertical the buildings would have collapsed.

The one link between Louis XV furniture and architecture is visible only in the few decorative elements that they share, such as various types of shells, little bouquets of flowers and heads of women and children. In addition, from the technical point of view, the craftsmen or artists had attained the greatest mastery of their arts. Their experience and precision enabled them to bend and manipulate around a hundred different kinds of wood at will, giving their imaginations free rein and creating geometric designs and floral or pictorial compositions, not to mention the Chinese and Coromandel lacquers with which they covered the carcases of their furniture.

This perfection and variety in furniture design was reinforced by the tastes of a society that displayed its wealth in the care and attention it gave to everything to do with the home, with no concern for expense.

Where the *Régence* style seems to have experienced a kind of crisis of construction in its short life, leaving us only a few buildings that bear its characteristic features, the Louis XV style seems to have been struck by a virulent epidemic of 'stone sickness'. The whole of France was overtaken by a taste for fine buildings: chateaux, taverns, squares and private houses were built all over the country. This led to a growth in the production of furniture, reflecting the importance given to the home. New pieces were invented: the *chiffonière* (a work table), the dressing-table, the haricot or kidney-shaped table (from the shape of the top), the secretaire, the table de nuit or night table, which had already made a brief appearance in the *Régence* period, and the bureau *à dos d'âne*.

There was also a great variety of different kinds of seating: the style saw the emergence of various kinds of bergeres, cabriolet and gondola armchairs and many other types of chair reflecting the various uses to which they were put.

But these new creations were not the only reasons behind the new expansion of cabinetmaking. Eighteenth century creativity was boosted by the favourable influence exerted over the arts by the golden age of the great royal favourites.

Louis XV is undoubtedly the figure who best represents the frivolity of a period which placed woman at the centre of the world. It is no coincidence that the French dictum 'What woman wants is what God wants' emerged at this time;

the king's most famous mistresses, the Marquise de Pompadour and Madame du Barry, were not 'objects' in the power of their sovereign; on the contrary (particularly in the case of the highly intelligent and refined Marquise de Pompadour), they were intensely involved in the country's political and cultural life. They paid close attention to every manifestation of fashion and were ready to use their prestige to encourage or suppress any new developments.

For example, when the Sèvres porcelain factory suffered a serious commercial crisis, it appealed to Madame de Pompadour, who, with the king's assent, organised a public sale of porcelain in the Versailles gardens. The nobility and wealthy bourgeoisie were invited to come and purchase large services and this they duly did, attracted not just because this was a society event but because they wanted to please their king and his mistress. This is a typical example of 18th-century public relations, where the aim was to foster a love of beautiful things while saving a porcelain factory, launching an artist or encouraging some other field of human activity. In addition the importance of women in the 18th century was such that writers, cabinet-makers, painters and miniaturists would dedicate their works to the great ladies of the time to ensure their patronage and support in society.

In this context furniture ceased to be a masculine preserve. It no longer served as proof of the social status of the master of the house. Furniture now became a tool in relationships between the sexes, intended to win the hearts of the women of a hedonistic, refined society. Women wanted their furniture to be graceful, practical, elegant and valuable. And what could be more elegant than the female body with its graceful, harmonious curves? This is why furniture was modelled on the female anatomy. The fronts of commodes, consoles and furniture in general alluded to the female body, if only symbolically.

The cabinet-makers started from a very simple principle: if a woman is as beautiful as the arrangement of her curves is harmonious, the same must be true of a piece of furniture. As a result the Louis XV style consists of a succession of curves whose flowing lines reflect the value of a piece of furniture, the degree of perfection it expresses. But to move beyond the feelings that came to life in the hands of some master cabinet-makers and get a more precise idea of all the factors that constitute the Louis XV style, we must consider the technical and decorative details that the new tastes dictated. We shall therefore examine these briefly.

The carcases of Parisian pieces had to be made of oak. Very occasionally some great master would use drawers in rosewood, mahogany or solid maple. The practice of using different woods for the carcases of pieces of furniture, sometimes found in the *Régence* period, disappeared.

Softwood or fruit trees were used only in the making of provincial furniture or pieces of the quality described as rustic in solid wood. In Paris beechwood and walnut were used for seating, while regional woods were used in the provinces.

Veneers were made from valuable, exotic woods such as amaranth, kingwood, tulipwood or rosewood and there was a preference for inlays of flowers, diamonds and geometrical designs. Different woods were used in the making of a single piece of furniture in order to create contrasts of colour, enhanced with ormolu mounts.

The most commonly-found decorative elements in either ormolu or wood were rushes, various kinds of shells, cartouches, bouquets of flowers on their stalks, musical and pastoral elements, symbols of love, doves, dolphins, monkeys and dervishes.

As well as the fashion for veneered furniture, the 18th century saw an explosion in the fashion for lacquered furniture with oriental motifs.

Lacquer panels that could be attached to furniture were imported directly from China until one of the Martin brothers developed a varnish to protect painted surfaces in Paris. Known as 'vernis Martin', it brought the brothers fame and led to their being wrongly regarded as the inventors of a perfected form of lacquer. There were also pieces of furniture painted with Coromandel lacquer. This was a type of lacquer in which the decorative motifs were engraved and painted in bas-relief.

Typical furniture

Having briefly discussed the main elements of the Louis XV style, let us now consider the most characteristic pieces of this multi-faceted production.

Commodes

Commodes became widespread during the *Régence* period, but were perfected by the Louis XV style. There are three different designs of commode.

The first type is simply a Louis XV version of the commode en tombeau, with veneer sometimes enhanced by a thread of pale wood running in a curving line around the outline of the drawers and fewer ormolu mounts. With a few exceptions this is a commode of a lesser value reflecting the last echoes of the *Régence* in the Louis XV style.

The second type includes a wide range of commodes of different sizes with two or three rows of drawers, with or without traverses, and cabriole legs.

The veneer or lacquer is enhanced with more or less extensive ormolu mounting. There are three main variants: a) the commode with a simple veneer in precious tropical wood, ormolu mounts and a marble top; b) the commode with inlaid geometrical designs (cubes or small squares), ormolu mounts and a marble top; c) the commode decorated with inlaid flowers or foliage with branches and stylised leaves, ormolu mounts and a marble top.

This third category itself includes: a) commodes in Chinese lacquer decorated with scenes from Chinese life (figures, pagodas, monkeys, landscapes, trees), ormolu mounts and marble tops; b) commodes decorated with Coromandel lacquer, showing scenes from Chinese life, the usual ormolu mounts and marble tops.

There is also a fourth type of buffet-commode with two doors in place of the two drawers and exactly the same decorations as the other commodes, but these are too rare to be listed.

Buffets and *dessertes*

These are generally made of oak or walnut, very occasionally of mahogany. They have two doors and are sometimes convex or bombe in shape, with short, cabriole legs and a marble top.

With the exception of rare examples of inlaid buffet-commodes, all the decorative elements of the period are carved into the solid wood, with an almost total absence of ormolu mounts.

Encoignures

Encoignures may have one or two doors, they have bombe fronts and three or four legs, the two or three front legs being cabriole. They are decorated in the same way as the commodes of the second and third type.

Consoles

There are two main types of console. The oak or natural wood console belongs to the first type. It may have four cabriole legs carved with leaf and flower motifs either all over or on the lower part; the legs are joined by stretchers consisting of curved elements that meet in the middle to form a kind of base enhanced with a decorative motif such as a seashell or a human or animal head.

The upper part of the legs are joined to a curving, decorated frieze that supports the marble top. When the console is gilt the same design may be made in different woods (beechwood, pine, etc.).

The second type of console, designed to stand against a wall, has only two curved legs linked by a stretcher and, again, a marble top. The decoration is of the same type as that found on the first type of console.

Bibliotheques

Veneered examples of these are rare since bibliotheques were generally integrated into the wood panelling of rooms intended as private offices. The veneered or lacquered designs differ in size; they have short, cabriole legs and one or two doors containing glass or grills, with curved mouldings. The pediment or surround is either serpentine or *à doucine* (curved inwards).

Armoires

Veneered or lacquered armoires are rare. Most were made of solid wood which was then engraved and carved with typical decorative elements of the period. They tend to be small with two doors, some rare examples having one door only.

In decoration and form they are similar to the bibliotheques, with one difference: the doors have neither glass nor metal grills and are entirely veneered or lacquered.

Tables

The dining table did not exist. At the time it was still customary to use planks set on trestles. However there was an indescribable variety of small salon tables and night tables, to which we can add the large writing table or bureau plat.

Bureaux plats

These almost always have a single row of three frieze drawers, the largest in the centre and a smaller drawer to either side. The four legs supporting the top are more tapered and curved than those of *Régence* period bureaux.

Instead of straight sides and rounded corners the top is now entirely curved and surrounded with ormolu. The bureau has ormolu handles and sabots and, on more valuable pieces, ormolu-mounted angles, bringing out the beauty of a piece which may be simply veneered, have floral inlays or be lacquered.

Small tables.

There are three kinds of small table: the night table (or bedside table), the small salon table and the work table. The top is usually square, oval, round or rectangular but all have delicate, tapering and curved legs.

Let us now consider each type in turn. Night tables almost always have a marble top under which there is either a small drawer or a space for holding books. Underneath this are one or two small doors concealing a space to put the chamber pot.

The small salon tables always have two or three small drawers under the marble top and sometimes also a small extending writing surface between the top and the first small drawer. Both night tables and small salon tables may have an undertier.

Small work tables resemble small salon tables, except that instead of marble they have veneered or lacquered tops. These can be lifted to reveal tiny compartments for needles, balls of wool and all the other items necessary to women's occupations. The front is either broken up by false drawers or has a side drawer under the compartments.

The small work table may also have an extending leaf just beneath the top or between the compartments and the small side drawer, which can be slid out, almost always from the front.

All small tables, without exception, have a rounded shape. When we speak of square or rectangular tables we are referring to their general appearance, as the lines that form the square or rectangle are serpentine. Small tables may be either veneered, have floral inlays or be lacquered; they may also be richly mounted with ormolu.

Small tables *à tambour* ('drum tables') or heart-shaped tables standing on only three cabriole legs are more rarely found.

Mirrors

Mirrors are almost always in giltwood. They have rectangular plates highly variable in size and stand on cabriole legs. The upper part is rounded, protruding slightly in the middle, where one of the characteristic elements of the style can be seen (shell, cartouche, flowers, leaves, human or animal head). Ormolu or gilt-lead mirrors are extremely rare.

There are as many types of mirror as there are characteristic decorative elements.

Beds

Two types of bed were very much in fashion during the reign of Louis XV: the *lit à la duchesse* ('duchess's bed') and the *lit d'ange* ('angel's bed').

Lits à la duchesse
These beds have a rectangular canopy of the same length, which is not supported by columns.

Lits d'ange
These beds have a head board and foot board, the head board being the higher, and a rectangular canopy without columns, which does not cover the entire length of the bed.

In addition to these main types of beds old designs were still produced and were adapted to the Louis XV style (*lit à la polonaise* ('Polish-style

bed'), *lit à la turque* ('Turkish-style bed'), *lit d'alcôve* ('alcove bed')).

Bureaux à dos d'âne, bureaux en pente

These are small pieces, each with a slanting leaf which, when lowered, reveals two rows of small drawers and a few compartments; one of these small drawers sometimes conceals a secret compartment reached by means of a sliding leaf. These bureaux are entirely curved in shape and stand on four cabriole legs. They are pieces *à toutes faces*, in other words they do not stand against the wall and therefore have veneer, floral inlays or lacquer on all sides. They may also be richly mounted with ormolu.

Bureaux *à dos d'âne* and all other pieces *à toutes faces* are familiarly known as *meubles à jour*.

Bureaux en pente are like bureaux *à dos d'âne*, but the back is not decorated as these bureaux stand against the wall.

Bureaux-à-cylindre ('roll-top bureaux')

This type of bureau first appeared in the reign of Louis XV, but it was during the reign of Louis XVI that it became widespread. It is therefore a very rare piece whose lower part, with its accentuated curves, is very similar to the *Régence* bureau with five drawers. The upper part consists of a marble top surrounded by an ormolu gallery supported by either one or three drawers forming a tier just above the curved front; the roll top itself is slotted into grooves on the inner surface of the sides, which are also curved at the front, to enable it to open and close. The bureau-à-cylindre may be veneered, have marquetry with floral motifs or be lacquered. One of the most famous bureaux-à-cylindre was ordered by Louis XV, begun by the famous master cabinet-maker Oeben and finished by Riesener. It is now preserved in the Louvre.

The secretaire *à abattant* ('fall-front writing desk')

Although these are not as rare as bureaux-à-cylindre they are also most commonly found in their Louis XVI version. This secretaire is large and narrow, taking its name from the *abattant* or fall-front in its upper part. When opened this serves as a writing surface and reveals small drawers and inner compartments. The secretaire has a marble top and (except for secretaires *à hauteur d'appui*) between the marble top and fall-front there may be a small drawer as wide as the front. The lower part has three rows of drawers or, more often, two doors.

The secretaire *à abattant* stands on short cabriole legs and in designs of higher quality, the angles are rounded or canted.

Like all other furniture of this period, secretaires *à abattant* were made using the typical Louis XV materials and ormolu mounts.

Semainiers

This type of piece looks like a much narrower version of the secretaire *à abattant*, but without fall-front or doors. It typically has seven drawers.

Coiffeuses (dressing tables)

Coiffeuses are small, with a shape reminiscent of the *Régence* period bureau plat. The difference lies not only in their size, but also in their overall shape, which is usually more serpentine, and in their upper part, which has three doors. When opened and tipped back slightly, the central door reveals a mirror. The two side doors conceal pigeonholes designed to hold small pots of cream, powder and perfume.

Coiffeuses are very graceful, whether veneered or lacquered, and do not have extensive ormolu mounting.

There are two types of coiffeuse: those de-signed for women and a larger type with more sober decoration for men.

Seating

In this period the use of curves was extended to the overall structure of all types of furniture and chairs of all kinds were no exception.

All chairs, with the exception of bergeres, have low backs which do not support the sitter's head. Seats and backs are generally padded, the padding being sometimes removable, or caned.

Armchairs, canapes, chairs and so on may be in natural wood carved with fashionable decorative elements, lacquered or gilt. There are five main types of armchair.

Fauteuils en cabriolet

Armchairs of this type are among the most enveloping and commonly-found of the Louis XV period.

Not only is the back rounded and violin-shaped, it is also concave, the better to fit the shape of the human anatomy. These were small salon armchairs, comfortable and practical.

Fauteuils en gondole

These are very similar to the Venetian gondola armchair.

The difference between the fauteuil en cabriolet and the *fauteuil en gondole* is that the former has armrests that are separate from the back, while the second has a far more concave back which includes the armrests. The back of the *fauteuil en gondole* is also much lower than all other backs.

Fauteuils de bureau

These are very rare pieces with backs similar to that of the *fauteuil en gondole*, but their legs are arranged in a more practical and unusual way, different from that of all other armchairs.

The seat is bow-fronted, with one leg joined

at the centre of the front, the two others on either side and set slightly back by comparison. There is a single leg at the back of the armchair.

Bergeres

These were very common in the reign of Louis XV. They are larger than the other armchairs with a higher back.

There are four main types: the bergere *en cabriolet*, the bergere *à dossier écusson* ('shield-backed bergere'), the bergere *à oreilles* ('winged bergere') and the bergere *à dossier plat* ('flat-backed bergere').

Marquises

These are very wide bergeres with lower backs than the rest. They look like small canapes.

Canapes à corbeille ('basket canapes')

These may have six or eight cabriole legs. The enveloping bombe sides include the armrests and form a piece with the long back.

Chairs

Like bergeres these take their name from the shape of their backs and the use for which they were intended. As well as chairs for everyday use we find: the *voyeuse* ('watcher's chair'), the *chauffeuse* ('warming chair'), the chaise *à coiffer* ('hair-arranging chair') and the chaise *à nourrice* ('nursing chair'), which has much shorter legs than the others.

Stools

These are rectangular in shape and variable in size, with serpentine lines and cabriole legs. Some X-shaped stools were made, adapting a Renaissance design to the Louis XV style. These are extremely rare.

Banquettes

These are shaped like rectangular stools, but are much longer and can be sat on by more people at once.

Duchesses brisées

These are chairs as long as the human body, in three parts: a bergere with a large, enveloping back, a large stool and a smaller bergere with a lower back. They may also be formed of two bergeres with gondola backs of different sizes and a very long seat.

Chaises longues

The chaise longue is a kind of day-bed, similar to the *duchesse brisée*, but all of a piece.

Parisian, rustic and provincial furniture

As we saw with decorations in the *Régence* style, the designs of Louis XV furniture enabled artists to give expression to their talents in a highly original way, abandoning pre-existing formulae.

To gain a more detailed understanding, we must now carefully distinguish between the different types of production in the Louis XV style, considering both their technical and aesthetic aspects. This is very important for the valuation of individual pieces.

Where aesthetic values are concerned, we must start by distinguishing three different types of furniture: a) Parisian furniture, which may be fine, classic or of good quality; b) rustic furniture, including both pieces used by the lower classes and more elegant, decorated pieces; c) provincial furniture, which may be veneered or inlaid with floral motifs.

The wood for making Parisian furniture was chosen very carefully and the regulations of the corporation of master cabinet-makers regarding the selection of woods were followed to the letter. The only regulation not to be followed was that relating to stamps, which we have already discussed.

A piece of furniture whose carcase and drawers are made of wood of a quality inferior to oak cannot be regarded as Parisian, whereas it is quite possible to find pieces with carcases of oak and drawers in far more valuable wood, such as mahogany or rosewood. Where the choice of wood was concerned, unlike the *Régence* style, which permitted a combination of valuable and less valuable woods in the carcase, the Louis XV style is absolutely intransigent. This enables us to distinguish Parisian from regional products.

Classic Parisian pieces are simply veneered and the ormolu mounts kept to an indispensable minimum, in other words the four sabots, handles and chutes.

The exception to this rule are the small *tables d'accouchée* ('tables for a woman lying down'), which have almost no ormolu mounts, to prevent them from weighing down too heavily on the bed. These should however be regarded as fine pieces because of their graceful shapes and because the master cabinet-maker had to use all his skill in order to create the impression of a small table made all of a piece.

Many classic pieces, even those of a simple, severe appearance (commodes, secretaires, small salon tables, small bureaux plats, bibliotheques), may be stamped. The reasons for this are the same as those we mentioned in the case of stamps on *Régence* furniture.

In the same way seats with no exceptional decoration or whose shape conforms to the usual precepts of the style are regarded as classic.

Fine or good quality furniture combines perfect shape with a decoration of lacquer or floral inlays, or with a veneer inlaid with geometric designs, sometimes with unusual ormolu mounts on part or all of the piece.

Where ormolu mounts are concerned, in addition to the comments made in the chapter on the *Régence* style, we should add that the manufacture of ormolu mounts for furniture was part of a different branch of artistic and commercial activity.

Just as there were furniture specialists, so there were specialists in chased ormolu and silvered bronze. Among these we must mention the famous Caffieri brothers, to whom we owe a great many ormolu mounts for furniture, lights and clocks of different kinds. They became so famous

that it often happened that any ormolu items stamped with a small letter 'c' with a crown above it were wrongly regarded as having been made by the Caffieri brothers; however the Caffieris only rarely stamped their works and always with their full name. In fact the crowned 'c' is the mark of a tax imposed on the corporation of gold and silversmiths between 1745 and 1749 by Louis XV. The stamp proved that the tax had been paid. However, although an enormous amount of furniture was being produced at the time, pieces with the crowned 'c' are comparatively rare, since, even in those days, tax evasion was an everyday practice.

In the time of Louis XV there were a great many makers of quality furniture, including the most prestigious. To discuss all of them would require a separate study, such as that provided by Alexandre Pradère in his book *Les ébénistes français - De Louis XIV à la Révolution* (Leonardo, 1990). Here we can only mention the most important names: Abraham Roentgen, Jean-François Oeben, Jean-Henri Riesener, Adam Weisweiler, Martin Carlin, the Pierre Migeons, all three of whom are very famous, and Pierre Roussel. The clientele of these master cabinet-makers included rulers and royalty from the whole of Europe.

In discussing seating, we should mention the pieces made by the members of the Tilliard family, which were never equalled. Armchairs, canapes and bergeres by the Tilliards are preserved in French museums.

Turning now to rustic furniture, the first thing to be said is that the makers of pieces of this type did not follow strict rules where the choice of wood was concerned. They used regional wood and, wherever possible, avoided expensive ormolu mounts. They did not use lacquer or veneer pieces with valuable tropical woods, preferring, for economic reasons, to make their designs in solid wood with appropriate shapes and decoration.

Two types of rustic furniture can be identified according to their quality. The first kind was used by the lower classes, the second is of an elegant or decorative type.

Furniture for use by the lower classes was made of regional wood, adopting only the shapes of the Louis XV style, with no valuable carvings or ormolu mounts. Pieces of this kind clearly have no great artistic or commercial importance. Their main value is historical and documentary, as examples of ordinary furniture from centuries gone by. These are poor, bare pieces, which are largely functional and do no more than ape the fashions that came in with the new times and trends.

However one can find elegant pieces of rustic furniture, made mainly in solid oak or walnut, whose makers did not confine themselves to imitating the shapes of the style, but chose also to carve them with decorative elements that would not have been possible had they used valuable wood veneers or ormolu mounts. A particularly well-made structure displays careful *modenatura* which accentuates its shape.

In addition, the style of the elegant rustic pieces that have been preserved reflects the designs of furniture formerly found in the chateaux and which the new styles rejected, gradually handing them down to the poorer social classes. In this way rustic furniture becomes valuable not only because it expresses rich and varied styles, such as those of the 18th century, but because it also inherited designs that the new styles no longer considered worthy of representation. The most obvious example is that of the Louis XV armoires, of which only a few lacquered or veneered examples of reduced size have survived, but of which there are very many large versions made in solid wood of various kinds, carved with period motifs.

There are aesthetic reasons for this phenomenon. The armoire, a functional, practical piece par excellence, could not manifest great elegance and grace of shape or decoration because its function required it to be made in particular shapes and sizes. This is why the Louis XV style tended to avoid trying to produce such pieces in a fine version, relegating them to the rustic cate-

gory. But the converse problem can also be found. The buffet, for example, in its most typical version with two doors, sometimes with a drawer above and a top of marble or wood, does not exist in fine versions. It was forgotten by the Louis XIV, *Régence* and Louis XV styles, but was present and very common in various regional rustic versions, in both elegant and ordinary variations. The Louis XVI style then inherited this piece and raised it to a new level of importance in a variety of designs of very high quality.

Of course elegant rustic furniture is more valuable than its ordinary counterpart, particularly if it is made in solid oak, walnut or, more rarely, mahogany.

We should add that one can find consoles in natural oak displaying fine carvings whose quality clearly raise these pieces to the level of art, although the same cannot be said of their simpler variants. These consoles should not be regarded as elegant rustic pieces.

Provincial furniture that is veneered or inlaid with floral motifs closely adheres to the rules for regional furniture of the *Régence* style where the wood used in making the carcase is concerned; on the other hand it displays decorative materials and motifs in wood and ormolu that clearly belong to the kaleidoscopic world of the Louis XV style. These differ from one region to the next – although not so much as Italian regional furniture – and there was no shortage of talented cabinet-makers. Among these we must mention one of the members of the Hache family of Grenoble, a name we have already referred to when discussing *Régence* furniture.

Although Pierre Hache preferred to make furniture in regional wood; his pieces are full of grace, with a wealth of decoration. His chairs and canapes were particularly pleasing to his Italian clientele, since the elegant shape of the seat was combined with rich carving, powerful *modenatura* and an unrelenting use of twisting shapes. These elements brought Hache closer to the heirs of the Italian baroque than to the academic French cabinet-makers.

A closer examination of the Louis XV style

The Louis XV style gave rise to furniture whose many characteristics can be summed up in a few essential points. We shall now consider these in detail.

Creative imagination

While the 18th century was indisputably the most imaginative century in the history of furniture, the Louis XV style marked the height of creativity of a period which managed to invent a piece of furniture for every kind of use, even those of a most ephemeral or transitory nature.

The origins of this great effervescence lay in a frivolous, flirtatious, sceptical society, which sought to express its taste for refined pleasures in everything, including furniture. The owners of the private residences and country houses that were springing up all over the place no longer wanted to display their wealth through furniture radiating pomp and solemn grandeur, as had been the case in the baroque period. Instead they tried to create the sense of a haven of intimacy and comfort, so that the art of making furniture as a whole took a new direction. The power and strength conveyed by Louis XIV furniture was replaced by the grace and comfort of a new style, which the Louis XV style perfected and continually updated to satisfy the demands of a new category of clients, who wanted an infinite variety of pieces.

So this period saw the emergence of the *fauteuil en cabriolet*, king of the salon armchairs and quintessential reflection of a world whose very existence revolved around conversation, both intelligent and banal. The Louis XV style fought against monotony, offering a remarkable range of bergeres and small day-beds and inventing the marquise, a piece that bridges the gap between the bergere and the canape.

But the Louis XV style was still not satisfied; it generalised what the *Régence* style had only begun, creating as many types of chairs as there were possible uses for them: the *fauteuil de bu-reau*, the coiffeuse, the nursing chair, a chair to pray in, a chair to warm oneself in and a chair from which to watch.

And because salon life was not just a matter of chat but also of intrigue, love affairs and hidden passions, the Louis XV style invented the bureau *à dos d'âne*, the bureau *à cylindre* and the secretaire *à abattant*, pieces with secret places where compromising documents, incriminating evidence or nothing more dangerous than a few perfumed love-letters could be hidden. Today the secret compartments in many pieces of furniture that long held the written expressions of the fears, hidden worries, passions and plotting of our ancestors, may seem to us to be nothing special, but this was not so when they were made. And very recently a few pieces were still holding treasures to be discovered by their buyers: antique gold coins, jewellery and writing that revealed the habits and customs of an entire period.

In addition, highlighting the importance of the role of women and the desire to please them, the style invented the little *table d'accouchée*, which allowed women to read, write or do their make-up from the comfort of their beds. Chinese lacquers were used to give pieces a different colour, a new aesthetic dimension to add to all the others that made up the multiform world of the Louis XV style.

A break with tradition: the triumph of curves and asymmetrical decoration

In the course of the development of furniture from the earliest times to the Louis XV style, there had been occasional attempts at creating curved shapes; however these were very few and far between. The 16th-century Italian coffer, for example, acquired a certain liveliness in its cover and base before disappearing altogether, but its contortions were no more than the death throes of funerary shapes and found no deeper echo, although they do constitute the very first desperate efforts to release furniture from the grip of rigid parallelepiped shapes. Both the Italian and French baroque – the former much more than the latter – began to give more sinuous shapes to the fronts of pieces and their carved decorations. In France in particular the Louis XIV style, which synthesises and reflects a very individualised baroque combiniong Italian, Flemish and Spanish influences, made very timid experiments with serpentine forms, confining curves to the stretchers and armrests of chairs and the fronts of commodes. In only a few examples of the heritage from that period can it at last be said that the style has truly absorbed curves into its structures.

The few examples of bureaux plats curved only in their four cabriole legs and consoles standing on sinuous supports were enough for the *Régence* style to develop a trend that had manifested only its first steps and stammerings in the Louis XIV style. Yet, as we have seen, the *Régence* was held back by its role as a transitional style and did not bring these developments to fruition.

And so we come to the Louis XV style, the most revolutionary in the history of furniture. Where it can be said that all styles had hitherto drawn on the structures and shapes of the architecture of their period, the trend under Louis XV was for furniture to free itself almost entirely from this long slavery. While some link with architecture may remain, the main point of reference is no longer stone but the curves of the female body. Indeed there is no more 'somatic' furniture than that of the Louis XV style.

So we are seeing here an almost total break with the traditions of the past in relation to shape. Moreover – and without mentioning the cartouches and shells placed at particular points on some pieces (consoles, mirrors and chairs), symbolising the female genitalia and providing an example of asymmetrical ornamentation – it can be said that decoration too was no longer required to remain prisoner of the rules governing the proportions of different parts of a piece. Such rules were, moreover, no more than the logical reflection of the old straight structures, in other words, as far as possible, decoration along straight lines for furniture with straight shapes.

In starting from a rejection of the paral-lelepiped shape the Louis XV style was obliged to adopt new decorative elements which, in order to follow the shapes dictated by the style, had themselves to become curved, freer and more varied, in a far more obvious way than they had done before. Thus we have the old, Louis XIV-style scallop shell which, in the new style, becomes irregular and affected. The same thing can be seen in relation to all the elements of the past, which the Louis XV present transformed and used in a new and different way. Decorative elements, both new and old, climb, twist and intertwine, with no respect for the old traditions and without limits or confines, concerned only to create light and highly imaginative designs. There was an effort to create compositions in which a human or animal figure would stand out among intertwined leaves and branches, in an alternation of movement and stillness. A profusion of inlaid flowers spread along the front and sides of a piece, seeming either to advance without going beyond the shape that contains them or to end without any sense of continuation, ignoring the new-grown twig, so full of life that it seems ready to escape. Elsewhere we find musical symbols inside a large cartouche with fluttering segments, tied with a knotted ribbon, decorating the top of a small salon table, completely ignoring the laws of symmetry.

To prove these observations we can draw two imaginary lines, one vertical and one horizontal, which meet at the centre of a Louis XV-style piece, dividing it into four sections. This will always reveal that both decoration and shape are divided into several asymmetrical parts.

The return of colour in furniture

From the early 16th to the late 17th century, with the exception of giltwood, furniture in general, both Italian and French, had abandoned painted decoration, leaving this to furniture termed rustic. The only permitted colour was that created by gilding.

Towards the end of the 17th century Venetian and Chinese lacquers offered a new kind of decoration based on colour, which had been forgotten for almost two hundred years. The lack of pictures decorating furniture had been much criticised, and in France much more than in Italy. The reasons for this lack should be sought in the later development of the pictorial tradition in France. This meant that for centuries France had been distanced from both the creative wealth of the multifaceted Italian school, and the technical perfection of the Flemish school. For although the tradition of painted furniture was widespread in Italy, being practised in the 13th, 14th and 15th centuries into the early 16th century, France had great difficulty assimilating and reproducing a decorative art it had not mastered.

The Louis XV style made up for this backwardness by producing a remarkable quantity of chairs coated in varnish of a single colour and furniture decorated with Chinese lacquers or vernis Martin.

It should be noted that the new furniture decorated with pictorial subjects did not take its inspiration from the Italian Renaissance alone. The themes chosen were no longer historical, biblical or mythological; there was a preference for landscapes of an oriental nature and compositions of exotic flowers.

But no matter what the subject, colour enters the history of French furniture in triumph, and with very singular accents.

Structural and decorative symbiosis

As we have already seen, the aesthetic aspect of a piece of furniture is based on the greater or lesser degree of harmony between two elements: its shape, or structures, and its decoration. But the results are not always the same, so that three different aesthetic judgements are possible. In the first the shape has more importance than the decoration; in the second the decoration has more importance than the shape; in the third there is some kind of balance between shape and decoration.

In those centuries when beautiful decoration was a prerogative of solid wood, one finds the harmonious beauty of early French and Italian gothic furniture or the beauty of Italian furniture at the dawn of the Renaissance, or the hybrid aspects of the French Renaissance. Then, with the advent of veneers and inlays of semiprecious stones, came the decorative grandiloquence of the Italian and French baroque. But nowhere do we find aesthetic perfection as great as that attained by Louis XV furniture.

With the Louis XV style it is no longer meaningful to speak of a dominant or harmonious relationship between two aspects which together give the piece its quality yet are each distinct and open to analysis. Louis XV furniture displays a kind of symbiosis in which shape and decoration merge to an extent that prohibits any kind of study involving their separation into two distinct aesthetic components.

For example, in terms of the three elements of which it is composed (its shape – the bombe oak carcase – and the two decorative elements consisting of its veneers in precious woods and mercury-gilt ormolu handles, chutes and sabots) the veneered commode forms a single, perfect whole. This phenomenon of the balanced, harmonious combination of several elements is the best demonstration of the technical and artistic maturity reached by 18th century furniture.

We can give an additional illustration of our argument with a comparative analysis of a gilt Louis XIV console and a Louis XV console. The first has some elements that are easy to distinguish: sinuous or straight angles, the stretcher and the frieze and top on which the marble rests. Examination of the structure reveals elements contributing to the overall decoration of the console, as there is a kind of separation between the architecture of the piece and its decoration.

If we now consider the Louis XV console, although it has cabriole legs, a stretcher and a frieze with sinuous lines on which the marble rests, its shape and decoration are so interdependent that it is no longer possible to distinguish them. We are looking at a body inside its skin and it is logically impossible to imagine or discuss a body without its skin or vice-versa.

Not all pieces of Louis XV furniture have the characteristics described above: secretaires, armoires, bibliotheques, day-beds, bureaux *à cylindre* and bureaux *à abattant* are to some extent prevented by their size from ever achieving a perfect fusion of structure and decoration. However the shapes of the small salon tables, bureaux *à dos d'âne*, commodes of various types, encoignures and chairs reflect the precepts of a style governed by a concern for harmony and artistic unity.

In the course of our history of furniture we have already noted, and shall note again, other elements of aesthetic value; yet we shall never again come across a style that achieves so harmonious a combination of its formal and decorative components and its numerous different materials (wood, ormolu, lacquer, veneer), giving them both unity and continuity. There is no doubt that this success is founded on the adoption of the 360° sinuous line, which alone can allow the structures of a piece to combine perfectly with its decoration. For, until the advent of the Louis XV style, furniture was contained in parallelepiped shapes, and these almost always contrasted with the decorative elements, which sometimes adopted sinuous lines. In other words, on the one hand were the rectangular, square and very occasionally round structures and on the other the round, oval, sinuous and curved decorations.

Clearly the vine and acanthus leaves and figures of angels and saints of the gothic style, not to mention the rosettes, could not be created using rigid geometrical lines; although gothic is stylised, it necessarily involved the use of curves. The same was true of the Renaissance, both in Italy and in France, with its pearls, festooning flowers and fruits, plaits and pictures showing historical, biblical or mythological themes; the baroque and *Régence* styles were still less ready to confine curves to their carved figures (caryatids, dolphins, fawns) and began to introduce sinuous lines into some parts of their furniture.

However, until the emergence of the Louis XV style, decorative elements had been forced to run, climb and contort themselves, bending to the rigid forms of the pieces on which they were placed. In this way beauty arose almost always out of the contrast between the straight lines of the shape and the less constrained decoration, which was forced to free itself from the rules by its very nature – although in practice it always respects symmetry and its elements are arranged directly on the shapes, in spaces defined by straight lines.

With the Louis XV style decoration was no longer obliged to wind along flat surfaces; it had simply to follow, penetrate and absorb shapes it had been dragging with difficulty from one piece of furniture to the next down the centuries. The symbiosis between the furniture's shapes and its decoration was thus achieved. The attempt that had failed under the *Régence* succeeded in the Louis XV style, which attained the peak of artistic maturity. The parabola reached its highest point. The Louis XV style was inexorably followed by a phase of decadence. The causes for this lie in the repercussions of political and social events on the art of furniture-making.

Meubles d'appui

Having discussed the general characteristics of the style, we must now rapidly identify the pieces that best typify the Louis XV style and those that reveal trends towards constantly evolving forms and decorations. We must first divide Louis XV furniture into two categories: *meubles d'appui* ('leaning furniture' or furniture that stands against a wall) and *meubles à toutes faces* ('furniture decorated or veneered on all sides').

Of all the meubles d'appui it is the commode which bears the most marked characteristics of the style within the limits of its possibilities. It has a bombe front and sides, but its role as *meuble d'appui* means that the part which stands against the wall and the marble top must follow straight lines, so that it cannot complete an imaginary circle. It is however undoubtedly the case that, of all the *meubles d'appui*, it is the commode that most forcefully manifests its identity and well-defined individual style, enabling it to reconcile its function with the art of the period.

The same cannot be said of armoires, bibliotheques and secretaires *à abattant*, whether veneered, lacquered or inlaid with flowers. These reflect the style in their decoration, but their large size means that they are tied from the outset to a world of straight lines, broken only by their short cabriole legs and concave or convex lower parts. These elements are not in themselves enough to enable us to state that in these creations the style was realised in all its aesthetic plenitude, ignoring the protestations of conservative elements and without looking to the past for inspiration. On this point we should remember that the Louis XV style was violently attacked by traditionalists and purists, who saw the furniture's evocation of female forms as an offence against classical culture. Furthermore, while bibliotheques and armoires tend to be in solid wood, the unavoidable lot of rustic furniture, secretaires made their appearance at a time when the style was being attacked with greater violence. These followed the discovery of examples of classical art during the excavations undertaken in 1738 at Herculanum, a city buried by lava in the 1st century BC. The secretaire is thought to have emerged around 1750, which would explain both its rarity and shape. Its shape is regarded as linking it more closely to the future or past than to its own time: to the past because of the straight lines it managed to retain at a period when every design was expected to be rounded; to the future because of the popularity of its Louis XVI versions.

The characteristic straight lines of the secretaire *à abattant* can also be noted in the semainier and the very rare bureau *à cylindre*: the very rare commode-buffet is an exception as, despite its bombe appearance, it foreshadows the great popularity of Louis XVI-style buffets and the emergence of a true dining-room in which trestle tables were no longer used. To a lesser extent the

encoignure is also an exception, as its compact shape enables it to be almost entirely contained within a sinuous line.

Meubles à toutes faces

The vast range of furniture *à jour* includes a variety of small salon tables, with square, rectangular, round or oval tops, in which the Louis XV style manifests itself fully and easily. The small size of these pieces and the possibility of giving them a serpentine outline all the way round provide the style with its best opportunity for synthesis through the successful 'encircling' of their shape and decoration. The piece is no longer contained and limited by the geometrical shape of the cube, adopting a series of circles instead.

The bureau *à dos d'âne* is one of the style's masterpieces. Larger than the small tables, but still graciously proportioned, unlike the console it succeeds in being both functional and decorative.

We could continue this presentation by citing all the *meubles à toutes faces* (the table d'accouchée, the coiffeuse, the work table, etc.) with similar characteristics. These are independent pieces, easily recognisable by their shapes and decorations, which are unique in the history of furniture. They cannot be confused with *Régence* furniture, as small *tables à toutes faces* appeared only briefly in that style; the *Régence* style did not have the variety of Louis XV furniture and, where shape is concerned, its creations show deplorable structural rigidity. They can in no way be confused with pieces from the Louis XV–Louis XVI transitional style, as these fall roughly into two categories during the slow return to straight forms and, as we shall see later, offer furniture of a hybrid beauty, using sinuous lines in its lower parts and straight lines above.

Where Louis XV seating is concerned, it is impossible not to fall into the descriptive commonplaces that apply to *meubles à toutes faces*, simply repeating that the sinuous line flows everywhere, from legs to the seats and backs of chairs. And as if that were not enough, the style offers us a detailed study of the habits and positions adopted by the seated human body, inventing corresponding designs, as we have seen.

The great technical and artistic maturity that seating quite suddenly reached is certainly surprising given its slow development in relation to other types of furniture.

Just a few decades earlier Louis XIV seating, with its intransigently rigid forms, had appeared enslaved by centuries of almost unchanged structures. Nothing in such pieces hints at the possibility that in so brief a time it would be possible to reach the comfort of Louis XV chairs. Later seating would return to straight forms, but without losing sight of the fact that its main object was the comfort of those using it.

The different versions of day-beds leave us perplexed and indifferent. They are long, take up too much space and appear to be a compromise between the armchair and the bed proper. Their function partially prevents any possibility for the style to manifest itself in all its grace and lightness.

To conclude on the Louis XV style, it can be said that its most particular and original components are the abandonment of the rule of the straight line, which had characterised furniture up until that time, and the whimsical asymmetry of the decorations. The construction techniques and materials used represent the synthesis of all preceding developments. In later years the arrival of mahogany seemed to suggest to the Louis XVI style, and still more to the Empire style, which wood they should use for most of their creations.

But the force with which the Louis XV style distanced itself from traditional concepts – due too to its unconditional rejection by both conservative sections of society and intellectuals who found the new developments too disturbing – also made it the determining cause of the return to the past that was to be the hymn of faith of all later styles.

Definitively speaking, the Louis XV style was the last stage in the historical evolution of furniture, just as the Louis XVI style was the first stage in its involution. Subsequent periods would brood nostalgically on what had been, unable to exist independently and break all ties with the past.

Copies and imitations

The Louis XV style undeniably marked the peak of refinement in the whole history of furniture-making. Its truly original and astounding shapes and the precious materials used and combined with balance and great good taste have certainly contributed to the fact that, in the intervening years, unscrupulous cabinet-makers and dealers have skilfully transformed and embellished more modest pieces, bestowing on them an artistic worth that the original versions certainly lacked. In addition, the mid-19th century saw the reproduction of all the styles of the past, and the Louis XV style was no exception. On the contrary, it was the most imitated of all, due both to a reaction against the straight shapes of the first half of the 19th century and the quantity of authentic Louis XV furniture available. But the real reason for this return to the past was almost certainly the fact that the 19th century was unable to develop an original, likeable style that could erase the memory of the perfection of 18th century decoration and that of the Louis XV style in particular.

The Empire style aside, the 19th century furniture styles of the *Restauration*, Charles X, Louis-Philippe and the Second Empire imitate old shapes and decorations, with a few new variations and a technical virtuosity that cannot hide their gothic, Renaissance or baroque inspiration. The furniture of the 19th century is marked by hybridism and a mixture of styles, with a return to the shapes of the past and a complete lack of originality.

The revival of styles began around 1840 and continued until the dawn of the 20th century. At first imitations of the Louis XV style were timid and there was a preference for the gothic, Louis

XIV and *Régence* styles, but as the years went by the manufacture of perfect Louis XV reproductions gradually but noticeably increased until it reached almost industrial proportions.

There are two types of reproduction: those that remain faithful to their classic or fine quality models and those made with a degree of stylistic freedom, with individualised ormolu mounts, accentuated shapes and additional lacquers decorated with imaginative motifs that differ from those of the Louis XV style.

Today both the perfect copies and approximate imitations are remarkably highly valued on the market, due not just to the high cost of labour which now precludes the reproduction of the furniture of the past, but also because of the technical precision and precious materials with which these pieces were made.

Their value lies partly in their artistic qualities, partly in their historical value and partly in the skill of their workmanship; in other words it is based on the real cost of making similar pieces today, something which is impossible in practical terms.

Transformations and fakes

Over the centuries many pieces of furniture have been restored or transformed as their surroundings demanded: this is true, for example, of the large pharmacist's cupboard transformed into a bibliotheque, or the 17th-century commode put on sale as a commode with a fall-front.

But we should first draw a distinction between innocent falsification at the owner's request and that which is skilfully carried out to deceive the buyer.

The most frequently-found transformations involve modifying the piece with the aim of giving it greater artistic, and therefore commercial value. For example we quite frequently find pieces of provincial French furniture which have been raised to the level of Parisian pieces simply by replacing softwood drawers with drawers of oak

and mercury-gilding the mounts, which had originally been merely cast. These changes substantially increase the valuation put on the piece.

Identifying reworked sections and regilt ormolu mounts is a difficult business. If the 'restorer' has taken the trouble to replace the drawer linings with oak taken from antique wood coverings or the underside of a period rustic piece of modest value, the task is no easy one, even for an expert in the field. But even the most perfect crime always leaves a few clues. It may be difficult to identify drawers that have been remade with great skill, yet, to the eye of the connoisseur, mounts that have had their mercury-gilding replaced will reveal that the piece has been transformed.

It should be remembered that mercury-gilding was used until the arrival of chemical and industrial gilding processes around 1840. Even after this, however, traditional craftsmen continued to hand down the secrets of this kind of gilding from father to son, as it is superior in quality to all other processes past and present. Although banned by law due to the toxic mercury fumes it produces, it is still practised in France by a few craftsmen.

But if the mercury-gilding on an ormolu mount has been carried out or replaced during the 19th or 20th century, the mount must first have been placed in a purifying bath of acid, without which it would not have been possible to cover it with a uniform coat of the amalgam of gold and mercury. While this acid bath creates the optimal conditions for gilding, it also removes any trace of patina on the bronze, in other words it takes away the characteristic colour visible on the inner part of the mount, which was fixed to the furniture without being gilt. One therefore only has to take off the ormolu mount and look carefully at the colour on its inner edge to see whether there is any presence of a true patina, or whether it has been skilfully recreated using chemicals. Furthermore, an ormolu mount that has been recently mercury-gilt shows a total lack of the natural signs of ageing that appear on the typical gilding of ormolu dating from the 18th century. An antiques expert will not be fooled by signs of ageing that have been artificially simulated. It should be said that one cannot turn oneself into an expert on the basis of theoretical knowledge in a field where practical experience acquired over many years spent studying and examining hundreds of pieces is more important than any theory.

Provincial bureaux plats have sometimes been transformed in such complex ways that only an artist could have carried them out. They look very similar to Parisian bureaux plats, but with a few differences: they are sometimes more squat , their legs are more solid and, though they may be more curved than those of the *Régence* period, the piece as a whole has a certain heaviness of shape. In such cases the transformation will consist of removing all the veneer and slimming down the piece to make it finer and lighter, reshaping the entire body. The original veneer is then replaced, oak drawers are substituted for the original softwood and, if necessary, the ormolu mounts are regilt. When the work is finished we will have before us a 'Parisian' bureau plat which has doubled or even tripled its commercial value compared to that of the provincial bureau plat. If the transformations have been skilfully carried out, only a knowledgeable expert will be able to identify them.

However lacquered bureaux plats or those covered with floral inlays cannot be modified in this way. The original floral inlay cannot be adapted to fit a new shape, nor can the lacquer be removed from the body without the risk that it will crumble. If a piece of furniture with a more slender body has been veneered and redecorated with floral inlays, the expert will easily recognise the artificial patina.

Some classic Parisian pieces are also subjected to embellishments, consisting of inserting floral inlays or inlays of geometric designs into the original plain marquetry, followed by the addition of extensive mercury-gilt ormolu mounting.

Rustic seats, which often faithfully reproduce the shapes of Parisian style furniture despite their larger proportions, can be given artistic value through skilful carving to make their structures more slender. Any wormholes revealed by this reshaping can be hidden with filler. To conceal the newly-cut surface the chair is painted with a pale-grey or pale-blue varnish, these being colours that were in fashion in the Louis XV period. As a finishing touch the new colour will be skilfully dirtied to make it look old.

We have revealed some of the most commonly-found faking processes used on Louis XV furniture. These should always be regarded with a certain degree of indulgence, since they are usually embellishments to true antiques, represent work of a kind that very few people are able to recognise and, with a few exceptions, do not affect the artistic worth of a piece. In practice, when the transformation has been skilfully carried out, it becomes unrecognisable in the space of twenty years and the piece is readily bought and sold on the basis of its new value.

Matters are very different when we are dealing with replicas and copies of Louis XV furniture made in the 19th century and more or less skilfully disguised to be sold as original pieces. Such cases are examples of real deception, which should be deplored and combated without reserve.

Let us now consider the main deceptions practised and how to identify them. First of all, the Louis XV style furniture made in the 19th century began to take on an industrial appearance, primarily in the uniformity of the precious wood veneer which covered the carcases. These veneers were indeed no longer cut by hand, as they had been in the 18th century, but using mechanical saws. And while 18th century veneers are almost two millimetres thick, those of the 19th century are never thicker than one millimetre.

The most frequently-used coverings in the 18th and 19th centuries were of tulipwood or kingwood. These veneers were obtained from tropical trees of the Indies and Americas. Over the centuries the action of atmospheric agents turns tulipwood from pinkish to light brown and kingwood from purplish to dark brown. This natural colour is called the patina and it is undeniably the case that veneered furniture made in the 19th century has a much lighter patina than that made in the 18th century.

This is the reason why the veneer on 19th-century Louis XV furniture was artificially 'aged' to obtain a similar colour to that of 18th century veneers. Industrially-gilt ormolu was also skilfully dirtied. After this the pieces could be put up for sale as authentic items. While it is possible for the uninitiated to confuse a sow's ear with a silk purse, the same is not true of a knowledgeable expert, who will be able to tell, if only from the thickness of the veneer, that the piece is a fake.

However we should not confuse a fake piece with an authentic piece whose veneer has been restored by incompetent craftsmen. If a piece of furniture has been cleaned several times with emery board its veneer will have been thinned down to the point that it will resemble that of a 19th-century piece. Again in such cases only a knowledgeable expert will be able to give a trustworthy judgement after examining various details.

Seating made in the 19th century was manufactured by an industrial process in which the different elements were cut with mechanical saws. They were then given an artisanal look by skilful gouging on the inner surface of the seats, in other words the part that was not finished in the 18th century as it was hidden from view. In addition, in the 18th century the wooden parts of seats had interlocking joints and were held in place by means of wooden nails known as pegs or linchpins. These fixed the wooden seat pieces in clefts in the legs and were quite visible. In the 19th century these pins were replaced by wooden reinforcements inside the seat, which held the different pieces in place by means of an iron screw and glue.

The person carrying out the fake would then make a hole right through the legs and insert wooden pins similar to those made in the 18th century. He did not even have to worry about removing the reinforcements inside the seat, since all antique seating which has been restored and reinforced at a later date shows the same modern reinforcing technique. To complete the fake, beechwood or walnut seats would be skilfully dirtied with chemicals to obtain an 18th century patina, or else the whole piece would be repainted using colours in fashion in the Louis XV period and an attempt would be made to give the new colour an antique look.

We have already mentioned that 19th-century copies have attained remarkably high valuations; nevertheless their value is half or two-thirds that of an original piece.

Lastly we should mention copies of pieces by famous 18th-century cabinet-makers which were produced in the following century in limited numbers and then faked, stamped and sold as authentic pieces. Such deception is now a thing of the past, since both originals and replicas are extremely rare on the art market. The very high price of such works, when they are authentic, means that they appear only very occasionally in the most famous salerooms and in the shops of dealers operating at a very high level.

How to find Louis XV furniture

Where Parisian furniture is concerned, pieces termed as 'classic' can still be found fairly easily in antiques shops and salesrooms in Paris and elsewhere in France, less easily in London and New York and occasionally in Italian cities. With the passing of the years these pieces clearly become rarer and more expensive. Although a certain range of commodes veneered in precious tropical wood veneer and soberly mounted with ormolu, a few *bergeres* of the cabriolet type, some armchairs and caned chairs can still be found in the cities mentioned above, it is only occasionally that one comes across a secretaire, bureau plat or one of the small tables that are so typical of the period's love of society gatherings in the salons. The same cannot be said of fine quality furniture, even pieces stamped with the most prestigious names in French cabinet-making. By and large such pieces have been scattered to the four corners of the earth by the best-known antiques dealers and by special departments in the internationally-renowned auction houses, whose wares are put on view mainly in the run-up to Christmas and Easter in order to draw the largest possible number of collectors from around the world.

Where rustic and provincial furniture is concerned, the same observations apply as for classic pieces. The more elegant items are of course rarer and more expensive than those designed for use by the less wealthy.

Seats of all kinds, from the plainest to the most elegant, skilfully shaped and elaborately carved, are even rarer than other types of furniture and are thus harder to find. Pairs of *bergeres*, sets of six or more chairs and identical armchairs are more or less absent from all markets. *Fauteuils en cabriolet* are found only in pairs or singly. On the other hand canapes en corbeille and all kinds of canapes and chaises longues are easier to find, as they are less in demand from collectors. They are regarded as too big to fit in today's apartments and tend to be replaced by modern padded divans.

Quality and valuation

Where the valuation of Louis XV furniture is concerned, the two main factors to be considered are rarity and quality.

The rarity of a piece depends on the quantity in which that type was produced in the style and subsequently appeared on the market. Quality depends on the precious materials used in making the piece (tropical woods, chased ormolu mounts, refined carving and inlays) and the precision and elegance of its shape. The combination of these factors logically determines the value of a work of art.

Let us now take a few practical examples as a guide. Classic Parisian commodes with two drawers, *sans traverse*, simply veneered, with a marble top and sober ormolu mounting, have a value that is proportional to their more or less perfect, elegant shape and the quality of the woods used in the veneer. Rosewood veneer is less highly valued than tulipwood or kingwood. A commode whose rows of drawers are separated by traverses will have a lower price than that which has no traverse visible between each drawer. A commode with traverses veneered in rosewood will have a lower value than the same piece veneered in tulipwood or kingwood.

When we speak of classic pieces, we are not referring to a type of furniture that has no value, but to an entire category of pieces produced, with a few variations, on a grand scale. These form the major part of the Louis XV heritage in private collections, past and present, and their owners should rightly be proud of them. For, although these may not be very rare items of very great value, they nevertheless fall into the category of antique furniture of internationally recognised value. A rosewood commode with traverses and soberly mounted with ormolu is worth between £10,000 and £30,000: if it has an oak carcase, three rows of drawers and a veneer of precious wood, it represents an excellent investment, which will increase its value as the years go by, and it will also be a functional and very spacious cabinet. Furthermore, its presence in an interior that is otherwise entirely furnished with modern pieces will create no problems of harmonisation. The same is true of all pieces that can be termed classic.

The most important thing when buying a classic Louis XV piece is to check that the insides of all the drawers are made of oak or walnut, this being synonymous with quality. If they are not, but are made instead of beechwood, poplar or some other wood, this means that the piece is provincial and, even if it dates from the Louis XV period, will have a lower value than that of a Parisian piece. In addition it is also important to make sure that the piece is not one of those described as 'late'. This is a familiar term much used by some antiques dealers to describe pieces in styles from any period that were made fifty or a hundred years after that period came to an end.

Moving now from classic Parisian commodes to fine commodes, decorated with floral inlays or lacquer and mounted with valuable ormolu, we must consider not just the quality but the fact that, given that they were created especially for a demanding, refined clientele, these pieces are inevitably very rare and costly.

If we want to reach the highest point on the scale of quality and rarity where commodes are concerned, we must consider the output of the major French cabinet-makers of the period, such as Jean-François Oeben, Antoine-Robert Gaudreaus, the Migeons, Jacques Dubois, BVRB and Mathieu and Antoine-Mathieu Criard. Commodes bearing the stamp of one of these people, or of other prestigious names in French cabinet-making, now appear only rarely on the international art market (Paris, London, New York), where they are very highly valued and easily attain prices of hundreds of thousands of pounds for a single piece.

The observations we have made in relation to commodes also apply to all the characteristic types of furniture in this style, whether lacquered or veneered: secretaires, encoignures, bureaux plats, bureaux *à dos d'âne* (very highly-prized as they are the most successful of the new Louis XV creations), bureaux *à cylindre*, small salon tables, small work tables, night tables, consoles, mirrors, armoires, semainiers and coiffeuses.

However in the case of lacquered pieces, in addition to the shape and ormolu mounts, the colour must be taken into account. French lacquered furniture is generally decorated with Chinese or floral subjects on a black lacquer background; those with a background of ivory, pale green or red lacquer are rarer and thus very highly sought-after and expensive. Among the lacquered and veneered pieces that reach very high valuations due to their rarity we should mention

small salon tables, work tables, bureaux *à dos d'âne*, bureaux plats and secretaires.

Given the quantity of mercury-gilt ormolu mounts used as a complementary decorative element on French furniture, we should briefly discuss the real importance of their gilding and their authenticity.

This is a question that has always given rise to great discussions and debates among the experts.

Let us consider the case of a classic secretaire. The ormolu mounts are confined to a few essential elements: sabots, chutes, escutcheons and apron. The fact that the gilding on these mounts looks 'very tired', to use a common term of antiques jargon, is of comparatively minor importance given that the secretaire's value is not determined by the ormolu mounts. On the contrary the ormolu mounts of a classic secretaire, or any other Parisian piece, are a complementary factor of modest aesthetic importance. The crucial factors remain the shape and veneer. In the same way, even if the ormolu mounts have been regilt or remade in the style, their presence has no noticeable effect on the price of the piece.

On the other hand, if we take a commode, bureau plat or secretaire, whether lacquered or veneered, whose shape is emphasised by a wealth of ormolu mounts, it is very important to check that these mounts are original and their mercury gilding must be replaced when they are 'very tired'. The reasons for this are obvious: in such cases the value of the piece is determined not only by the shape and veneer, but also by the ormolu mounts.

In some cases such decoration is more important than the veneer itself as an indicator of value and quality; as a result, in the final analysis the value of such a piece is determined almost entirely by the shape and the ormolu mounts. Where high quality furniture is concerned, attention should also be paid to the quality of the chasing of the ormolu mounts themselves. However, with a few very rare exceptions, in Louis XV furniture this does not attain the degree of finesse and precision that we shall find in the Louis XVI style.

Turning now to rustic furniture, only decorated pieces are valued at levels worthy of interest. There is however a fair degree of demand for plain rustic pieces, or those destined for use by the lower classes, as certain types of commode, buffets and chairs of this type are priced only slightly above contemporary pieces of a similar nature and, unlike the latter, are more solid and will retain their value down the years. Provincial pieces with veneer or floral inlays are valued well, particularly in their place of origin, although they do not have a value on the international market. The exception to this are stamped pieces or those that are attributed to the great provincial cabinet-makers such as Hache of Grenoble.

Where seats are concerned, given their greater rarity, mentioned above, they are always valued very highly. A set of six chairs or six *fauteuils en cabriolet* can attain exorbitant sums in international salesrooms. When chairs stamped by Delanois, Avisse, Gourdin or the very famous Tilliard are put up for auction, they reach record sums. The artistic, social and financial repercussions of these sales send ripples through newspapers and specialist magazines.

The same can be said of rustic seats, whose prices tend to level off at values more closely reflecting their craftsmanship, without artistic pretensions. This makes them more accessible to clients who are interested in acquiring a piece that is simply pleasant and functional rather than rare and valuable.

Generally speaking, the state of preservation is an important factor in the value of any kind of seat. Chairs, stools and canapes in natural wood (beech or walnut) that are badly worm-eaten are not advisable purchases and their value in comparison to a similar piece that has been excellently preserved is noticeably lower.

Gilt seats are valued at lower prices than those in natural waxed wood of similar artistic quality. For example, six *fauteuils en cabriolet* in natural waxed beechwood with Aubusson tapestry showing motifs from La Fontaine's fables are worth far more than they would be if they were gilt. In general there is a low level of demand for gilt furniture of any period. This is a question of fashion rather than of style or aesthetics, and may be a good reason to buy quality pieces at prices that are still affordable. Far from diminishing the elegance of furnishings, gilt brings a touch of colour to the whole and may, in the long term, prove to have been an excellent investment. Finely carved and gilt consoles do not look out of place in a hall or drawing-room and they are currently valued at lower levels than consoles in natural oak. Antique pieces should not be regarded only as safe investments, so that one purchases only the most sought-after pieces and sometimes runs the risk of paying over the odds. It is important to use discernment, caution and common sense when buying, sometimes opting for a piece that is not currently in great demand but which may soon become so.

In the antiques trade general rules are useful only in assessing the clearest and most commonly-found cases. The exceptions and quantities produced, not to mention each producer's imaginative interpretations, are such that each piece must be analysed, studied and valued on its own merits. In doing this the three main factors that determine both its artistic and economic value, and should always be borne in mind, are shape, materials and type of decoration.

As we have noted, Louis XV furniture is very highly valued and sought-after throughout France and the world as a whole. It is, without question, a safe investment. Yet, paradoxically, it is very often valued more highly in the London auction houses than in Paris. This does not mean that the French do not appreciate the true value of their artistic heritage, but it is undeniably the case that in London the art market has risen beyond all expectations. The quality and prestige of 18th-century French decoration are such that they have given rise to flourishing markets even outside their own country.

It is in London, and less frequently in Monte Carlo, that the most precious pieces reach the highest values. This phenomenon is confined to public auctions, where the competitive spirit of the buyers is often the main cause of this sometimes irrational inflation where prices are concerned.

In Italy on the other hand, for the last decade or so no quality Louis XV furniture has been imported. This has prevented the development of a taste for things French among Italian collectors. The exception to this rule are the Piedmontese, whose culture and affinities bring them closer to their transalpine 'cousins'. The same is true of an elite of collectors on the international level, whose tastes have been cultivated in the museums of Europe and the world's best-known antiques shops, without any provincialism or silly chauvinism.

Today in Italy the trade in Louis XV furniture of the classic type, most of which comes from for-mer private collections, is starting to flourish. Nor is there any lack of quality pieces, which sometimes appear in antiques shops and salesrooms.

In Italy valuations are much lower than they are in France. The French dealers are well aware of this, since they go to Italy to buy and, ironically, it is not uncommon for an exceptional commode or secretaire on display in a shopwindow in Rome, Milan or Turin to cross back over the Alps to take pride of place in the shop of a dealer in Paris or London, before returning some time later, in the possession of an Italian buyer, to Rome, Milan or Turin. Of course in the meantime the piece has acquired its proper value.

But, anecdotes aside, it is undeniably the case that, with a few exceptions, in Italy French furniture is valued at less than its true value.

Fine two-drawer commode *sans traverse*, with *brèche d'Alep* marble top. The front has three segments with floral inlays. The sober ormolu mounting and elegant shape make this a piece of very high quality.
Sold in Paris in 1970: £ 3,100, $ 5,300.
1984 valuation: £ 23,200, $ 30,780.
Current valuation: collector's price.

Fine small commode in black and polychrome Chinese lacquer, extensively mounted with ormolu, bearing the stamp of P. Roussel.
Sold in Paris in 1970: £ 5,750, $ 9,900.
1984 valuation: £ 27,500, $ 36,480.
Current valuation: collector's price.

Below: Fine commode of exceptional quality, with two drawers sans traverse, tulipwood veneer and floral inlays in kingwood, bearing the stamp of P. Roussel. The harmonious, flowing lines of this commode are a quintessential reflection of the Louis XV style in its finest interpretation.
Current valuation: collector's price.

Fine commode extensively mounted with ormolu, floral inlays and *brèche d'Alep* marble top. Of particular note are the ormolu mounts giving the impression that the commode has doors in place of drawers. Sold in Paris in 1970: £ 10,600, $ 18,400.
1984 valuation: £ 29,200, $ 38,760. Current valuation: collector's price.

Fine commode with two drawers sans traverse and a *brèche d'Alep* marble top. The tulipwood and amaranth decoration is enhanced with refined foliate inlays. The sober ormolu mounting makes this a quality piece. Sold in Paris in 1975: £ 6,200, $ 12,800. 1984 valuation: £ 21,500, $ 28,500. Current valuation: collector's price.

Below: extremely rare, fine buffet with a marble top. Kingwood and amaranth veneer, the side and front panels with losenge inlays. Soberly mounted with ormolu. This buffet is regarded as the ancestor of the Louis XVI buffet and half-moon commode.
Current valuation: collector's price.

Classic commode with two drawers sans traverse and a marble top. Kingwood and tulipwood veneer with a cube design, little sought-after by collectors. Soberly mounted with elegant chased ormolu and bearing the stamp of Dubois. 1984 valuation: £ 4,300, $ 5,700. 1991 valuation: £ 9,000, $ 15,900.
Current valuation: £ 10,200, $ 16,900, € 15,250.

Below: small three-drawer commode with traverses. The fairly common shape is enlivened with floral inlays and soberly mounted with ormolu, partially mitigating its classic aspect. Sold in Paris in 1972: £ 1980, $ 3400. 1984 valuation: £ 7,740, $ 10,260. 1991 valuation: £ 20,000, $ 35,400.
Current valuation: £ 15,300, $ 25,350, € 22,880.

Fine small commode with two drawers sans traverse and a *brèche d'Alep* marble top. The commode is given great finesse by a delicate floral decoration in black and polychrome Chinese lacquer.
1984 valuation: £ 25,800, $ 34,200.
Current valuation: collector's price.

Fine small commode having two drawers with traverse and a marble top, veneered in kingwood and tulipwood with an exuberant floral motif. Sold in London in 1976: £ 3,600, $ 7,500. 1984 valuation: £ 8,600, $ 11,400. 1991 valuation: £ 20,000, $ 35,400.
Current valuation: £ 15,300, $ 25,350, € 22,880.

Fine commode with a marble top, two drawers *sans traverse* and exuberant floral decoration. The slightly rustic floral inlay partially reveals its 17th-century Flemish origins. It bears the stamp of Rubestuck. Sold in Paris in 1974: £ 5,500, $ 11,400. 1984 valuation: £ 27,500, $ 36,480. Current valuation: collector's price.

Fine commode with two drawers sans traverse and a *brèche d'Alep* marble top. The precious wood veneer has a rich floral decoration with an inlaid scrolled surround. The chased ormolu mounts are marked with a crowned 'c', indicating a tax imposed on the corporations of chasers and bronze gilders by Louis XV between 1745 and 1749. There is a notable absence of ormolu handles, which would overload the marquetry. Sold in Paris in 1973: about £ 5,200, $ 11,000. 1984 valuation: £ 32,250, $ 42,750. Current valuation: collector's price.

Fine commode bearing the stamp of Criard. The geometrical decoration is still in the *Régence* style, although the shape of the commode and the ormolu mounts suggest that it is a creation of the early Louis XV style. Sold in Paris in 1972: £ 19,800, $ 35,500. 1984 valuation: £ 21,500, $ 28,500. 1991 valuation: £ 46,000, $ 81,400. Current valuation: £ 51,000, $ 84,500, € 76,250.

Fine commode veneered in tulipwood and rosewood, with floral inlays and a *brèche d'Alep* marble top. 1984 valuation: £ 34,400, $ 45,600. Current valuation: collector's price.

Fine commode with two drawers *sans traverse* and a *brèche d'Alep* marble top. Kingwood and amaranth veneer. The commode has an elegant decoration of inlaid foliage and flowers. The ormolu mounting is sober but refined. The commode bears the stamp of Hansen. 1984 valuation: £ 25,800, $ 34,200.
Current valuation: collector's price.

Fine commode with two drawers *sans traverse* and a marble top. The shape, veneer in precious exotic woods, floral inlays and extensive chased ormolu mounting make this a very high quality piece. Sold in New York in 1976: £ 17,000, $ 35,000. 1984 valuation: £ 77,400, $ 102,600. Current valuation: collector's price.

Fine commode with two drawers *sans traverse*. The proportions, lightness of the designs on the veneer and sober, refined ormolu mounting are of particular note.
Current valuation; £ 91,800, $ 152,100, € 137,250.

Fine commode with a *brèche d'Alep* marble top. It has two drawers sans traverse, a curved shape and finely executed marquetry and is extensively mounted with ormolu. Current valuation: collector's price.

Fine Chinese lacquered encoignure, one of a pair, with a marble top. The beauty of these encoignures stems from their extremely rich ormolu mounting. 1984 valuation: £ 43,000, $ 57,000. Current valuation: collector's price.

Fine encoignure, one of a pair. The curved shape, floral inlays and ormolu mounts enhance its value. 1984 valuation: £ 25,800, $ 34,200. Current valuation: collector's price.

Extremely rare, fine encoignure with clock, veneered in satinwood and extensively mounted with ormolu, bearing the stamp of J. Dubois. The valuation reached by this commode can be attributed to the variety and quality of the ormolu mounts, which dominate and almost obscure its shape. (Photo Sotheby Parke Bernet).
Sold in Monte Carlo in 1979: £ 846,300, $ 1,980,500. A record price for furniture at that time.
Current valuation: collector's price.

Encoignure, one of a pair, partly classic and partly fine quality, with a marble top. The floral inlay covers three panels, enhancing the shape of the piece. Sold in Milan in 1973: £ 4,000, $ 7,400.
1984 valuation: £ 17,200, $ 22,800.
1991 valuation:, £ 26,000, $46,000.
Current valuation, £ 30,600, $ 50,700. € 45,750.

B*elow*: important fine quality console with red breccia top. A curved shape in wood carved with shells, leaves and flowers. It stands on four curved supports, joined by a stretcher decorated with animals. Sold in Paris in 1971: £ 4,400, $ 7,600.
1984 valuation: £ 12,900, $ 17,100.
Current valuation: collector's price.

Coromandel lacquered encoignure, one of a pair. The polychrome decorative subjects are enhanced by elegant ormolu mounts.
1984 valuation: £ 25,800, $ 34,200.
Current valuation: collector's price.

Fine encoignure, one of a pair, with a marble top. The contrast of colours between the exuberant floral decoration on a tulipwood ground and the kingwood surround is of particular note. Sold in 1970: £ 2,000, $ 3,400. 1984 valuation: £ 17,200, $ 22,800. 1991 valuation: £ 37,000, £ 65,500. Current valuation £ 25,500, $ 42,250, € 38,100.

Classic encoignure, one of a pair, with a marble top. The plain veneer and sober ormolu mounting make this an ordinary piece, but its purity of style makes it worthy of consideration. 1984 valuation: £ 6,450, $ 8,550. 1991 valuation: £ 17,000, $ 30,100. Current valuation: £ 5,100, $ 8,450, € 7,600.

Fine encoignure, one of a pair, with a marble top and kingwood and tulipwood veneer. The slightly rustic floral inlays partly reveal its 17th-century Flemish origins. It bears the stamp of Jacques Dubois. Sold in Paris in 1972 : £ 3,300, $ 6,000. 1984 valuation: £ 17,200, $ 22,800. 1991 valuation: £ 37,000, .$ 65,500. Current valuation: £ 30,600, $ 50,700, € 45,750.

Fine encoignure, one of a pair, with a marble top. The beaty of this piece stems from its curved shape, emphasised by ormolu mounts, and foliate inlays. Current valuation: collector's price.

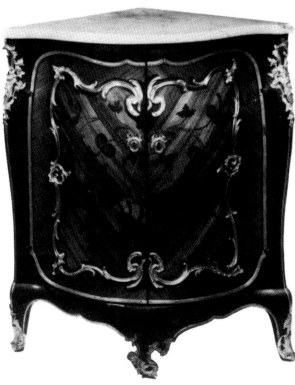

Fine salon furniture consisting of six armchairs with flat backs known as *fauteuils à la reine* ('queen's armchairs') and a *canapé à oreilles* of excellent quality. Covered in period tapestries representing fables by La Fontaine. Of particular note are the elegant shape, unusual carvings and 'whiplash' armrests. Bearing the stamp of Père Gourdin, master carpenter in Paris in 1737. Provenance: Château de Condé, collection of the Marquis de Sade.
Current valuation: collector's price.

Fine commode from the first period of the Louis XV style, attributed to Carel, in Chinese lacquer and vernis Martin lacquer with floral and bird motifs. Richly mounted with chased ormolu. Attributed to Carel due to the similarity of its ormolu mounts and shape with those of other, signed commodes, now held in private collections.
Sold by Sotheby's in Monte Carlo in 1992: £ 387,590, $ 680,170.
Current valuation: collector's price.

Fine commode in black lacquer with red and gold landscape in the Chinese fashion. Sold by Sotheby's in New York in 1993: £ 170,500, $ 256,100. Current valuation: collector's price.

Two almost identical, fine commodes of exceptional quality from the Louis XV period, bearing the stamp of BVRB (Bernard II Van Risen Burgh, died c. 1765), master cabinet-maker in Paris in 1737, in Chinese lacquer with a red ground and a decoration of landscapes.

Pieces in red or beige lacquer are particularly rare and highly-prized by collectors. There are slight differences between the ormolu mounts and side panels on the two commodes. Sold by Sotheby's in Monte Carlo in 1996: £ 1,168,800, $ 1,818,400.
Current valuation: collector's price.

Fine commode of exceptional quality in black Chinese lacquer with landscape motifs, bearing the stamp of J. P. Latz, special cabinet-maker to Louis XV. Of particular note is the extensive ormolu mounting, which Latz had chased in his own workshop. In so doing he contravened the regulations imposed by the casters' corporations, which ordered a seizure in 1749. However Latz's ormolu mounts were imitated and reproduced by other cabinet-makers. Few lacquered pieces by this artist are known. Sold by Etude Tajan in Paris in 1996: £ 282,780, $ 440,000.
Current valuation: collector's price.

Fine commode of exceptional quality with floral inlays on a tulipwood ground. Noteworthy for the extensive ormolu mounting enhancing all the structures of the piece.
Current valuation: collector's price.

Fine, rare table à mécanismes, with floral inlays in imitation tortoise-shell on a ground of satinwood, bearing the stamp of J. F. Oeben, master cabinet-maker in 1761 and cabinet-maker to the king in 1754.

Sold by Sotheby's in Monte Carlo in 1996: £ 314,200, $ 488,800. Current valuation: collector's price.

Fine writing table in tulipwood and amaranth veneer, the top with floral inlay.

Sold by Sotheby's in London in 1991: £ 50,000, $ 88,500, at the same time as another very similar piece dating from the 19th century. Current valuation: collector's price.

Fine secretaire of exceptional quality, bearing the stamp of BVRB (Bernard II Van Risen Burgh), master cabinet-maker in Paris around 1737. The secretaire is veneered in tulipwood inlaid with a floral motif in kingwood. Of particular note are the refined chased ormolu mounts, which enhance both the shape and decoration. This secretaire was bought in 1763 by the merchant Poirier for the Count of Coventry. Sold by Sotheby's in Monte Carlo in 1996: £ 565,570, $ 879,900. Current valuation: collector's price.

Pair of fine encoignures in European imitation Chinese lacquer, with landscape motifs and extensively mounted with ormolu, bearing the stamp of J.B. Hedouin, master cabinet-maker in Paris in 1738.

Sold by Etude Tajan in Paris in 1996: £ 157,100, $ 244,400. Current valuation: collector's price.

Fine encoignure, one of a pair, in tulipwood with floral inlay and *brèche d'Alep* marble top, bearing the stamp of J. Holthausen, master cabinet-maker in Paris in 1764.

Sold in Paris in 1975: £ 9,100, $ 18,700. Sold in Milan in 1983: £ 15,170, $ 22,970. Sold in 1990: £ 25,800, $ 45,900. Current valuation: £ 35,700, $ 59,000, € 53,380.

Fine console in carved giltwood. Of particular note for the finesse of its carvings, which in no way detract from the sinuous shapes.

Sold by Etude Tajan in Paris in 1996: £ 56,550, $ 87,990. Current valuation: collector's price.

Rare, fine bureau plat in Chinese lacquer and satinwood of exceptional quality, bearing the stamp of BVRB (Bernard II Van Risen Burgh), master around 1735. Made of oak, with three walnut drawers with runners underneath; the drawer fronts and sides are decorated with Chinese lacquered panels and satinwood bands extending over the entire surface of the legs. Extensively mounted with ormolu. Current valuation: collector's price.

Fine secretaire in tulipwood and amaranth, with floral inlays and *brèche d'Alep* marble top, bearing the stamp of F. Rubestuck, master cabinet-maker in Paris in 1766. Of particular note is its shape, reminiscent of a violin, which is extremely rare and prized by collectors.

Sold in Paris in 1984: £ 21,500, $ 28,500.
Current valuation: £ 30,600, $ 50,700, € 45,750.

Fine bureau of exceptional quality in tulipwood and amaranth veneer with inlaid flower-covered branches. The piece is stamped twice with the initials BVRB (Bernard II Van Risen Burgh), master cabinet-maker in Paris around 1735. Richly mounted with chased, mercury-gilt ormolu mounts.

Sold by Sotheby's in London in 1991: £ 300,000, $ 507,000. Current valuation: collector's price.

Rare pair of fine commodes with serpentine facades and two drawers *sans traverse*, fine floral inlays in panels on a ground of tulipwood, double surrounds in kingwood with foliate motifs. The commodes are extensively mounted with rocaille ormolu, including fixed handles and chutes with a small central cartouche. They bear the stamp of REIZELL. Louis XV period.
Current valuation: collector's price.

Important bureau plat with a serpentine apron in satinwood veneer with floral panels on an amaranth ground; fine rocaille ormolu mounts and exceptional scrolled sabots. The bureau bears the stamp of LATZ. Louis XV period.
Current valuation: collector's price.

Rare commode of exceptional quality with two drawers *sans traverse*, decorated with Chinese motifs on a ground of yellow lacquer. Of particular note is the extensive ormolu mounting surrounding the lively scenes. The commode bears the stamp of Rubestuck.

(Photo: Tajan, Paris). Sold in Paris in 1975: £ 61,700, $ 127,400. 1984 valuation: £ 86,000, $ 114,000. Current valuation: collector's price.

Fine Louis XV commode with two drawers *sans traverse*, decorated with Chinoiseries on a black lacquered ground.
Sold in London in 1988:, £ 205,750, $ 365,760.
Current valuation: collector's price.

Exceptional commode in kingwood veneer, with floral inlays and extensively mounted with ormolu.
Sold in Paris in 1984: £ 95,100, $ 126,000.
Current valuation: collector's price.

Opposite: commode of exceptional quality in black and gold Chinese lacquer, with two drawers *sans traverse*. The ormolu mounts which enclose the lively scenes are extremely fine. This detail of decorative technique, highly prized by collectors, gives the piece its value. (Photo: Tajan, Paris). Sold in Paris in 1978: £ 97,000, $ 218,000.
Current valuation: collector's price.

Commode of exceptional quality in satinwood and amaranth veneer, extensively mounted with ormolu, bearing the stamp of BVRB.
Sold in Paris in 1981: £ 52,440, $ 105,540.
1984 valuation: £ 64,500, $ 85,500.
Current valuation: collector's price.

Fine commode with two drawers *sans traverse*, in tulipwood veneer, with floral inlays and elegant ormolu mounts, bearing the stamp of C. Maclard, master cabinet-maker in Paris in 1742.
Sold in 1986: £ 43,650, $ 64,000. Current valuation: collector's price.

Below: rare, fine commode of exceptional quality in red lacquer (vernis Martin), decorated with Chinoiseries. This commode is remarkably elegant, with two drawers sans traverse and very fine chased ormolu mounts enhancing its every detail. (Photo: M. Meyer, Paris). Current valuation: collector's price.

Rare, fine commode of exceptional quality in tulipwood and kingwood veneer, with floral inlays in coloured wood, bearing the stamp of M. Criard, master cabinet-maker in Paris in 1738. Of special note are the curves and wealth of chased ormolu mounts enhancing its every detail. Current valuation: collector's price.

Fine commode with two drawers *sans traverse*, in amaranth and tulipwood veneer with floral inlays in coloured wood, surrounded by large cartouches. The ormolu mounts and the balance of the curved shape are remarkably elegant.
Current valuation: collector's price.

Below: fine commode with two drawers sans traverse, in tulipwood veneer with cartouche surrounds in amaranth. The floral decoration is in horizontally-cut kingwood. The harmonious, flowing curves give the commode a perfectly elegant shape.
Current valuation: collector's price.

Rare, fine small commode with two drawers *sans traverse*, in tulipwood and kingwood veneer with floral inlays in coloured wood, bearing the stamp of P. Roussel. The piece is enhanced by a wealth of chased ormolu mounts.
Current valuation: collector's price.

Fine encoignure, one of a pair, in amaranth veneer with floral inlays. Of particular note is the wealth of ormolu mounting enhancing the contours of the piece, which bears the stamp of J.P. Latz. These encoignures come from the Château d'Eu and were part of the collection of the Duc de Vendôme, then of the collection of André-Vincent and lastly of the collection of Comte Moulin de Rochefort. (Photo: Sotheby Parke Bernet).

Sold in Monte Carlo in 1979: £ 300,000, $ 685,000.

Current valuation: collector's price.

Pair of fine, small cabinets in rosewood veneer, with *brèche d'Alep* marble tops, bearing the stamp of Wolff. (Photographed from front and back). Provenance: the collection of Prince Paul of Yugoslavia, sold with the furniture of the Villa Demidoff in 1969. Current valuation: collector's price.

Fine commode with two drawers *sans traverse*, in kingwood veneer with floral inlays in pale wood, bearing the stamp of N. Tuard, master cabinet-maker in Paris in 1741. The wealth of chased ormolu mounts emphasises the shape of the piece. Current valuation: collector's price.

Fine bureau plat with its *cartonnier* ('filing cabinet'). Kingwood veneer decorated with Chinese lacquered panels with motifs of landscapes and flowers. The presence of the *cartonnier* is rare and raises the price of bureaux plats. This bureau bears the stamp of Dubut. Jean-François Dubut must have had the king as his patron, since he was able to stamp his creations as a cabinet-maker without acquiring a master's qualification. Provenance: Hamilton Rice collection (Photo: Tajan, Paris). Sold in 1974: £ 81,300, $ 160,000. Current valuation: collector's price.

Opposite bottom: rare, fine bureau plat, bearing the stamp of BVRB (Bernard II Van Risen Burgh), one of the greatest cabinet-makers in the reign of Louis XV. The bureau has three drawers and a veneer of *file de rose* tulipwood (a particular cut of the wood creating the effect of many threads) inlaid with a foliate motif. Of particular note is the rich, asymmetrical ormolu mounting characteristic of the style and particularly the five-sided cabriole legs, a design detail that considerably raises the financial and aesthetic value of the piece. Sold in Paris in 1974: £ 50,600, $ 99,400.
Current valuation: collector's price.

Fine bureau plat, with tulipwood and amaranth veneer and fine chased ormolu mounts, bearing the stamp of Criard, master cabinet-maker in Paris in 1738. The inlaid losenge design is characteristic of the *Régence* period. (Photo: M. Meyer, Paris).
Current valuation: collector's price.

Fine bureau plat of exceptional quality in Chinese lacquer with a black and gold ground and gold decorative motifs of figures, flowers, birds and fruit. The harmoniously curved shape and extensive chased ormolu mounts are particularly fine. (Photo: M. Segoura, Paris). Provenance: Goldschmidt-Rothschild sale, Berlin 1931.
Sold in Paris in 1983: £ 239,600, $ 362,800.
Current valuation: collector's price.

Fine bureau plat in tulipwood and amaranth veneer with floral inlays in green-coloured wood. Mounted with elegant, refined, chased ormolu. The vertical and horizontal curves of the overall shape are typical of the Louis XV style.
Current valuation: collector's price.

Below: bureau plat of high quality, in precious, exotic wood veneer, richly mounted with chased ormolu.
Sold in Paris in 1981: £ 39,200, $ 79,000.
Current valuation: collector's price.

Fine bureau plat of exceptional quality, in black lacquered wood, red tortoiseshell veneer and brass foliate inlays. Stamped in ink under the top, 'LATZ FECIT MDCCXLIV' (1744). J.P. Latz was awarded the title of special cabinet-maker to the king, which allowed him to ignore the rules imposed by his corporation and to stamp his creations without paying the accompanying tax. (Photo: Tajan, Paris).
Sold in Paris in 1990: £ 768,700, $ 1,368,000.
Current valuation: collector's price.

Fine bureau plat in tulipwood and kingwood veneer, richly mounted with chased ormolu, bearing the stamp of H. Hansen, master cabinet-maker in Paris in 1747. The ormolu mounts have a crowned 'c' mark (1745-1749). (Photo: M. Meyer, Paris).
Current valuation: collector's price.

Below: rare bureau plat of exceptional quality, with satinwood and amaranth veneer, bearing the stamp of BVRB. (Photo: Sotheby Parke Bernet). Provenance: Rodolphe Kann, Paris; Yale University; Winston Guest collection; Parke Bernet sale 1967. Sold in Monte Carlo in 1979: £ 275,400, $ 645,000.
1984 valuation: £ 180,600, $ 239,400.
Current valuation: collector's price.

Fine bureau plat of exceptional quality, with satinwood veneer and kingwood floral decoration and extensively mounted with chased ormolu marked with a crowned 'c'. The bureau bears the stamp of Jacques Dubois, master cabinet-maker in Paris in 1740. (Photo: M. Meyer, Paris).
Current valuation: collector's price.

Fine bureau plat of exceptional quality, in satinwood and rosewood veneer, the floral decorations with tulipwood surrounds. The refined ormolu mounting emphasises and enhances the overall value of the piece.

It bears the stamp of Latz, master cabinet-maker by royal decree. Current valuation: collector's price.

Small table of exceptional quality in tulipwood and amaranth veneer, with fine inlays, bearing the stamp of J.P. Latz. Of particular note are the curved front and half-moon back. This fine piece is one of the few examples of asymmetry in shape. In Louis XV furniture as a whole, asymmetry was generally used in the ormolu mounts and lacquered or inlaid decoration. (Photo: M. Segoura, Paris).
1984 valuation: £ 32,000, $ 42,500.
Current valuation: collector's price.

Opposite: bureau *dos d'âne* of exceptional quality, in tulipwood veneer with black lacquered panels showing polychrome motifs of flowers, foliage and birds of oriental inspiration. It bears the stamp of E. Doirat, master cabinet-maker in Paris under Louis XV. The refined ormolu mounts enhance the shape of the piece.
Current valuation: collector's price.

Rare, fine bureau *à cylindre* of exceptional quality, in the late Louis XV style, with sycamore veneer and marquetry in several woods and coloured woods showing Chinese figures, parrots, flowers and ribbons. With its harmonious shape that draws the eye, this bureau is undoubtedly the work of David Roentgen. (Photo: M. Segoura, Paris). Provenance: Abdy collection.
Sold in Paris in 1984: £ 308,100, $ 408,400.
Current valuation: collector's price.

Fine bureau *dos d'âne* in Chinese lacquer with a black and gold ground and motifs of oriental figures and landscapes. Elegant chased ormolu mounts. It bears the stamp of Dubois, master cabinet-maker in Paris in 1742. (Photo: M. Meyer, Paris).
Current valuation: collector's price.

Rare, fine small table in tulipwood and kingwood veneer with floral inlays in coloured wood. On one side the drawer conceals a small leather-bound writing surface, on the other a mirror. The curved shape is exceptionally elegant.
Current valuation: collector's price.

Rare, fine small salon table, in exotic walnut and amaranth veneer with motifs of flowers and chinoiseries. All its profiles are in ivory. Chinese motifs are particularly prized by collectors.
Current valuation: collector's price.

Rare, fine small table in tulipwood veneer, with floral inlays in kingwood. The sliding top hides a drawer with a *pupitre* or reading stand. This table is particularly noteworthy for its concave front and convex back, an asymmetry typical of the Louis XV style.
Current valuation: collector's price.

Extremely rare games table of exceptional quality. The top has a removable lid in tulipwood veneer inlaid with a snakes and ladders board, and contains a trictrac board. (Photo: Sotheby Parke Bernet). Sold in Monte Carlo in 1979: £ 13,200, $ 90,800. 1984 valuation: £ 11,180, $ 14,800. 1991 valuation: £ 17,500, $ 30,975. Current valuation: £ 40,800, $ 67,600, € 61,000.

Below left: fine trictrac table in tulipwood and kingwood veneer with a chessboard inlaid in the top. The table's elegant shape is of particular note. 1991 valuation: £ 23,000, $ 40,700. Current valuation: £ 18,360, $ 30,400, € 27,450.

Right: rare, fine small table, in tulipwood and amaranth veneer, with floral inlays in coloured wood on all surfaces. The four canted corners give the table great elegance. Current valuation: collector's price.

Fine encoignure, one of a pair, with a *brèche d'Alep* marble top. The ormolu mounts, curved shape and floral inlays enhance the elegance and rarity of this pair of encoignures.
Current valuation: collector's price.

Rare, elegant small giltwood console. 1984 valuation: £ 3,180, $ 4,200. 1991 valuation: £ 7,000, $ 12,400.
Current valuation: £ 6,600, $ 10,980, € 9,900.

Encoignure of exceptional quality, one of a pair, in Chinese lacquer with a top of *brèche d'Alep* marble. Lacquer with a red ground is rare and precious. Of particular note are the decorative Chinese scenes with pagodas, enhanced by elegant ormolu mounts.
Sold in Paris in 1973: £ 5,680, $ 10,550.
Current valuation: collector's price.

Rare, fine console in natural oak with a marble top.
1984 valuation: £ 6,400, $ 8,550.
1991 valuation: £ 19,000, $ 33,600.
Current valuation: £ 18,360, $ 30,400, € 27,450.

Fine console d'appui, one of a pair, in giltwood with a purple breccia marble top. Consoles of this type are very rare, expensive and highly-prized by collectors for the display of Chinese objects, statuettes, porcelain etc. 1984 valuation: £ 4,900, $ 6,500.
1991 valuation: £ 7,500, $ 13,270.
Current valuation: £ 15,300, $ 25,300, € 22,880.

Classic bureau plat. This piece lacks elegance and balance, despite its curved shape. 1984 valuation: £ 17,200, $ 22,800.
1991 valuation: £ 39,000, $ 69,000.
Current valuation: £ 35,700, $ 59,100, € 53,380.

Fine bureau plat with extensive ormolu mounting.
Current valuation: collector's price.

Fine small salon table with floral inlays and refined ormolu mounts. It bears the stamp of BVRB. Current valuation: collector's price.

Fine small bureau with sober ormolu mounting. Sold in Paris in 1972: £ 7,400, $ 13,300. 1984 valuation: £ 25,800, $ 34,200. 1991 valuation: £ 55,000, $ 97,300. Current valuation: £ 51,000, $ 84,500, € 76,250.

Fine bureau plat extensively mounted with chased ormolu. Bureaux plats were designed for the elite and, with rare exceptions, are not found in a more sober, modest, classic version. 1984 valuation: £ 43,000, $ 57,000. Current valuation: collector's price.

Fine bureau plat in kingwood and tulipwood veneer, bearing the stamp of Jean-Charles Saunier. Sold in Paris in 1974: £ 11,700, $ 23,000. 1984 valuation: £ 27,950, $ 37,000. Current valuation: collector's price.

Rare, fine bureau plat extensively mounted with minutely chased ormolu. Current valuation: collector's price.

Below: fine bureau plat in kingwood veneer, bearing the stamp of Jean-Charles Saunier. Sold in Paris in 1974: £ 11,700, $ 23,000. 1984 valuation: £ 36,550, $ 48,450. Current valuation: collector's price.

Rare, unusual trictrac table in kingwood veneer with a removable black lacquered top decorated with polychrome and gold birds of paradise, flowers and foliage. Sold in Paris in 1974: £ 5,700, $ 11,100. 1984 valuation: £ 8,600, $ 11,400. 1991 valuation: £ 9,200, $ 16,280. Current valuation: £ 20,400, $ 33,800, € 30,500.

Rare, small *en cas* table in tulipwood veneer with a double Spanish brocatelle marble top. The table could be moved easily using the clover-leaf handles on its sides and it is to this particularity that it owes its name of *en cas* ('in case') table. 1984 valuation: £ 6,450, $ 8,550. 1991 valuation: £ 7,000, $ 12,400. Current valuation: £ 10,200, $ 16,900, € 15,250.

Rustic bureau *de pente* in natural walnut with ormolu handles. 1984 valuation: £ 6,450, $ 8,550. 1991 valuation: £ 11,500, $ 20,355. Current valuation: £ 10,200, $ 16,900, € 15,250.

Fine large kidney-shaped table with *pupitre* in kingwood and amaranth veneer inlaid with geometric designs. The top consists of a central *pupitre* and two compartments hidden by flaps. Three frieze drawers. The ormolu profiles elegantly enhance the table's shape. It bears the stamp of Mathieu Criard. Sold in Paris in 1971: £ 10,300, $ 18,100. 1984 valuation: £ 21,500, $ 28,500. Current valuation: collector's price.

Classic bureau dos d'âne with a curved shape and kingwood veneer. 1984 valuation: £ 12,900, $ 17,100. 1991 valuation: £ 8,000, £ 14,160. Current valuation: £ 10,200, $ 16,900, € 15,250.

Fine bureau *dos d'âne*, veneered on all sides in kingwood and tulip-wood bands. Exuberantly inlaid with flowers and foliage; the legs and frieze are outlined with ormolu. 1984 valuation: £ 25,800, $ 34,200. Current valuation: collector's price.

Fine small *en cas* table, one of a pair, of very high quality. Two small, rosewood-veneered doors have been added. The edges and bands are in kingwood. 1984 valuation: £ 21,500, $ 28,500. Current valuation: collector's price.

Classic coiffeuse in rosewood and tulipwood veneer. The top has three opening leaves, the central leaf conceals a mirror. The piece has four drawers and a writing surface in the frieze. 1984 valuation: £ 6,450, $ 8,550. 1991 valuation: £ 7,000, $ 12,400. Current valuation: £ 9,180, $ 15,200, € 13,700.

Fine bureau *dos d'âne* with kingwood veneer on all sides and amaranth bands, inlaid overall with foliage and flowers.
Sold in Paris in 1971: £ 9,300, $ 16,400. 1984 valuation: £ 25,800, $ 34,200. Current valuation: collector's price.

Fine large bureau *à cylindre*. This type of piece is fairly rare in the Louis XV style, becoming very popular in the Louis XVI style. The item shown here is attributed to Dubois and is an example of the late Louis XV style. 1984 valuation: £ 6,500, $ 8,600. 1991 valuation: £ 20,000, $ 35,400.
Current valuation: £ 30,600, $ 50,700, € 45,750.

Classic bureau *dos d'âne* from the early Louis XV period, in kingwood veneer inlaid with a design of squares. The curves and lightness of the piece give it a degree of prestige despite its few ormolu mounts. 1984 valuation: £ 10,750, $ 14,250.
1991 valuation: £10,000, $ 17,700.
Current valuation: £ 15,300, $ 25,350, € 22,880.

Classic bureau *dos d'âne* extensively mounted with ormolu. Generally speaking Louis XV bureaux *à dos d'âne* are curved, but bureaux with two rows of drawers are heavier, less elegant and therefore less sought-after, with a lesser value. Sold in Paris in 1973: £ 2,880, $ 5,360. 1984 valuation: £ 10,750, $ 14,250. 1991 valuation: £ 28,000, $ 49,560. Current valuation: £ 20,400, $ 33,800, € 30,500.

Fine rare kidney-shaped table, attributed to Migeon, in *bois de fil* tulipwood decorated with scrolls. Sold in Paris in 1970: £ 4,000, $ 7,050. 1984 valuation: £ 12,900, $ 17,100. Current valuation: collector's price.

Fine giltwood mirror with flowers and foliage.
1984 valuation: £ 4,300, $ 5,700. 1991 valuation: £ 18,400, $ 32,570.
Current valuation: £ 18,870, $ 19,400, € 28,200.

Fine *lit à la polonaise* in wood painted grey and carved with little flowers. Sold in Paris in 1971: £ 10,300, $ 18,160. 1984 valuation: £ 2,580, $ 3,420. 1991 valuation: £ 11,500, $ 20,355 .
Current valuation: £ 10,200, $ 16,900, € 15,250.

Classic bed in natural beechwood, carved with little flowers and foliage. 1984 valuation: £ 4,300, $ 5,700.
Current valuation: £ 9,200, $ 16,280.
Current valuation: £ 10,200, $ 16,900, € 15,250.

Fine *lit à la polonaise* in natural beechwood, carved with little flowers and foliage. The hangings contribute to the overall value of these beds, which are too large for modern houses and are therefore not much in demand. Prices quoted for them are lower than their real value. Sold in Paris in 1974: £ 2,150, $ 4,300. 1984 valuation: £ 4,300, $ 5,700. 1991 valuation: £ 14,000, $ 24,780. Current valuation £ 12,240, $ 20,280, € 18,300.

Classic secretaire with kingwood veneer and a marble top, bearing the stamp of P. Roussel. Despite its classic appearance, the curve of the *doucine* and the veneer in the form of several panels of woods of contrasting colours are fine touches. Sold in Paris in 1972: £ 1,900, $ 3,360. 1984 valuation: £ 19,350, $ 25,650.
1991 valuation: £ 15,000, $ 26,550.
Current valuation: £ 16,300, $ 27,000, € 24,400.

Classic secretaire *à doucine*, with butterfly kingwood veneer and ormolu mounts, bearing the stamp of Lardin. 1984 valuation: £ 19,350, $ 25,650. 1991 valuation: £ 15,000, $ 26,550.
Current valuation: £ 16,300, $ 27,000, € 24,400.

Fine secretaire with tulipwood veneer inlaid with flowers, surrounded by curving rosewood bands, bearing the stamp of Manchon. The chased ormolu mounts are remarkably elegant.
1984 valuation: £ 19,350, $ 25,650.
Current valuation: collector's price.

Fine small armoire, with tulipwood and kingwood veneer and a *brèche d'Alep* marble top. Sober ormolu mounting. The shape is rather too rigid in relation to the sinuosity of the inlaid designs, which suggests this armoire dates from early in the Louis XV period. Sold in Paris in 1973: £ 4,300, $ 7,900. 1984 valuation: £ 8,600, $ 11,400. 1991 valuation: £ 15,000, $ 26,550.
Current valuation: £ 16,300, $ 27,000, € 24,400.

Fine bibliotheque with kingwood and amaranth veneer, elegantly mounted with ormolu. The curved sides are a rare technical detail, making this piece more valuable.
Sold in London in 1972: £ 4,800, $ 8,600.

1984 valuation: £ 15,050, $ 19,950.
1991 valuation: £ 36,000, $ 63,700.
Current valuation: £ 40,800, $ 67,600, € 61,000.

Fine bibliotheque with grills to the doors, tulipwood veneer and amaranth bands. Of particular note are the elegant outline of the doors and the shelves edged in the same veneer as the bibliotheque as a whole. 1984 valuation: £ 8,600, $ 11,400.
1991 valuation: £ 12,000, $ 21,240.
Current valuation: £ 20,400, $ 33,800, € 30,500.

Fine Louis XV secretaire *à doucine*, with kingwood veneer and a marble top. Curved sides are particularly rare in secretaires and increase their value considerably. 1984 valuation; £ 34,400, $ 45,600.
Current valuation: collector's price.

Fine secretaire *d'appui* with a *brèche d'Alep* marble top. The magnificent floral decoration of the facade is contained within a single panel and shows large roses scattered on a ground of kingwood outlined in tulipwood. 1984 valuation: £ 21,500, $ 28,500.
Current valuation: collector's price.

Fine secretaire in Chinese lacquer with a top in *brèche d'Alep* marble, soberly mounted with ormolu. The piece has a red and gold decoration showing figures, pagodas and scenes on a ground of black lacquer. 1984 valuation: £ 30,100, $ 39,900.
Current valuation: collector's price.

Fine secretaire known as a secretaire *d'appui* (from the French s'ap-puyer, meaning 'to lean'). Pieces of this type were designed to allow a person to stand with one elbow resting on the marble top, which was lower than usual for secretaires. This piece bears the stamp of J. Baumhauer. 1984 valuation: £ 21,500, $ 28,500. 1991 valuation: £ 41,000, $ 72,570 . Current valuation: £ 35,700, $ 59,150, € 53,380.

Fine secretaire *d'appui* bearing the stamp of Macret. Sober ormolu mounting. 1984 valuation: £ 25,800, $ 34,200. Current valuation: £ 25,500, $ 42,250, € 38,100.

Rare, fine secretaire *à doucine* bearing the stamp of Pierre Migeon. Its violin shape is rare and very highly-prized. Sold in Paris in 1973: £ 4,300, $ 7,900. 1984 valuation: £ 32,250, $ 42,750. Current valuation: collector's price.

Fine secretaire *à doucine* with a marble top. The floral decoration is still rustic, revealing the influence of the 17th-century Flemish inlay-ers. The piece is admirable for the pleasantly contrasting colours of the wood and sober ormolu mounting. 1984 valuation: £ 21,500, $ 28,500. Current valuation: £ 25,500, $ 42,250, € 38,100.

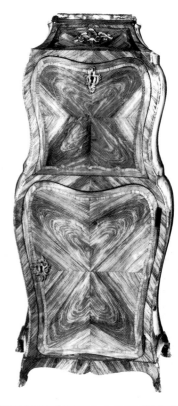

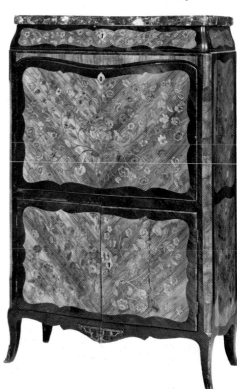

Rare, fine, small *en cas* cabinet, so named because it could easily be moved when necessary. The rounded front slides open. Sold in Paris in 1973: £ 2,900, $ 5,400. 1984 valuation: £ 8,600, $ 11,400. 1991 valuation: £ 18,400, $ 32,570. Current valuation: £ 15,300, $ 25,350, € 22,880.

Fine bonheur-du-jour with tulipwood veneer, soberly mounted with ormolu. Louis XV versions of this piece are fairly rare; it was more frequently produced in the Louis XVI style. Current valuation: £ 66,300, $ 109,850, € 99,140

Rare, fine secretaire with a *brèche d'Alep* marble top. The curved upper part and sides, rich floral decoration and exuberant chased ormolu mounting make this item a superior work of cabinet-making. Current valuation: collector's price.

Fine small lacquered fall-front bureau with a green ground and small polychrome flowers. It has two drawers beneath the fall-front and two further side drawers in the undertier. Sold in Paris in 1970: £ 4,400, $ 7,600. 1984 valuation: £ 10,750, $ 14,250. 1991 valuation: £ 36,000, $ 63,700. Current valuation: £ 35,700, $ 59,150, € 53,380.

Classic tulipwood vitrine, bearing the stamp of Schmidt. Sold in Paris in 1971: £ 600, $ 1,100. 1984 valuation: £ 8,600, $ 11,400. 1991 valuation: £ 8,000, $ 14,160. Current valuation: £ 10,200, $ 16,900, € 15,250.

Fine, rare small cabinet with kingwood and tulipwood veneer, bearing the stamp of P. Roussel. Sold in London in 1977: £ 11,800, $ 2,500. 1984 valuation: £ 12,900, $ 17,100. 1991 valuation: £ 30,000, $ 53,100. Current valuation: £ 30,600, $ 50,700, € 45,750.

Classic vitrine with glass doors, bearing the stamp of L. Boudin. Sold in Paris in 1971: £ 680, $ 1,200. 1984 valuation: £ 8,600, $ 11,400. 1991 valuation: £ 19,000, $ 33,630. Current valuation: £ 20,400, $ 33,800, € 30,500.

Exceptional, rare bureau *dos d'âne*, with satinwood and kingwood veneer and floral inlay. The rich chased ormolu mounting brings great refinement to this masterpiece by J. Dubois. Current valuation: collector's price.

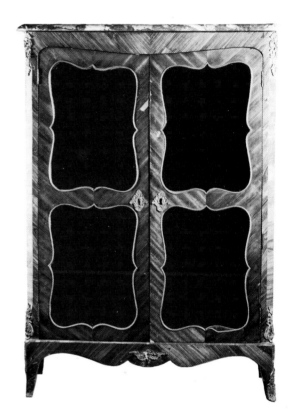

Very rare, fine *cartonnier* bearing the stamp of Hervé. Veneered in kingwood and surmounted by an ormolu clock. This piece in two sections is given great elegance and refinement by its chased ormolu mounts. Cartonniers are highly sought-after and make only fleeting appearances on the art market.
Current valuation: collector's price.

Gilt, flat-backed armchair , one of a set of four, of exceptional quality. Carved overall with seashells, garlands of flowers and foliage. It bears the stamp of Heurtaut, one of the most prestigious names in the history of seating in France. These armchairs are said to have been made for Louis XV. (Photo: Tajan, Paris). Sold in Paris in 1975: £ 7,000, $ 14,400. Current valuation: collector's price.

Rare fine coffer with a rounded shape and extensive chased ormolu mounting. Sold in Paris in 1973: £ 10,700, $ 19,900. 1984 valuation: £ 3,180, $ 4,200. 1991 valuation: £ 11,500, $ 20,355.
Current valuation: £ 15,300, $ 25,350, € 22,880.

Rare pair of fine armchairs made in Parma for Madame Infante (Louise Elisabeth de France, daughter of Louis XV and Marie Lecsinska). The giltwood frames are very richly carved with acanthus leaves, cartouches, scrolling foliage, reeds, palmettes, agrafes and rocaille on an *amati* ground. The padded backs are flanked by C scrolling, the curved armrests are carved with rocaille and garlands. The festooned apron is very richly carved with cartouches, foliage and flowers. The scrolled cabriole legs end in outscrolled feet.

They bear the following marks: branded CR with a closed royal crown in the centre for Casa Reale (Royal House); marked C 611/2 and C 611/3, relating to the furniture store of the palace of Colorno; a small, black, handwritten mark C 611/2; branded M L with a double royal crown in an oval cartouche for the furniture store of Marie-Louise of Austria, marked after 1815. Attributed to Nicolas-Quinibert Foliot. (Doc: Tajan, Paris). Current valuation: collector's price.

Fine bureau *dos d'âne* with precious, exotic wood veneer inlaid with flowers, bearing the stamp of Hache Fils of Grenoble. (Photo: Tajan, Paris). Sold in Paris in 1976: ₤ 15,000, $ 30,400 1984 valuation: ₤ 21,500, $ 28,500. 1991 valuation: ₤ 50,000, $ 88,500.
Current valuation: collector's price.

Opposite: bureau *dos d'âne* of exceptional quality, extensively mounted with ormolu and bearing the stamp of BVRB. The lock to the fall-front is marked with two intertwined 'L's, suggesting a mark of royal origins; however the absence of any inventory number or chateau mark rule out the possibility of identifying its origins. There is however a great resemblance between this piece and the double secretaire now in the Paul Getty Museum, which was exhibited in the Hotel de la Monnaie in Paris in 1974.
Current valuation: collector's price.

Fine coiffeuse with tulipwood and amaranth veneer, inlaid with flowers in kingwood, attributed to Wolff. The value of the piece is enhanced by its curves and admirably harmonious shape.
Current valuation: collector's price.

Fine bureau *dos d'âne*, with tulipwood
and amaranth veneer inlaid with flowers,
bearing the stamp of RVLC: Roger Vandercruse,
known as Lacroix, master cabinet-maker
in Paris in 1755.
1984 valuation: £ 36,550, $ 48,450.
Current valuation: collector's price.

Fine small bureau veneered in satinwood
with sober ormolu mounting.
(Photo: Tajan, Paris).
Sold in Paris in 1977: £ 24,300, $ 53,000.
1984: £ 32,250, $ 42,750.
Current valuation: collector's price.

Fine bureau *dos d'âne* with tulipwood veneer inlaid with kingwood, attributed to BVRB. The refined ormolu mounts enhance each part of this bureau. Sold by Sotheby's in London in 1988: £ 68,930, $ 122,500. Current valuation: collector's price.

Fine bureau *dos d'âne* veneered in tulipwood and kingwood inlaid with flowers in kingwood. Of particular note for its chased ormolu mounts, elegant shape and fine marquetry. The design can be attributed to the famous cabinet-maker BVRB.
Current valuation: collector's price.

Rare, fine bureau *dos d'âne*, veneered in tulipwood and kingwood with a floral inlay in coloured wood. The elegance of the shape stems from its harmoniously alternating curves.
Current valuation: collector's price.

Rare, classic, small bureau *dos d'âne* with tulipwood veneer and green-coloured wood bands. Its reduced size suggests this bureau was designed for a young person. 1991 valuation: £ 7,000, $ 12,390. Current valuation: £ 9,180, $ 15,210, € 13,700.

Rare fine secretaire with tulipwood and amaranth veneer and a floral design in kingwood, bearing the stamp of Wolff. The curved sides give it a certain prestige.
Current valuation: collector's price.

Below: fine *meuble d'entre-deux* or 'between cabinet' in tulipwood veneer inlaid with flowers in kingwood. The *Régence* style shape has Louis XV-style inlay and ormolu mounts (with the exception of the ormolu profiles on the base). The piece bears the crowned 'c' stamp, signifying the tax on ormolu mounts imposed between 1745 and 1749, and the stamp of BVRB. It was made for J.C. Machault

d'Arnouville, French minister in 1749. It has 42 internal compartments designed to hold a collection of minerals and was certainly made using the carcase of an existing piece. It was not rare for pieces to be adapted, even by the great cabinet-makers, in order to meet the demands of the new owner. (Photo: Tajan, Paris). Sold in Paris in 1970: ₤ 667,400, $ 1,157,000. Current valuation: collector's price.

Rare fine secretaire *d'appui* with tulipwood and amaranth veneer inlaid with flowers in coloured wood. The top is *brèche d'Alep* marble.
Current valuation: collector's price.

Extremely rare *écritoire* of exceptional quality, with tulipwood and amaranth veneer. The extensive, refined ormolu mounting emphasises every detail of the piece.

Provenance: Alphonse de Rothschild collection, Vienna. (Photo: Sotheby Parke Bernet). Sold in Monte Carlo in 1979: £ 301,000, $ 705,800. 1984 valuation: £ 258,000, $ 342,000. Current valuation: collector's price.

Fine regulateur de parquet veneered in amaranth and richly mount-ed with ormolu, bearing the stamp of Lamy and dated 1767 on the face. Sold in Paris in 1981: £13,500, $ 27,200. 1984 valuation: £ 18,900, $ 25,000. Current valuation: collector's price.

Exceptional regulateur de parquet veneered in amaranth, inlaid with flowers and opulently mounted with ormolu, attributed to Latz. (Photo: Tajan, Paris). Sold in Paris in 1984: £ 47,000, £ 62,400. Current valuation: collector's price.

Fine console of exceptional quality, in elegantly carved giltwood. Its curves and fine carving make this console a masterpiece. Sold in London by Sotheby's in 1988: £ 51,800, $ 92,400.
Current valuation: collector's price.

Fine console of exceptional quality, veneered in kingwood and richly mounted with chased ormolu, bearing the stamp of Hubert Hansen, master cabinet-maker in Paris in 1747. This piece comes from the shop of Darnault, a Parisian furniture dealer known in the 18th century, and bears his original label. Sold by Sotheby's in London in 1988: £ 116,400, $ 206,970.
Current valuation: collector's price.

Rare fine, giltwood console and its accompanying mirror, also in carved giltwood. The light elegance of the shape and finesse of the carvings are admirable.
Current valuation: collector's price.

Fine chaise longue *à oreilles* in elegantly carved natural beechwood. 1984 valuation: £ 4 300, $ 5,700. 1991 valuation: £ 9,000, $ 15,900. Current valuation: £ 8,670, $ 14,360, € 12,960.

Fine *bergere*, one of a pair, in carved walnut. Gros point tapestry decorated with figures and animals. 1984 valuation: £ 8,600, $ 11,400. 1991 valuation: £ 20,000, $ 35,400. Current valuation: £ 25,500, $ 42,250, € 38,100.

Finely carved giltwood armchair of exceptional quality, one of a pair, bearing the stamp of Nicolas Heurtaut, master cabinet-maker in Paris in 1775. The shape is very elegant and the carving remarkably fine. Only masterpieces of gilt seating, such as the item shown below, are valued very highly. (Photo: Tajan, Paris).
Sold in Paris in 1984: £ 38,700, $ 51,300.
Current valuation: collector's price.

Fine chair in natural, waxed beechwood, one of a set of twelve. The decorative carving enhances the entire structure. Sets of twelve chairs are extremely rare. Current valuation: collector's price.

Right: fine armchair in elegantly carved natural beechwood, one of a set of six. It is always more difficult to find six identical armchairs. Current valuation: collector's price.

Fine armchair in waxed natural beechwood, one of a set of six, covered in Royal Aubusson tapestries and bearing the stamp of NDLP (Nicolas de la Porte). Of particular note are the lightness and curved shapes of these chairs and the different oriental themes of the tapestries, which are far rarer than those based on themes from La Fontaine's fables. Current valuation: collector's price.

Left: fine *bergere* in carved beechwood, one of a pair. Traces of a stamp have been identified, probably that of Courtois.
Current valuation: collector's price.

Armchair of exceptional quality in waxed natural walnut, from the early Louis XV period, one of a pair, covered in Aubusson tapestry. The decorative carving enhances the chair's structure and raises its overall value. 1984 valuation: £ 13,670, $ 18,140.
Current valuation: collector's price.

Below: Fine cabriolet armchair in elegantly carved natural beech-wood, one of a set of four. The chair's valuation reflects the quality of the carving and its perfectly harmonious, flowing curves.
1991 valuation: £ 15,000, $ 26,550.
Current valuation: £ 20,400, $ 33,800, € 30,500.

Right: Fine rare *bergere* in finely carved natural walnut, one of a pair of which one bears the stamp of Nogaret of Lyon.
1991 valuation: £ 15,000, $ 26,550.
Current valuation: £ 18,360, $ 30,400, € 27,450.

Fine cabriolet armchair of exceptional quality, in waxed natural beechwood, one of a set of four. Two of the four bear the stamp of M. Beauve, a celebrated carpenter in Paris in 1754. The admirably fine carving, which extends even to the chair backs, makes them true masterpieces. Current valuation: collector's price.

Fine *bergere* in elegantly carved beechwood, one of a pair.
1991 valuation: & 23,000, $ 40,700.
Current valuation: & 20,400, $ 33,800, € 30,500.

Below: fine, rare *banquette* in elegantly carved natural beechwood.
1991 valuation: & 11,500, $ 20,355.
Current valuation: & 10,200, $ 16,900, € 15,250.

Fine *bergere* in delicately carved walnut, one of a pair. The elegantly curved shape is particularly noteworthy.
1991 valuation: & 23,000, & 40,700.
Current valuation: & 20,400, $ 33,800, € 30,500.

Fine *bergere* in elegantly carved beechwood, one of a pair. It bears the stamp of E. Meunier, the most famous member of a family of carpenters working under Louis XV.
Current valuation: collector's price.

Fine stool in elegantly carved natural beechwood with an admirably harmonious shape. 1991 valuation: £ 7,000, $ 12,400.
Current valuation: £ 7,140, $ 11,800, € 10,680.

Fine cabriolet armchair, one of a set of four which, with two chairs created by the same ébéniste, make up a set of Louis XV salon furniture. Of particular note are the perfect shape and delicacy of the finely carved elements. Attributed to P. Pluvinet, master cabinet-maker in Paris in 1754. 1991 valuation: £ 20,000, $ 35,400.
Current valuation: £ 25,500, $ 42,250, € 38,100.

Pair of fine cabriolet armchairs in carved natural walnut, bearing the stamp of Nogaret. 1984 valuation: £ 7,740, $ 10,260 .
1991 valuation: £ 23,000, $ 40,700.
Current valuation: £ 20,400, $ 33,800, € 30,500.

Fine *fauteuil de bureau* in natural beechwood, caned and carved with shells and foliage. *Fauteuils de bureau* are rare and expensive for the same reasons as bureaux plats, which were generally made for wealthy clients. 1984 valuation: £ 3,440, $ 4,560.
1991 valuation: £ 10,000, $ 17,700.
Current valuation: £ 10,200, $ 16,900, € 15,250.

Cabriolet armchair, partly fine, partly classic, in carved natural beechwood, one of a pair. Sold in 1981: £ 4,100, $ 8,270.
1984 valuation: £ 3,870, $ 5,100.
1991 valuation: £ 6,000, $ 10,600.
Current valuation: £ 7,650, $ 12,670, € 11,440.

Fine caned beechwood chair carved with rocailles, flowers and branches, bearing the stamp of Saint-Georges. Sold in Paris in 1973: £ 740, $ 1,380. 1984 valuation: per chair, £ 860, $ 1,140. For the set of six £ 7,740, $ 10,260. 1991 valuation: per chair, £ 2,300, $ 4,070. For the set of six £ 28,000, $ 49,560. Current valuation: for the set of six, collector's price.

Fine giltwood stool with floral carving. Sold in Paris in 1969: £ 180, $ 300. 1984 valuation: £ 645, $ 855. 1991 valuation: £ 6,000, $ 10,600. Current valuation: £ 6,120, $ 10,140, € 9,150.

Important fine *canapé corbeille* in grey-painted wood, carved with cartouches and foliage. 1984 valuation: £ 3,440, $ 4,560.
1991 valuation: £ 11,500, $ 20,355.
Current valuation: £ 18,360, $ 30,420, € 27,450.

Fine *canapé corbeille* in natural walnut carved with small flowers and foliage. This canape can be attributed to the workshop of Nogaret. 1984 valuation: £ 3,000, $ 4,000.
1991 valuation: £ 14,000, $ 24,780.
Current valuation: £ 15,300, $ 25,350, € 22,880.

Fine small *canapé corbeille* in natural beechwood carved with small flowers and branches, bearing the stamp of Jean-Jacques Pothier. The shape of the canapé corbeille is the most elegant and highly-prized of the Louis XV style, and so commands the highest prices. Sold in Paris in 1970: £ 11,000, $ 19,160.
1984 valuation: £ 4,300, $ 5,700.
1991 valuation: £ 14,000, $ 24,780.
Current valuation: £ 13,770, $ 22,800, € 20,590.

Rare pair of *fauteuils d'angle* ('corner armchairs') in natural beech-wood, bearing the stamp of L. Delanois. Sold in Paris in 1969: £ 2,100, $ 3,600. 1984 valuation: £ 14,600, $ 19,380. 1991 valuation: £ 18,500, $ 32,750. Current valuation: £ 18,360, $ 30,400, € 27,450.

Pair of armchairs, partly classic, partly fine, with flat backs, carved with garlands of flowers and foliage. The seats are covered with Royal Aubusson tapestries showing branches and flowers. 1984 valuation: £ 5,160, $ 6,840. 1991 valuation: £ 23,000, $ 40,700. Current valuation: £ 20,400, $ 33,800, € 30,500.

Fine *fauteuil de bureau* in white-painted wood with floral carving. The very broad, flowing shape of the back, which is usually too functional to come into the fine category, nevertheless gives it elegance. Sold in Paris in 1972: £ 680, $ 1,200. 1984 valuation: £ 3,000, $ 4,000. 1991 valuation: £ 10,000, $ 17,700. Current valuation: £ 13,260, $ 21,970, € 19,800.

Fauteuil de bureau in natural beechwood, caned and carved with small flowers, bearing the stamp of Meunier. Sold in Paris in 1970: £ 440, $ 760. 1984 valuation: £ 2,150, $ 2,850. 1991 valuation: £ 17,000, $ 30,100. Current valuation: £ 13,260, $ 21,970, € 19,800.

Pair of classic cabriolet armchairs, covered with tapestries with a design of flowers and ribbons. 1984 valuation: £ 2,580, $ 3,420. 1991 valuation: £ 8,500, $ 15,050. Current valuation: £ 10,200, $ 16,900, € 15,250.

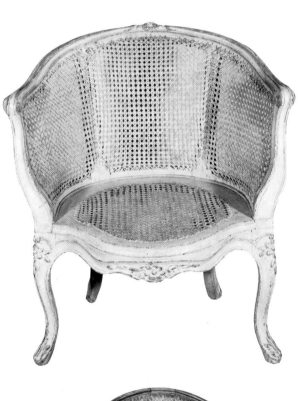

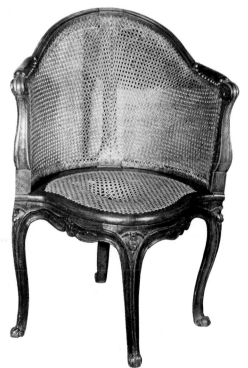

Fine cabriolet armchair, one of a pair, in natural walnut and attributed to Nogaret. Sold in Milan in 1971: £ 2,680, $ 4,740.
1984 valuation: £ 7,740, $ 10,260.
1991 valuation: £ 18,500, $ 32,750.
Current valuation: £ 20,400, $ 33,800, € 30,500.

Fine *canapé corbeille* in beechwood, carved with small flowers and branches. iIs flowing curves are enhanced by a rich polychrome tapestry depicting pastoral scenes.
Current valuation: collector's price.

Fine flat-backed, giltwood armchair, one of a pair, carved with cartouches, shells, flowers and foliage and bearing the stamp of G. Sené. Sold in 1970: £ 5,300, $ 9,200. 1984 valuation: £ 7,740, $ 10,260. 1991 valuation: £ 18,500, $ 32,750.
Current valuation: £ 20,400, $ 33,800, € 30,500.

Important giltwood armchair, one of a pair, elegantly carved with branches and flowers. Sold in London in 1972: £ 7,250, $ 12,990.
1984 valuation: £ 11,180, $ 14,820.
1991 valuation: £ 23,000, $ 40,700.
Current valuation: £ 25,500, $ 42,250, € 38,100.

Canape, partly classic, partly fine, in grey painted wood carved with small flowers and branches.
1984 valuation: £ 2,580, $ 3,420.
1991 valuation: £ 7,000, $ 12,400.
Current valuation: £ 7,140, $ 11,830, € 10,680.

Fine armchair, one of a pair, in carved natural walnut and bearing the stamp of Nogaret. 1984 valuation: £ 8,600, $ 11,400.
1991 valuation: £ 18,500, $ 32,750.
Current valuation: £ 18,360, $ 30,400, € 27,450.

Fine, large canape in carved natural beechwood, bearing the stamp of Tilliard. Current valuation: collector's price.

Fine canape, carved and gilt overall. 1980 valuation: £ 3,560, $ 8,280. 1991 valuation: £ 11,500, $ 20,350. Current valuation: £ 10,200, $ 16,900, € 15,250.

Important giltwood canape carved with small flowers and foliage with Beauvais tapestry. The seat is decorated with a hunting scene and the back shows children playing in parkland. Sold in London in 1973: £ 2,300, $ 4,300. 1984 valuation: £ 3,870, $ 5,100. 1991 valuation: £ 14,000, $ 24,780. Current valuation: £ 18,360, $ 30,400, € 27,450.

Classic flat-backed, giltwood armchair, carved with shells, garlands of flowers and leaves. The Beauvais tapestry shows themes from La Fontaine's fables. 1984 valuation: £ 2,150, $ 2,850. 1991 valuation: £ 4,500, $ 7,970. Current valuation: £ 6,120, $ 10,140, € 9,150.

Classic *bergere* with a concave (cabriolet) back, one of a pair, in natural beechwood carved with flowers and foliage. Sold in Paris in 1969: £ 3,550, $ 6,140. 1984 valuation: £ 6,880, $ 9,100. 1991 valuation: £ 13,000, $ 23,000. Current valuation: £ 16,320, $ 27,000, € 24,400.

Small classic canape in natural beechwood carved with small flowers and foliage. There is more demand for the small, two-seater canapes than for larger styles and they are therefore more expensive. 1984 valuation: £ 3,180, $ 4,200. 1991 valuation: £ 7,000, $ 12,400. Current valuation: £ 7,140, $ 11,800, € 10,680.

Pair of fine *bergeres* bearing the stamp of N. Heurtaut. Sold in Paris in 1970: £ 6,200, $ 10,700. 1984 valuation: £ 15,050, $ 19,950. 1991 valuation: £ 39,000, $ 69,000.
Current valuation: collector's price.

Fine *bergere à oreilles* in carved natural beechwood. Sold in Paris in 1969: £ 3,000, $ 5,300. 1984 valuation: £ 3,400, $ 4,560. 1991 valuation: £ 14,000, $ 24,780.
Current valuation: £ 12,240, $ 20,280, € 18,300.

Fine stool in carved wood, one of a pair, reflecting the early Louis XV style. Sold in Milan in 1972: £ 2,400, $ 4,350 the pair. 1984 valuation: £ 3,180, $ 4,200. 1991 valuation: £ 5,500, $ 9,700.
Current valuation: £ 6,100, $ 10,100, € 9,150.

Classic chairs in carved beechwood. Original petit point tapestry covers showing flowers and foliage. Sold in Paris in 1973: £ 3,250, $ 6,050. 1984 valuation: £ 3,000, $ 4,000. 1991 valuation: £ 4,600, $ 8,140. Current valuation: £ 4,080, $ 6,760, € 6,100.

Fine chair in elegantly carved natural beechwood. 1984 valuation: for one, £ 1,300, $ 1,700. The pair £ 3,440, $ 4,560. 1991 valuation: The pair £ 9,200, $ 16,280. Current valuation: The pair £ 8,160, $ 13,500, € 12,200.

Rare fine *bergere* in white painted wood carved with cartouches, foliage and garlands of flowers. Its sinuous elegance is enhanced by the refined carving. The seat bears the stamp of J.B. Tilliard, one of the most prestigious names of all the French carpenters. Current valuation: collector's price.

Rare fine *fauteuil de bureau* in natural beechwood and caned, impressively carved with flowers and foliage. 1984 valuation: £ 2,580, $ 3,400. 1991 valuation: £ 10,000, $ 17,700. Current valuation: £ 12,240, $ 20,280, € 18,300.

Rare giltwood *bergere* which converts into a *prie-dieu*. This is a very costly design, highly-prized by collectors. Sold in London in 1983: £ 1,700, $ 2,600. 1984 valuation: £ 3,180, $ 4,200. 1991 valuation: £ 8,300, $ 14,700. Cuurent valuation: £ 8,160, $ 13,500, € 12,200.

Fine *chaise longue* in natural beechwood carved with small flowers, bearing the stamp of I. Avisse. Admirable for its elegant curves and refined carvings. Sold in Paris in 1974: £ 6,600, $ 13,000. 1984 valuation: £ 6,000, $ 8,000. 1991 valuation: £ 8,300, $ 14,700. Current valuation: £ 8,670, $ 14,360, € 12,960.

Rare *chaise-bidet* in natural beechwood. 1984 valuation: £ 2,300, $ 3,000. 1991 valuation: £ 3,200, $ 5,660. Current valuation: £ 3,570, $ 5,900, € 5,340.

Fine coiffeuse in tulipwood veneer with floral inlay and sober ormolu mounting, bearing the stamp of RVLC, Roger Vandercruse, known as Lacroix, master cabinet-maker in Paris from 6 February 1755. The curved shape of this coiffeuse is remarkably elegant. Exceptionally, the original accessories have been retained. These include boxes, brushes in vernis Martin, Sèvres porcelain jars and crystal flasks. Sold in Paris in May 1984: £ 18,060, $ 23,940.
1991 valuation: £ 30,000, $ 53,100.
Current valuation: £ 35,700, $ 59,150, € 53,380.

Fine *fauteuil de bureau* in elegantly carved beechwood, attributed to Meunier. Despite its shape, which lacks aesthetic qualities, this type of armchair is always highly valued due to its specific function and rarity. Sold in Paris in May 1984: £ 7,740, $ 10,260.
1991 valuation: £ 10,000, $ 17,700.
Current valuation: £ 13,770, $ 22,800, € 20,600.

Fine gilt armchair, one of a pair, bearing the stamp of Heurtaut. The tapestry shows themes from La Fontaine's fables. If these armchairs were in natural wood their value would be doubled. Sold in Paris in 1978: £ 11,600, $24,800. 1984 valuation: £ 9,460, $ 12,540.
1991 valuation: £ 28,000, $ 49,560.
Current valuation: £ 25,500, $ 42,250, € 38,100.

Rare fine two-seater *canapé corbeille* in elegantly carved natural beechwood. 1991 valuation: £ 9,200, $ 16,280. Current valuation: £ 10,200, $ 16,900, € 15,250.

Fine giltwood *canapé à oreilles,* of exceptional quality. The carving is so energetic and precise that it almost outweighs the functionality of the piece. The canape bears the stamp of Heurtaut. (Photo: Tajan, Paris). Sold in Paris in 1975: £ 23,940, 49,200. 1984 valuation: £ 15,000, $ 20,000. Current valuation: collector's price.

Classic caned cabriolet armchair, one of a pair, in carved walnut.
1984 valuation: £ 3,000, $ 4,000.
1991 valuation: £ 9,200, $ 16,280.
Current valuation: £ 9,380, $ 15,550, € 14,000.

Fine *bergere* in natural beechwood, carved with branches and flowers. 1984 valuation: £ 3,180, $ 4,200 .
1991 valuation: £ 9,200, $ 16,280.
Current valuation: £ 8,160, $ 13,500, € 12,200.

Fine, rare *chaise longue* gilt and carved with shells and foliage. Of particular note are the unusual shape and long backless seat, which lightens the structure. 1984 valuation: £ 2,150, $ 2,850.
1991 valuation: £ 9,200, $ 16,280.
Current valuation: £ 10,200, $ 16,900, € 15,250.

Small classic commode reflecting the early Louis XV style, with two drawers with traverse and a marble top and bearing the stamp of J.C. Ellaume. The piece is veneered in rosewood and kingwood and has asymmetrical ormolu mounts typical of the style. However, although slightly curved, the shape recalls some details of the *Régence* style while the ormolu is clearly Louis XV. Although pleasing to the eye, this piece cannot be regarded as a masterpiece of cabinet-making. The drawers are separated by a traverse which reduces its value. Commodes with two drawers sans traverse are more highly valued.
1984 valuation: £ 4,300, $ 5,700.
1991 valuation: £ 10,000, $ 17,700.
Current valuation: £ 8,160, $ 13,500, € 12,200.

Rare and unusual small console with a *brèche d'Alep* marble top, kingwood and rosewood veneer and a frieze drawer. It has two cabriole legs joined by a stretcher. Sold in Milan in 1972: £ 1,350, $ 2,400. 1984 valuation: £ 6,450, $ 8,550.
1991 valuation: £ 17,500, $ 30,980.
Current valuation: £ 15,300, $ 25,350, € 22,880.

Fine commode with two drawers *sans traverse* and a marble top.
Current valuation: collector's price.

Classic commode with two drawers sans traverse and a marble top. Tulipwood and amaranth veneer. The piece has a decoration of cubes, which is not highly regarded and reduces both its value and beauty. 1984 valuation: £ 15,000, $ 19,950.
1991 valuation: £ 34,000, $ 60,180.
Current valuation: £ 30,600, $ 50,700, € 45,750.

Rare fine armchair which can be attributed to Tilliard, or at least to his style. It was part of a set of salon furniture consisting of four identical armchairs, two smaller armchairs and a canape. All the pieces are in gilt beechwood carved with ribbons, shells, roses and cartouches on a ground engraved with a chequered pattern. Sold in Paris in 1969: £ 26,500, $ 46,000. Current valuation: collector's price.

Canape with armrests, partly classic, partly fine, and a pair of armchairs, bearing the stamp of E. Meunier.
1984 valuation: £ 8,600, $ 11,400.
1991 valuation: £ 34,000, $ 60,180.
Current valuation: £ 30,600, $ 50,700, € 45,750.

Pair of fine, giltwood armchairs carved with cartouches and flowers. The tapestry shows scenes from La Fontaine's fables. Sold in Paris in 1973: £ 2,100, $ 3,900. 1984 valuation: £ 3,440, $ 4,560.
1991 valuation: £ 23,000, $ 40,700.
Current valuation: £ 23,460, $ 38,870, € 35,000.

Fine, large stool in carved wood, one of a pair. The elegance of the overall shape and carvings and the skill and precision with which the stool is made are attributed to the famous cabinet-maker and sculptor Cresson. 1984 valuation: £ 6,450, $ 8,550 .
1991 valuation: £ 23,000, $ 40,700.
Current valuation: £ 20,400, $ 33,800, € 30,500.

Pair of fine stools in carved beechwood. Sold in Paris in 1970: £ 6,200, $ 10,700. 1984 valuation: £ 3,440, $ 4,560.
1991 valuation: £ 11,500, $ 20,350.
Current valuation: £ 10,200, $ 16,900, € 15,250.

Fine stool, carved and gilt, one of a pair. Sold in Paris in 1973: £ 2,300, $ 4,300. 1984 valuation: £ 3,870, $ 5,130.
1991 valuation: £ 11,500, $ 20,350.
Current valuation: £ 10,200, $ 16,900, € 15,250.

Pair of chairs, partly classic, partly fine, in beechwood carved with foliage and flowers, bearing the stamp of J.B. Lerouge. Sold in Paris in 1973: £ 2,300, $ 4,300. 1984 valuation: £ 2,150, $ 2,850.
1991 valuation: £ 5,500, $ 9,700.
Current valuation: £ 5,100, $ 8,450, € 7,600.

Small classic table with a wooden top, three drawers with traverses and an undertier. The piece is veneered in tulipwood and amaranth. The top and undertier have a refined floral decoration. Small tables veneered *à toutes faces* are known as *tables de milieu* ('middle tables') or tables à jour ('day tables'). 1984 valuation: £ 7,740, $ 10,260. 1991 valuation: £ 8,000, $ 14,160. Current valuation: £ 10,200, $ 16,900, € 15,250.

Classic chiffonnier. A typical piece of bedroom furniture, designed to contain lingerie. Sold in Paris in 1973: £ 2,100, $ 3,900. 1984 valuation: £ 6 ,450, $ 8,550. 1991 valuation: £ 10,000, $ 17,700. Current valuation: £ 8,160, $ 13,500, € 12,200.

Fine small table with three drawers sans traverse, amaranth and tulipwood veneer, inlaid overall with flowers, foliage and birds and bearing the stamp of Delorme. Sold in Paris in 1970: £ 5,300, $ 9,200. 1984 valuation: £ 17,200, $ 22,800. Current valuation: collector's price.

Classic eight-drawer chiffonier *à doucine*, in rosewood veneer with a marble top and sober ormolu mounting. Sold in Paris in 1972: £ 780, $ 1,400. 1984 valuation: £ 3,440, $ 4,560. 1991 valuation: £ 5,000, $ 8,850. Current valuation: £ 6,630, $ 10,980, € 9,900.

Rare fine small table in two sections forming a bidet, in tulipwood veneer with ormolu side handles and bearing the stamp of Migeon.

This type of furniture is very highly-prized by collectors of curiosities and rare objects. Current valuation: collector's price.

Canape *à oreilles* in natural walnut carved with small flowers and foliage. The tapestries show scenes from La Fontaine's fables. This canape was part of a large set of fine salon furniture also comprising ten armchairs and two stools. The set bears the stamp of Nogaret, who preferred walnut to beech, the wood more commonly used in Paris. Sold in Paris in 1973: £ 23,300, $ 43,270.
1984 valuation: £ 32,250, $ 42,750.
1991 valuation: £ 86,000, $ 177,000.
Current valuation: collector's price.

Fine example of a painted chaise longue, gilt and carved with small flowers. 1991 valuation: £ 7,000, $ 12,400.
Current valuation: £ 6,630, $ 10,980, € 9,900.

Fine bureau dos d'âne of exceptional quality, in tulipwood and kingwood veneer with floral inlay. Of particular note are the harmonious curves that give it its perfect shape and the extensive ormolu mounting. Sold in Paris in 1996: £ 188,500, $ 293,300.
Current valuation: collector's price.

Important fine bureau *de pente* with a curved shape and satinwood, amaranth and rosewood veneer inlaid with branches and flowers in *bois de bout*. The front opens to reveal six drawers, a secret compartment and four pigeonholes. The lower part has two doors concealing three drawers.

The legs are decorated with chutes with acanthus leaves, with sabots on the feet. The bureau bears the stamp of Dubois. (Photo: Tajan, Paris). Sold in Paris in 1996: £ 113,100, $ 175,980. Current valuation: collector's price.

Rare fine cabinet with a curved shape and wood veneer, inlaid with tulipwood and coloured wood flowers on a squared ground and amaranth surrounds. A sliding top reveals a drawer with pigeon-holes and a pupitre.

The lower part has a sliding door concealing four drawers. Cabriole legs. The cabinet bears the stamp of L. Boudin. (Photo: Tajan, Paris). Sold in Paris in 1994: £ 329,800, $ 504,900.
Current valuation: collector's price.

Fine armchair, one of a set of six, in giltwood moulded and carved with scrolled foliage, cartouches and acanthus leaves. Provenance: the collection of the Duke of Hamilton at Hamilton Palace, Lord Leconfield and Dutasta. (Photo: Couturier Nicolay). Sold in Paris in 1995: £ 56,360, $ 86,980.
Current valuation: £ 102,000, $ 169,000, € 152,500.

Commode with a curved shape in black and gold Chinese lacquer and European lacquer with a polychrome design of landscapes in aventurine surrounds. It has two drawers sans traverse and cabriole legs. Chased ormolu mounts including chutes, handles and sabots. *Brèche d'Alep* marble top. The commode bears the stamp of I. Dubois, admitted as master cabinet-maker in 1742. Provenance: the collection of the Chateau du Luat. (Photo: Tajan, Paris).
Sold in Paris in 1995: £ 54,540, $ 84,180.
Current valuation: £ 61,200, $ 101,400, € 91,500.

Fine commode with a curved shape in European imitation Chinese lacquer with a polychrome design of pagodas, landscapes and figures on a black and gold ground. Two drawers to the front. Richly mounted with chased ormolu with the crowned 'c' mark, including foliate scrolled chutes, surrounds, escutcheons and sabots.

Brèche d'Alep marble top. This commode bears the stamp of Mewesen, a Swedish-born cabinet-maker, admitted as master in 1766. (Photo: Tajan, Paris). Sold in Paris in 1996: £ 209,260, $ 325,500. Current valuation: collector's price.

The Louis XV–Louis XVI transitional style

The transition from the Louis XV style to the Louis XVI style can be dated approximately between 1755 and 1770.

Like all transitional styles, it produced pieces with a hybrid appearance, whose shape and decorative elements were partly in the Louis XV style and partly heralded the precepts of the Louis XVI style. The 'cultural production' of the style took place mainly at the French Academy in Rome, meeting place for a dozen young artists who were challenging the Louis XV style. On their return to Paris these artists, who had been inspired by the remains of the ancient civilisation and influenced by the publication of the engravings for Piranese's *Roman Antiquities* (1756), fought to bring about a return to classicism in art. This cultural movement, known as neoclassicism, spread from Paris throughout the whole of Europe, the only exception being England. Here the scene was dominated by the Adam brothers, who laid down the rules for a very particular form of neoclassicism with specific characteristics.

This cultural aspect aside, there was also an elite of buyers in Paris who rejected outright what they regarded as the excessive forms and outlandish decorations of the Louis XV style. So there were plenty of influential people who had remained faithful to Louis XIV furniture, particularly those designs by the great cabinet-maker Charles Boulle, and were encouraging a love of traditional art. For a good part of the 18th century Boulle's sons continued to make his designs, and were consequently known as 'their father's apes'.

To the factors mentioned above we should add the passion for archaeological excavation which was gaining ground throughout the 18th century. The items brought to light from the ancient Greek and Roman civilisations fuelled salon discussions of the artistic problems of the day. One of the greatest controversies concerned beauty: could it and should it arise from rationality and the straight lines of ancient art or did it lie in the imaginative, asymmetrical eccentricities of the new Louis XV style? Passionate arguments were made against the illogical aspects and formal excesses of a style which had broken ties with the past and with tradition, in the same way that many people today rail against furniture made of metal or plastic. Such a comparison may seem extreme, but not once we try to enter into the atmosphere of the Louis XV period, with its ceaseless passion for all kinds of novelty. The inevitable reaction against a style that had received so much criticism and was at the same time so widespread could only take the form of a return to the old sources of classical inspiration.

It was once again in Paris, where the precepts of fashion were still as keenly followed, that the furniture of the transition period found the select clientele that was fashion's most efficient transmitter. So the transition style can be said to have been conceived in Rome and baptised in Paris, where it took its first steps.

However the new style did not find expression in all types of furniture. Commodes, small salon tables and secretaires were the most affected by the new turmoil. All these pieces now had cabriole – in other words Louis XV – legs, but rectangular or square bodies, foreshadowing the Louis XVI style.

The materials did not change, but where decoration was concerned the new preference was for inlays of small bouquets or garlands of flowers on square or rectangular panels enhanced by a *grecque* (a decorative element harking back to the Renaissance), or a simple band of paler wood surrounding the motifs. At the same time inlays of classically-inspired vases or amphora began to appear on furniture, alongside pastoral scenes and, less frequently, landscapes with ancient ruins. Inlays of flowers bound by love-knots (ornamental motifs consisting of a single or double knot), which had fluttered when they made their rare appearances on Louis XV pieces, became more stylised, linear and sensible.

Mahogany was used more frequently. Until the transition period it had made only an occasional appearance in 18th-century furniture and had been used mainly for making nautical items and

Louis XV *rafraîchissoirs* (cabinets with metal recipients for keeping drinks cold).

The transition period style invented nothing new (apart from the fairly rare half-moon commode), but it made great use of the secretaire, the bureau *à cylindre* and the bonheur du jour (a lady's small bureau). In these pieces curves were confined to the legs, on which was set a rectangular top with a drawer and a straight-edged upper section, slightly overhung by the top. Half-moon commodes also made their appearance and this typical shape was to become one of the most prized elements of Louis XVI furniture.

Ormolu mounts gradually returned to decorative subjects that had been used since the Renaissance (grecques, pearls, small vases, amphora, festooned handles, entrelacs, etc.).

There was a growing fashion for pieces mounted with inlaid Sèvres porcelain plaques decorated with rosebuds.

This gives us an overview of the elements that make up the transition period style, although they are not always so apparent or frequent as to enable them to be recognised immediately. In practice the furniture of the transition period can be identified by a number of factors, affecting either shape, decoration or both; however to gain an understanding of these, the illustrations are more useful than a description of each of the different kinds of furniture.

We should also bear in mind the acceleration and creative diversity of 18th-century fashions, which offered an infinite number of different variations on the same kind of piece. As we approach the Louis XVI period transition period furniture, which was in a constant process of development, accentuates the formal and decorative characteristics that make it possible to pass from one style to the next.

This is not true, however, where seating is concerned. We have only a few vague examples of chairs, armchairs, *bergeres* and canapes from the transition period. Their rarity can perhaps be attributed to the fact that the Louis XV style had invented the shapes that were not only the most elegant, but also and above all the most comfortable. As a result they were obliged to remain bound to the curves that faithfully follow the anatomy of the human body. This does not mean that seating suddenly passed overnight from the Louis XV style to that of Louis XVI, but it was certainly difficult to find an appropriate new shape.

In terms of shape, transition period seating seems to have developed in the opposite direction from that of the *Régence* period, which was orientated towards the conquest of the curve. At the same time in the transition period decoration used subjects inspired by Antiquity, which were then reworked using more modern materials and techniques.

Typical furniture

As we have already noted, the style of the Louis XV-Louis XVI transitional period produced furniture of a hybrid appearance. Some links with the past became more tenuous and here and there rules re-emerged that were to form the future Louis XVI style. It might seem, therefore, that the revolution that was under way was entirely similar to that of the *Régence* style, but with different results. In fact, however, it was quite different.

The *Régence* style had indicated to the future Louis XV style the need to adopt rounded shapes and asymmetrical, richly imaginative decoration, freed of all ties to the past. In its development it had created typical shapes (the *arbalète*) and decorations (asymmetrical shells, female heads with hair, exotic subjects) that were easily recognisable. In other words it had presented itself as a style of conquest, richly creative and orientated towards the future.

The transition period style, on the other hand, turned with renewed enthusiasm to the past, which it tried to rework in an original way. It did not suggest anything new, it simply sought to adapt more modern techniques and materials to old shapes and subjects. This was a style not of conquest, but rather of re-development. Its main problem was to express the old classic themes of shape and decoration using new materials, such as veneer and ormolu. Its creativity was expressed through the experiments and technical virtuosity with which it reproduced vases, amphora, garlands of flowers, grecques, pearls, olives, the omnipresent acanthus leaf, *feuille d'eau*, new love-knots, symbols of love or entrelacs. These elements could no longer be reproduced in solid wood, for to do so would have been simply to imitate Renaissance art in a monotonous, nostalgic way. The originality and value of the transition style must be sought in the process by which it redeveloped elements from the past and in its tasteful choice, through much experimentation and reworking, of elements from Antiquity that could be best expressed using the new materials. In this way it cleared the ground for the development and maturity of the Louis XVI style.

If the style of the transition period has no more precise or definable features, this is also due to the vast quantity of elements inspired by the past. There is no type of furniture which sums up or typifies some of its precepts or archetypes, as is the case with the classic commode en tombeau of the *Régence* period.

Let us take the example of transition period commodes, whose variants can rapidly be described in the following way: commodes of a Louis XV shape, with floral inlays and ormolu mounts foreshadowing the Louis XVI style; rectangular (Louis XVI) commodes on short, cabriole (Louis XV) legs with a simple veneer of precious, exotic wood; veneered rectangular (Louis XVI) commodes with short cabriole legs and slightly serpentine (Louis XV) fronts; rectangular (Louis XVI) commodes on long cabriole legs, with extensive floral inlays which may be inspired by either the Louis XV or the Louis XVI styles, or both at once. There are a many variants within these categories, to which should be added other designs whose originality puts them beyond the scope of a brief list.

The transition period style explored decorative

aspects far more than it did shape. The new trend and the ideas carried forward to the future Louis XVI style seem more obvious in relation to shape, where there was a return to symmetry and to straight lines. Where decorative motifs are concerned, the selection process was longer and more laborious. However, given that there has never been a style that did not bequeath an indelible heritage to the future, we should note that oval and round shapes did not disappear and that the transition period style adopted them in small salon tables, whose legs were less obviously curved than those of the Louis XV designs. These pieces, more than any others, reveal the goals of the new style and the remains of the old: they manifest the most complete return to symmetry, as long as it is broken by round and oval medallions made with all kinds of materials (wood, ormolu, porcelain). A further example of what we are describing can be seen in seating, where the best Louis XVI designs have medallion backs (round or oval).

In conclusion, in comparison to the Louis XV style, the transition period style led the future Louis XVI style towards a total rejection of bombe shapes. Where decoration was concerned, it weighed up the past and suggested continuing to express beauty in furniture by means of veneers, floral inlays and many other decorative elements used in the neoclassical manner.

As a consequence of the new artistic credo aesthetic values in furniture were no longer determined by a symbiosis of form and decoration, as had been the case in the Louis XV style, but by the balance or contrast between the shape and the sum of the decorative elements.

In judging the transition period style as a whole, we have to acknowledge that it has an irrefutable historical value: it marks the beginning of creative decadence in furniture, the exhaustion of imagination and an inability to find new, original and unexplored directions. It was the beginning of the continual reworking of the styles of the past as the sole source of inspiration, apart from a few decorative elements and the occasional invention of new pieces.

At this decisive turning point in the history of furniture, we should very briefly mention two components which can be present in either shape, decoration or both and which have always been present in the furniture of every period. These are round and oval shapes and decorations. These two geometrical forms, which are among the most perfect that exist, had never entirely disappeared (for example in the round or oval table of the gothic, Renaissance or baroque periods). We shall frequently come across them in the later history of furniture in general and in that of the Louis XVI style in particular, which is partly based on decorations set in round or oval medallions. The transition period style both passed on and fostered such decorations.

Fakes and copies

The style of the transition period has bequeathed us a remarkable number of commodes, small salon tables and bonheur-du-jour and, even today, such pieces are easier to find on the market than bureaux *à cylindre*, fall-front bureaux or any kind of seating.

Among the cabinet-makers who distinguished themselves in creating the most elegant designs of the transition period we should mention Jean-François Oeben, who died in Paris in 1763, and his two best pupils, Jean-François Leleu and Jean-Henri Riesener. It seems certain moreover that the latter two stamped their work with the name of their dead master in order to increase sales of the pieces produced by the workshop.

This in itself provides further evidence of the comparative unimportance of the stamp. We do not mean by this that it has no value at all, we simply observe that the quality of a piece of furniture remains the same no matter who made it. The value of the work is determined by the precision with which it is made, the quality of the wood and mounts used and the elegance of its shape. These are the factors which, in combination, enable us to distinguish a masterpiece from a more modest piece.

Martin Carlin, another original cabinet-maker, popularised the art of making furniture with inlaid Sèvres porcelain plaques. His creations are masterpieces of high cabinet-making, whose current values are proportionate to the difficulty of finding them.

No matter what the commercial value of works by the great cabinet-makers of the transition period style, one thing is abundantly clear: the precepts of this style are almost entirely absent from furniture known as rustic. This phenomenon is easy to explain.

Paris, the centre of all 18th century fashions, influenced the other great European capitals, which were receptive to any new cultural or artistic trend. The intellectual elite and select clientele of the French capital facilitated innovative developments shaped by the most sophisticated tastes. Rustic furniture, on the other hand, always tended more or less openly to recreate precise styles. It remained open to the influences of historical formulae and revealed an indifference to and indeed an inability to imitate intermediate designs, in other words transitional styles. Furthermore the craftsmen in the smaller urban centres of France were more traditionalist, less demanding and less given to enthusiasm for the new. They needed more time to pass from one style to the next and transitional styles, by their very nature, had too brief an existence to spread to the provinces. The only exception to this is the *Régence* style, which marks the passage from the Louis XIV to the Louis XV styles and which was also adopted by the makers of rustic furniture.

But the *Régence*, king of the transitional styles, benefitted from an exceptionally long period in relation to its historical bounds and succeeded in creating shapes and decorations whose revolutionary aspect could not fail to influence rustic furniture. The comparatively fine commode en tombeau, which was made throughout the first half of the century in every part of France, provides the most significant example of this: it was not a beautiful piece, but from the stylistic point of view it reflected the new and original directions in which tastes were moving. The Louis XV–Louis XVI transitional style on the other hand did not have any avant-garde characteristics and offered no innovations: its output was scattered and its gestation and maturation period too short in comparison to those of the *Régence*. As a result its influence on rustic furniture was negligible, as we have noted.

On the other hand some rustic pieces may reveal a mixture of different styles. These are the typical pieces of particular poor regions, such as Brittany, which were culturally isolated and removed from the main routes of communication and exchange. Artisanal production in these regions sometimes lagged far behind in its grasp of the shapes and decorative elements of the different styles, combining them all after the event, without distinction of style or chronology, in commodes, buffets, armoires, beds or chairs. Over the centuries in this way the traditions of past periods were combined with the conceptions of the present.

We have spent a little time describing some unusual aspects of the history of rustic furniture in order to justify our lack of discussion of the transformations and embellishment of specific rustic pieces. Practically speaking it is not possible to embellish pieces which, to all intents and purposes, do not exist.

Nor is it possible to speak of fakes in this context since, with the exception of a few pieces of very high quality, the transition period did not create typical pieces whose characteristics were reproduced and which could provide models for the fakers. This is not to deny the existence of any transition period pieces which have been transformed, embellished or faked, but simply to note that they are absent from the current antiques market.

When the period of reproduction furniture in past styles of all kinds began in the 19th century (around 1840), the most common designs of the transition period were left out. Instead only the most celebrated pieces were reproduced, and these in limited quantities. They included fine commodes on long cabriole legs, decorated with inlaid flowers and medallions and exuberantly mounted with ormolu.

It is not impossible that, in the past, some of these items were faked to appear as original period pieces.

But faked masterpieces of any kind are hard to sell today, given their notoriety, the very high prices they reach and the serious guarantees that collectors require. Furthermore, the extensive studies which continually appear in the public domain make such deception even more risky.

In conclusion we can say that transition period furniture offers the best guarantees of authenticity, if only because it is difficult to pin down its style.

How to find transition period furniture

The transition period style produced a kind of furniture of undisputed historical importance, irrespective of its artistic value. Just like the *Régence* style, it reflects the gradual change in taste of a whole society.

Today, and particularly in Paris, it is still possible to find many pieces in this style, both in the shops of antiques' dealers and in the salesrooms. There is no lack of commodes, small oval or round tables, semainiers and secretaires; seats of any kind are less frequently found. The most magnificent pieces are also available, although there are not many of them. These are represented by rare commodes with two or three rows of drawers *sans traverse*, inlaid with medallions with pastoral motifs and enhanced by rich ormolu mounting. There are also bonheur-du-jour and, rarely, bureaux *à cylindre*.

In London and New York the transition period style appears only occasionally in the form of its most significant and very high quality pieces, particularly in the most high-profile sales. In Italy transition furniture is very rare and finding it is a pure matter of luck. Turin, Milan and Rome are of course the main cities in which it may be possible to find an important piece.

Quality and valuation

In its twenty years the transition period style produced a lesser quantity of pieces than the Louis XV and Louis XVI styles. As a result valuations for commodes, small tables, bureaux, veneered or lacquered secretaires and seats in natural wood or gilt are fairly high, noticeably less than those for Louis XV pieces and more than those for Louis XVI.

Among the finest pieces we must mention the rare, elegant bonheur-du-jour, either inlaid with flowers or simply veneered or lacquered and enhanced with valuable ormolu mounts. These pieces are not too large and have great personality, which makes them easy to accommodate. Their aesthetic qualities immediately make them an important element in any interior and they are therefore highly-prized by women buyers, who tend to prefer small, graceful pieces. It is true that where antique furniture is concerned, rarity and quality almost always mean very high prices, but any financial sacrifice will reap its rewards over time.

Among the rare, valuable pieces, we should mention the lacquered secretaires decorated with oriental motifs and enhanced with extremely finely chased ormolu mounts, superior in their precision to Louis XV mounts.

At the same level of quality are the commodes with three rows of drawers, two *sans traverse*, with long, slightly cabriole legs, chased mercury-gilt ormolu profiles and fronts split into several panels by splendid ormolu mounts. Generally speaking a central ormolu medallion contains a pastoral scene, landscape or scene of ruins; on either side of this bouquets of flowers or other decorative elements such as amphora, Medici vases or figures are inlaid inside ormolu sur-

rounds. These are the most significant and sought-after pieces of this style, for obvious reasons: the transition period adopted the most refined techniques and materials, characteristic of the 18th century, to create pieces that were still linked to the Louis XV style through their long cabriole legs, which lend a touch of eccentricity. This type of commode represents the synthesis of three mutually-reinforcing qualities: beauty, rarity and originality.

Where new designs, or rather new shapes are concerned, pride of place goes to the half-moon commode with slightly cabriole legs. Such pieces are fairly rare and rightly prized by collectors. Most sought-after are those whose half-moon shape is slightly concave at the sides. This detail, which may at first sight seem insignificant, represents a refinement of technique and construction typical of the great master cabinet-makers.

Turning now to seating, pieces of this type appear on the antiques market only occasionally and it is impossible to identify all the variations, which are manifest more in stylistic details than in typical, frequently-reproduced shapes. We cannot therefore describe them precisely. Seats should be assessed individually, remembering that chairs, armchairs, *bergeres* and canapes (whether or not they are covered with Aubusson, Gobelins or Beauvais tapestry) are more fragile pieces and more subject to wear than other types of furniture. This makes them rare and they almost always reach very high prices.

Clearly, when discussing the finest pieces, we are referring to a precise category which, even when produced in large quantities, comprises the most original designs and thus those that are most highly valued by the market.

The consoles and gilt seats of the transition period follow the same rules as those of the Louis XV style; however as these pieces are currently less fashionable, they may be bought for better prices. This is a step worth taking, as fashions change but antique furniture remains and genuine period pieces acquire a dual advantage with the passing of time: they bring refinement to an interior and are also a good investment.

Moving now from the rarest pieces to the more common, and therefore simpler items, forming the basic output in this style, we can say that the pieces described above can be bought on the honourable antiques market in more modest versions, without too great a degree of sacrifice. Such pieces can easily be integrated into a creatively arranged interior, alongside Louis XV and Louis XVI pieces, even in spaces of a very modern design. We should add that commodes, bureaux, secretaires, small tables, chairs, *bergeres* and canapes which do not aspire to the highest pinnacles of art have never been a favourite target of the fakers. For reasons of vanity and, above all, greed, such people proceed like gourmets, selecting only the rarest, most expensive dishes.

Even the many reproductions of furniture of every 18th-century style and period seem to have avoided transition period furniture, particularly the most commonly found. Those reproductions there are copy only the most prestigious pieces, and in very small numbers compared to the other styles.

Turning now to the limited production of provincial furniture, which should not be ignored even when the carcases are made with regional woods (fruitwood, beechwood, walnut), valuations are slightly lower than those for Parisian pieces. For the French, a cabinet that does not have oak drawers is not worthy of consideration. Such severity is perhaps unfair, given that many provincial pieces have the same technical details, shapes and veneers as their Parisian counterparts. And because there is precisely no qualitative difference from the aesthetic point of view, and because prices are always very affordable, we would not hesitate to advise in favour of purchase.

Furniture of the transition period is very highly valued throughout France, particularly in Paris, where the most significant pieces of all styles and periods are found. Furthermore, the tastes of the clientele are formed by reading books and specialist magazines, visiting antiques exhibitions and studying the pieces themselves. We should add to this that the French academic rigour in both style and construction assists in making these works better known, so that interest is sustained, and this favours the seller.

In Italy, on the other hand, like most foreign styles characterised by nuances and hybrids of past and future elements, the transition style is not very well known. Italians have not developed a taste for this style of furniture because the comparable Italian phenomenon of the passage from the Barocchetto to the neoclassical styles is even harder to identify and more nuanced from the stylistic point of view.

Italian antiques dealers prefer better-known and more highly-prized pieces such as classic Louis XV and Louis XVI furniture. The few examples that do appear on the Italian market generally come from old private collections and do not usually reach very high prices.

For all these reasons we can buy transition period furniture anywhere in Italy with the exception of Piedmont, where an affinity with the style and culture of France means that such pieces are recognised and receive a more appropriate assessment and valuation.

Fine commode with rounded angles, three rows of drawers, two *sans traverse* and a *brèche d'Alep* marble top. The piece is veneered in precious, exotic woods and divided overall into panels richly mounted with ormolu surrounds, to which can be added the imposing ormolu frieze around the top drawer and the mounts along the profiles of the legs. Such elements add value to all such types of commode from the Louis XV–Louis XVI transition period.
Current valuation: collector's price.

Fine commode with three rows of drawers, two *sans traverse*. The rich ormolu mounting enhances the overall shape and decoration of the piece. Current valuation: collector's price.

Below: fine commode with rounded angles, three rows of drawers, two sans traverse, and a white marble top. In this piece, veneered in rosewood, tulipwood and amaranth, the beauty and refined precision of the inlays combines with the rich exuberance of the ormolu mounts. It is without question a masterpiece of French cabinet-making. Sold in London in 1972: £ 12,680, $ 22,700.
Current valuation: collector's price.

Classic commode with two drawers with traverse and a marble top, veneered in tulipwood and kingwood with sober ormolu mounting. The Louis XV style is present only in the cabriole legs.
1984 valuation: about £ 7,740, $ 10,260.
Current valuation: £ 13,260, $ 21,970, € 19,800.

Partly classic, partly fine commode with three rows of drawers and a *brèche d'Alep* marble top; inlaid with cubes in rosewood and tulipwood. The rich ormolu frieze across the top drawer and around the sides partly distracts attention from the banality of the cube decoration. 1984 valuation: £ 17,200, $ 22,800.
Current valuation: £ 30,600, $ 50,700, € 45,750.

Fine commode with canted angles, two drawers *sans traverse* and a Saint-Anne grey marble top. It is veneered in kingwood with elegant inlays of various motifs enhancing its value and refinement. Sold in Paris in 1972: £ 5,400, $ 9,700.
1984 valuation: £ 21,500, $ 28,500.
Current valuation: collector's price.

Classic commode with canted angles, three rows of drawers, two *sans traverse*, and a Saint-Anne grey marble top; it is veneered in tulipwood and amaranth and has a medallion inlaid with flowers at the front, reflecting its aspirations to the fine category.
1984 valuation: £ 15,000, $ 19,950.
Current valuation: £ 22,440, $ 37,200, € 33,550.

Bottom left: commode in mahogany with canted angles, two drawers with traverse and a grey veined marble top. The decoration engraved in the mahogany suggests that this is an artisanal piece made in the Bordeaux region. Sold in 1973: £ 3,250, $ 6,060.
1984 valuation: £ 8,600, $ 11,400.
Current valuation: £ 10,200, $ 16,900, € 15,250.

Fine, rare bibliotheque of exceptional quality in the shape of a commode, veneered in burr walnut and amaranth and inlaid with hearts on the sides. It bears the stamp of J.F. Oeben.

Sold by Sotheby's in Monte Carlo in 1996: £ 879,780, $ 1,368,700. Current valuation: collector's price.

Fine commode of exceptional quality with three rows of drawers, two *sans traverse*, in tulipwood and amaranth veneer, inlaid with motifs of vases of flowers and pastoral scenes, mounted with elegant chased ormolu surrounds. It bears the stamp of P.A. Foullet, master cabinet-maker in Paris in 1765. Sold by Sotheby's in London in 1984: £ 107,500, $ 142,500.
Sold by Christie's in New York in 1993: £ 235,170, $ 353,300.
Current valuation: collector's price.

Fine commode in tulipwood and sycamore veneer with elegant or-
molu mounts. The refinement of the inlaid pastoral scene and still lifes is so perfect that they seem to be painted.
Current valuation: £ 91,800, $ 152,100, € 137,200.

Fine secretaire in tulipwood with floral inlays and ivory, attributed to Daniel Deloose, master cabinet-maker in Paris by royal privilege in 1767. In shape the piece still reflects the Louis XV style, while the small ivory vase and inlaid four-leafed clover enhanced with ivory are from the Louis XVI period.

Sold in Milan in 1980: £ 152,480, $ 35,500.
Current valuation: £ 76,500, $ 126,750, € 114,400.

Fine jewel-case of exceptional quality in tulipwood and sycamore veneer, richly decorated with Sèvres soft paste with floral motifs. The extensive, refined ormolu mounting enhances the structure of the piece, which bears the stamp of Martin Carlin, master cabinet-maker in Paris in 1766.

Provenance: Marie-Antoinette, dauphine, 1770.
Sold by Etude Tajan in Paris in 1996: £ 282,780, $ 440,000.
Current valuation: collector's price.

Classic breakfront commode with rounded angles. It is veneered in tulipwood inside amaranth surrounds with a double band of boxwood or olivewood. It has two large drawers sans traverse, with a row of three drawers above. Chased ormolu mounts with laurel and acanthus leaves, channelled and scrolled chutes, clawed sabots, ribboned escutcheons, *cul de lampe* and mouldings with movable ring handles. The top is of moulded, white-veined grey marble.

The commode bears the stamp of R. Lacroix. Roger Vandercruse, known as Lacroix, admitted as master on 6 February 1755, with the master's mark. (Photo: Tajan, Paris).
Sold in Paris in 1995: £ 37,570, $ 58,000.
Current valuation: £ 45,900, $ 76,000, € 68,600.

Commode of exceptional quality in satinwood and amaranth veneer, with fine chased ormolu mounts. It was made for queen Marie-Antoinette, to be placed in the Petit Trianon. It is regarded as being of national importance.

Sold in Paris in 1981: £ 105,970, $ 213,280.
1984 valuation: the same.
Current valuation: collector's price.

Fine commode in tulipwood veneer, richly mounted with ormolu, attributed to Topino. Sold in Monte Carlo in 1979: £ 25,600, $ 60,000. 1984 valuation: £ 36,120, $ 47,880.
Current valuation: collector's price.

Facing page, top: commode of excellent quality, in tulipwood and satinwood veneer. The rich ormolu mounting and medallions inlaid with figures (peasants and musicians), typical of the Louis XVI style, are of particular note. Sold in Monte Carlo in 1983: £ 60,690, $ 91,890. 1984 valuation: the same.
Current valuation: collector's price.

Facing page, bottom: fine commode of excellent quality, in tulipwood veneer. Inlaid with scenes in the Chinese fashion, showing themes from pictures by François Boucher. The piece has three drawers, two sans traverse and with the central section of each protruding. The breakfront shape in both the transition and Louis XVI styles is a detail of construction and technique that noticeably raises the value of these pieces. This commode bears the stamp of Christophe Wolff. (Photo: Tajan, Paris). Provenance: the collection of F. de Panague. Sold in Paris in 1983: £ 32,900, $ 49,880.
1984 valuation: the same. Current valuation: collector's price.

Facing page: exceptional commode with a top of Spanish brocatello marble, bearing the stamp of Dautriche. The piece is veneered in tulipwood inlaid with a rich pattern of stylised daisies.
Current valuation: collector's price.

Fine commode in tulipwood and kingwood veneer, with profiles in green-coloured wood, inlaid with small four-leafed clover and ivory flecks. It bears the stamp of D. de Loose, master cabinet-maker in 1767. The piece has an elegant shape, with sides slightly curved where it touches the wall. The refined mercury-gilt ormolu mounts are combined with the inlaid sections with great skill and to harmonious effect. Current valuation: collector's price.

Fine commode of exceptional quality, in tulipwood and amaranth veneer, inlaid with flowers and vases. It bears the stamp of N. Grevenich, master cabinet-maker in 1768. A few similar examples have variants showing landscapes treated pictorially with elements in ivory. Current valuation: collector's price.

Fine commode in tulipwood and amaranth veneer with mercury-gilt ormolu profiles enhancing the entire structure.
Current valuation: £ 51,000, $ 84,500, € 76,250.

Fine commode in tulipwood veneer, inlaid with floral motifs. It is soberly mounted with mercury-gilt ormolu.
Current valuation: £ 51,000, $ 84,500, € 76,250.

Small salon table in tulipwood veneer inlaid with utensils, with an undertier. Attributed to G. Topino. (Photo: Tajan, Paris).

Sold in Paris in 1980: £ 12,900, $ 30,000. 1984 valuation: £ 15,050, $ 19,950. Current valuation: collector's price.

Fine bonheur-du-jour in tulipwood veneer inlaid with utensils. Attributed to G. Topino.

1984 valuation: & 21,500, $ 28,500.
Current valuation: collector's price.

Fine small table in tulipwood and amaranth veneer, richly decorated with musical motifs and vases of flowers. The musical elements, neo-classical vases and rectangular band of the drawer decorations already reflect the Louis XVI style, while the cabriole legs reflect the Louis XV style. These small salon tables are now very rare in all versions of the different styles, which explains why they are valued at a collector's price.
Current valuation: collector's price.

Fine small salon table in tulipwood veneer, inlaid with landscapes and flowers in coloured woods. Sober chased mercury-gilt ormolu mounting. This piece is also known as a *table de milieu* ('middle table') because it is decorated back and front.
1984 valuation: & 17,200, $ 22,800.
Current valuation: collector's price.

Left: fine small salon table in tulipwood veneer, inlaid with flowers in green-coloured wood. The transition period is reflected in the rectangular shape of the top and inlaid medallion. Rectangular and oval shapes are precepts of the Louis XVI style, while the ormolu mounts and curved legs denote the Louis XV style.
Current valuation: collector's price.

Fine small table in tulipwood veneer, with an ormolu frieze of grecques. The Louis XV style persists in the highly cabriole legs, while the Louis XVI style manifests itself in the ormolu grecques, which are one of its frequently-reproduced features. The piece bears the stamp of RVLC, master cabinet-maker in Paris in 1755. Sold in London in 1988 by Sotheby's: about £ 43,400, $ 77,200.
Current valuation: collector's price.

Below: fine small table veneered in tulipwood and amaranth and decorated in the Chinese manner with landscapes and birds, bearing the stamp of J.F. Oeben, cabinet-maker to the king in 1754. This table should be dated to the beginning of the transition period, since it reflects the Louis XV style in shape and decoration, except for the geometrical inlays on its body, which has opening drawers. (Photo: Tajan, Paris). Sold in Paris in 1990: £ 56,750, $ 101,000.
Current valuation: collector's price.

Fine *bonheur-du-jour* in tulipwood veneer inlaid with vases of flowers and utensils, bearing the stamp of J.G. Schlichtig, master cabinet-maker in Paris in 1765. It is decorated with refined chased mercury-gilt ormolu mounts.
Current valuation: collector's price.

Fine *bonheur-du-jour* in tulipwood and kingwood veneer, inlaid with vases of flowers and utensils. It bears the stamp of C. Topino, master cabinet-maker in Paris in 1773. It is mounted with chased mercury-gilt ormolu. Inlays of utensils are characteristic of Topino and his pupils. Current valuation: collector's price.

Fine *coiffeuse* of exceptional quality, bearing the stamp of Léonard Boudin, master cabinet-maker in Paris in 1761. It is veneered in tulipwood with surrounds of grecques in green coloured wood and inlaid with bouquets and baskets of flowers, musical instruments and symbols of love.

This design is typical of the last phase of the transition style; the Louis XV style survives only in the curved legs.
Sold in Paris in 1990: £ 221,860, $ 394,800.
Current valuation: collector's price.

Fine *coiffeuse* in tulipwood and amaranth veneer, inlaid with flowers and musical motifs in coloured woods, bearing the stamp of C. Wolff (Paris 1720–1795). Current valuation: £ 35,700, $ 59,150, € 53,380.

Rare pair of fine cabinets of exceptional quality with sliding doors, in tulipwood veneer with amaranth profiles; richly mounted with chased mercury-gilt ormolu. The top is of *brèche d'Alep* marble. Current valuation: collector's price.

Rare fine small secretaire in tulipwood and amaranth veneer, richly inlaid with musical motifs and flowers on stalks, bearing the stamp of N. Petit, master cabinet-maker in Paris in 1761. The piece dates from the early transition period; all the elements of shape and decoration reflect the Louis XV style, with the exception of the musical motifs on the fall front. Current valuation: collector's price.

Fine secretaire in tulipwood and amaranth veneer inlaid with flowers and musical instruments. Still perfectly Louis XV in shape, the piece shows essentially Louis XVI decoration (small bouquets of flowers bound with ribbons, musical instruments surmounted by

drapery). It bears the stamp of Nicolas Petit, master cabinet-maker in Paris in 1765.
1984 valuation: £ 25,800, $ 34,200.
Current valuation: £ 25,500, $ 42,250, € 38,100.

Fine small secretaire *d'appui* in tulipwood, amaranth and coloured wood veneer, inlaid with vases of flowers. Soberly mounted with chased, mercury-gilt ormolu. The top is of *brèche d'Alep* marble and the secretaire bears the stamp of C. Saunier, master cabinet-maker in Paris in 1752, at only eighteen years of age.
Current valuation: £ 35,700, $ 59,150, € 53,380.

Fine bibliotheque of exceptional quality in kingwood veneer, richly mounted with ormolu. (Photo: Tajan, Paris). Sold in Paris in May 1984: £ 51,600, $ 68,400. 1984 valuation: the same. Current valuation: collector's price.

Classic commode, one of a pair, in tulipwood veneer with kingwood profiles and cartouches. The flattened shape and Louis XVI decorative ormolu mounts reflect the transition period. Sold in Paris in 1984: £ 51,600, $ 68,400. Current valuation: collector's price.

Fine commode with rounded angles, two drawers *sans traverse* and a grey Saint-Anne marble top. The piece has a polychrome and gold lacquer with birds and flowers. Of particular note are the elegant ormolu contours of the facade, containing the decoration of both drawers within a single surround. Sold in Paris in 1973: £ 4,650, $ 8,760. 1984 valuation: about £ 15,050, $ 19,950. Current valuation: collector's price.

Fine small commode with rounded angles, two drawers *sans traverse* and a white marble top, bearing the stamp of J. Bircklé. Of particular note are the rich and refined inlays of doves, vases and flowers which enhance the value of this commode. 1984 valuation: £ 21,500, $34,200. Current valuation: collector's price.

Classic commode with rounded angles, two drawers *sans traverse* and a Spanish brocatello marble top. The rosewood and tulipwood cube inlay, which is not currently seen as desirable, detracts from the elegant ormolu mounting. 1984 valuation: £ 4,300, $ 5,700. Current valuation: £ 17,340, $ 28,700, € 25,900.

Giltwood console with *brèche d'Alep* marble top. The supports and stretcher are in the Louis XV style, but the decoration overall, carved with foliage, pearls, rosettes and laurel leaves, is manifestly Louis XVI. Sold in Paris in 1974: £ 26,380, $ 51,750.
1984 valuation: £ 4,300, $ 5,700.
Current valuation: £ 10,200, $ 16,900, € 15,250.

Below: fine commode in lacquer on a black ground, with rounded angles, three rows of drawers, two sans traverse, and a *brèche d'Alep* marble top, bearing the stamp of Boudin. It has a polychrome and gold decoration of figures, flowers, leaves and landscapes. Sold in Paris in 1975: £ 5,260, $ 10,860. 1984 valuation: £ 10,750, $ 14,250.
 Current valuation: collector's price.

Rare fine half-moon commode with three drawers, two *sans traverse*, and slightly concave sides with doors. The top is in veined white marble. Kingwood veneer surrounded by green wood profiles and rich ormolu mounting. The commode bears the stamp of Topino. Sold in Paris in 1971: £ 13,400, $ 23,680. Resold at auction in 1980: £ 30,500, $ 71,000. 1984 valuation: £ 38,700, $ 51,300. Current valuation: collector's price.

Pair of fine encoignures in lacquer with a black ground and *brèche d'Alep* marble top. Polychrome and gold decoration of figures, landscapes and pagodas.

Sold in Paris in 1975: £ 3,800, $ 7,900.
1984 valuation: £ 15,050, $ 19,950.
Current valuation: collector's price.

Fine oval salon table. It is veneered in tulipwood with amaranth profiles and richly decorated with inlays of losenges and four-leafed clover. It bears the stamp of RVLC. The undertier has an ormolu gallery. Sold in Paris in 1970: £ 4,070, $ 7,050.
1984 valuation: about £ 8,600, $ 11,400.
Current valuation: £ 20,400, $ 33,800, € 30,500.

Rare fine small commode, one of a pair, with rounded angles, two drawers *sans traverse* and a white marble top, inlaid with musical motifs and entwined leaves and bouquets of flowers, bearing the stamp of F. Rubestuck. Sold in Paris in 1973: £ 14,240, $ 26,480.
1984 valuation: about £ 34,400, $ 45,600.
Current valuation: collector's price.

Classic salon table in tulipwood veneer with undertier. Sold in Paris in 1975: £ 2,870, $ 5,900. 1984 valuation: about £ 5,160, $ 6,840. Current valuation: £ 10,200, $ 16,900, € 15,250.

Rare fine small commode in lacquer with a black ground, with rounded angles, two drawers *sans traverse* and a white marble top. It has a decoration of landscapes in polychrome and gold and bears the stamp of F. Bircklé. Sold in Paris in 1971: £ 3,100, $ 5,500.
1984 valuation: about, £ 6,450, $ 8 550.
Current valuation: £ 20,400, $ 33,800, € 30,500.

Fine small oval table standing on four legs with an undertier, in tulipwood and amaranth veneer. The piece is inlaid with utensils, a motif much used by Topino, whose stamp it bears.
1984 valuation: ₤ 17,200, $ 22,800.
Current valuation: collector's price.

Rare small oval salon table in precious, exotic wood inlaid with four-leafed clovers contained within losenges and bearing the stamp of J.P. Dusautoy. Sold in Paris in 1971: ₤ 5,200, $ 9,150.
1984 valuation: about ₤ 12,900, $ 17,100.
Current valuation: collector's price.

Rare fine small salon table, in kingwood veneer with sober inlays. The ormolu profiles follow the shape of the piece. Sold in Paris in 1970: ₤ 4,770, $ 8,300. 1984 valuation: about ₤ 10,750, $ 14,250.
Current valuation: collector's price.

Classic small salon table without undertier. Sold in Milan in 1971: ₤ 4,770, $ 8,300. 1984 valuation: about ₤ 4,300, $ 5,700.
Current valuation: ₤ 5,100, $ 8,450, € 7,600.

Rare small round salon table, fine in quality, with one drawer and an undertier. It is veneered in tulipwood with a delicate floral inlay, elegantly mounted with ormolu and bears the stamp of C. Topino. Sold in Paris in 1970: £ 7,960, $ 13,800.
1984 valuation: about £ 38,700, £ 51,300.
Current valuation: collector's price.

Bureau, partly classic, partly fine. It is still Louis XV in style, however the contours with grecques enhancing the kingwood veneer and the ormolu gallery to the table top, also with grecques, denote the transition style. 1984 valuation: about £ 19,350, $ 25,650.
Current valuation: £ 35,700, $ 59,150, € 53,380.

Rare rafraîchissoir, one of a pair, in mahogany and bearing the stamp of J.C. Canabas. These pieces are not very fine in quality; however they are very highly valued for two reasons: their rarity and the stamp of Canabas, regarded as one of the most prestigious of French cabinet-makers for mahogany. Sold in Paris in 1973: £ 11,170, $ 20,770. Current valuation: collector's price.

Rare, fine, ovoid work table, in amaranth inlaid with losenges in pale wood. Attributed to J.H. Riesener. Sold in Paris in 1973: £ 11,170, $ 20,770. Current valuation: collector's price.

Secretaire of excellent quality in tulipwood and kingwood veneer. The curved front and sides and the drawer *à doucine* above the fall-front are typical of the Louis XV style, while the decorative grecques on the profiles reflect the Louis XVI style.
1984 valuation: about £ 21,500, $ 28,500.
Current valuation: £ 20,400, $ 33,800, € 30,500.

Important bureau *à cylindre* in tulipwood veneer decorated with cubes and losenges. This piece is manifestly Louis XV in style, but is placed in the transition period due to its ring handles, typical of the Louis XVI style, and the ormolu gallery around the top, which has ovoid elements. The bureau bears the stamp of J.H. Riesener.
Current valuation: collector's price.

Centre: small fine drum table, one of a pair, in tulipwood and amaranth veneer inlaid with vases, flowers and leaves.
1984 valuation: about £ 19,350, $ 25,650.
Current valuation: collector's price.

Classic semainier with canted angles and *brèche d'Alep* marble top. The piece is veneered in butterfly kingwood.
1984 valuation: about £ 8,600, $ 11,400.
Current valuation: £ 7,650, $ 12,700, € 11,440.

Classic large semainier with canted angles and Saint-Anne grey marble top. The piece is veneered in kingwood and tulipwood and is stamped P. Desfriches. Sold in Paris in 1972: £ 2,700, $14,250.
1984 valuation: about £ 10,750, $ 14,250.
Current valuation: £ 12,750, $ 21,150, € 19,000.

Fine secretaire with rounded angles and a *brèche d'Alep* marble top. It is richly inlaid on a kingwood ground with the musical instruments, vases of flowers and utensils typical of the Louis XVI style, while the Louis XV style is manifest in the short cabriole legs. Attributed to Topino. Sold in Paris in 1971: £ 3,580, $ 6,300.
1984 valuation: £ 21,500, $ 28,500.
Current valuation: £ 20,400, $ 33,800, € 30,500.

Fine small *canapé corbeille*, gilt and of excellent quality. The refined carving follows and decorates the entire structure of the piece, which bears the stamp of Pothier.
1984 valuation: about £ 8,600, $ 11,400.
Current valuation: collector's price.

Fine armchair, one of a set of four, in carved natural wood.
Current valuation: £ 18,360, $ 30,400. € 27,450.

Armchair in wood, painted white and gilt. The shape is typical of the Louis XV style, while the medallion decoration with festooned leaves and flowers on the back and seat already denote the Louis XVI style.
1984 valuation: £ 1,500, $ 2,000. 1991 valuation: £ 2,700, $ 4,780.
Current valuation: £ 2,040, $ 3,380. € 3,050.

The Louis XVI style

The Louis XVI style became dominant in Paris around 1770 and persisted for a few years after the death, in 1793, of the king who gave it its name. Having influenced a large part of Europe, and Italy in particular, it faded more quickly than the other 18th-century styles, being swept away by the French Revolution. It represents the continuation and logical outcome of the transitional style which, as we have seen, advocated a return to classical sources of inspiration.

Commodes, bureaux, small tables and *bergeres* no longer imitated the whimsically distorted shapes of the Louis XV style; on the contrary they tended to straighten all that had hitherto been gracefully bent or curved.

Once curves and rounded structures were abandoned, the late 18th century saw the return of traditional parallelepiped shapes, with decorative elements taken from Greek, Roman and Renaissance art and sometimes from the Louis XIV style. We should not forget that the ancient city of Pompeii was excavated in 1763, having been buried by the eruption of Vesuvius in AD 79. This event provided new material to the intellectual elite of the time, who were engaged on a search through the traces of the past for ideas to create a new form of art.

On this basis one might have expected Louis XVI furniture to be a monotonous expression of classical art, reflecting a sterile return of that style. In reality, however, things were quite different. It is true that the style drew its inspiration from the past, and from every period of the past, but it succeeded in avoiding any slavish imitation by reworking old themes in original ways, using a range of modern techniques and materials. This is easy to appreciate when we remember that the great periods for furniture (gothic, Renaissance and part of the baroque) had not had the rich variety of 18th-century materials at their disposal and used mainly solid wood (oak, walnut).

To get a better look at this return to the past, we shall now analyse the decorative elements taken from antiquity and given new life in Louis XVI fur-

niture. The list of the most frequently used, created in ormolu and the different woods, worked using the techniques of engraving, carving and marquetry, is as follows: grooved plaques, female heads, incense burners, pine cones, rosettes, garlands, trophies, urns, *entrelacs*, rosettes entwined with crowns, olive leaves, acanthus leaves, vine leaves, *oronges*, grecques and knots.

The veneers, inlays and lacquers were the same as those used on Louis XV furniture, but the interpretation of the style was entirely different.

In floral inlays there was a preference for small bouquets and vases of flowers in a stylised, restrained arrangement, quite unlike the decoration of Louis XV furniture, with its invasions of exuberant, disordered flowers, whose roses became Louis XVI rosebuds. The decorative images of Louis XVI inlays portray bucolic scenes, echoes of a life lived closer to nature, which can also be heard in the literature of the time.

The Chinese lacquers and vernis Martin reflect the same subjects as the Louis XV style, but the scenes of oriental life unfold on flat surfaces, framed by straight surrounds of ormolu or bands of wood.

The decoration of furniture (particularly secretaires and commodes), with round or oval medallions enhanced with typical elements of the style (female heads, floral inlays, musical instruments, children) and surrounded by rich ormolu mounts or inlays, is another typical aspect of the Louis XVI style. Many pieces have inlaid round, oval or rectangular porcelain plaques, others are decorated with simple metal mounts, with some channelling on the legs and drawer traverses, as we shall see from the illustrations on the following pages.

Let us now turn from the most commonly-found decorative elements to the shapes that typify the style, its preferred materials and the innovations it introduced.

As we have seen, bombe shapes disappeared and straight lines reasserted themselves. But to avoid excessive rigidity, the cabinet-makers used a great many rounded or canted angles in their designs for commodes, secretaires, semainiers and so on; they avoided straight angles wherever possible and the half-moon shape became a typical Louis XVI form, having previously made only occasional appearances in a few console tables of the rustic type (such as the round table used in convents, consisting of two half-moon console tables) and, more rarely, in transition furniture. Many commodes, consoles, tables and *dessertes* were made in this shape.

The construction materials were practically the same, but, in addition to all the woods previously used, we should now note the vast production of pieces in either solid mahogany or with mahogany veneer; not only do these typify an aspect of the style, they bring the status of art to a wood which the Louis XV style used only for pieces of minor importance (rafraîchissoirs, jardinières).

Typical pieces

The Louis XVI style was not particularly inventive in spirit, but as heir to all the innovations of the Louis XV style, it interpreted this inheritance in its own language and popularised the bureau *à cylindre*, secretaire and bonheur-du-jour. The latter was first presented in 1750 and very soon became fashionable. However this style's specific creations are the table bouilllotte, the *commode desserte* and the *console desserte*.

The table bouillotte

This is a round table with a diameter of about 70 cm, consisting of a marble top surrounded by an ormolu gallery, with two drawers and two sliding surfaces in the frieze. It is generally made of mahogany and has four legs. It takes its name from the card game known as *bouillotte*, which was invented in the reign of Louis XVI. It usually has a removable round top, one side of which is bound in leather and the other covered in green baize for playing card games.

The commode desserte and console desserte

The commode desserte is a kind of half-moon-shaped commode, with three rows of drawers in the centre-front, the frieze drawer at the top being smaller than the lower two. The two convex side sections contain shelves level with the drawers. Sometimes the commode desserte has only a single row of drawers in the frieze and two shelves beneath. In this case it is known by the more appropriate name of 'console desserte'. This is a far rarer piece than the commode desserte, but consoles dessertes with a single shelf are very common.

Sometimes the desserte has a shape that we can broadly describe as 'flattened half-moon': the central section at the front is straight and only the two side sections are concave or convex.

Where all the other pieces are concerned (commodes, bureaux, small vitrines, bibliotheques, etc.), it is better to go directly to the illustrations and captions, which give a better understanding of the new style.

Half-moon commodes

These commodes have a characteristic shape, with a marble top and three rows of drawers at the front, with or *sans traverse*. The curved sides have two doors. This piece made its first, timid appearance with the Louis XV–Louis XVI transitional style.

Seating

We should start by noting that seats reached the peak of their development with the Louis XVI style in a remarkable range of different designs, although they did lose some of the comfort of the Louis XV chairs.

Even in this domain, the Louis XVI style transformed earlier designs (both those for summer use with caned seats and backs and the padded versions designed for winter) and presented them in new versions. In addition there was a remarkable increase in the numbers of types of chairs, which take their names from the shapes of their backs, whether round, oval or medallion-shaped, horseshoe-shaped, straight, trapezium-shaped (with the smallest side between the angles near the seat), lyre-shaped, curved, or montgolfière ('hot-air balloon-shaped', after the balloon in which the *Montgolfier* brothers made the first ascent by human beings in 1783).

Chair legs generally take the form of a small column, tapered at the bottom. The most common variations are legs with channelling, small *rudenté* pilasters (whose channelling includes a semi-circular, twisted element up to a certain height), helicoidal legs and legs *à asperge* ('asparagus legs', after the channelling which, up to a certain height, includes an element reminiscent of an asparagus tip).

Almost all legs end in bun feet, while the upper part narrows before ending in a cube, known as the *dé de liaison* or 'linking die' between leg and seat. This element can be either smooth or decorated with various motifs (rosettes, pearls, acanthus leaves, etc.). Seats generally have a semi-circular front.

Armchairs follow this pattern very closely, with backs that are either straight or *en chapeau de gendarme* ('shaped like a gendarme's hat', in other words straight, but slightly rounded at the top), medallion-shaped, trapezium-shaped, etc.. Whatever the outline of their backs, both armchairs and *bergeres* are known as *à la reine* or 'the queen's' when the back is flat and en cabriolet when it is concave. Canapes are straight or gondola-shaped.

But there are so many types of seating that it is better to refer to the illustrations to present a complete panorama of Louis XVI production, including the elegant banquettes and designs created by the great cabinet-makers, which invariably defy crude categorisation.

To get a more precise idea of the level of technical and artistic perfection reached by Louis XVI seating, it should be understood that three different people might be involved in making a single piece: the master carpenter would give the chair, armchair or *bergere* its shape; the master decorator or sculptor was responsible for the decoration and the master of gilt and lacquer would coat it with wax, gilt or lacquer.

These few elements may explain why so many beautiful, refined mahogany armchairs and *bergeres* were produced.

We should add that seats made in traditional woods might be painted in the fashionable colours of the period (green, white, sky-blue, beige) or gilt if they were intended for a salon or drawing-room.

Like Louis XV furniture, Louis XVI pieces must be divided into specific, detailed categories in order to be described more easily, for the output of Louis XVI furniture was quite remarkable. Let us take the archetypal example of the famous cabinet-maker Delanois, whose workshop produced no less than fourteen thousand pieces between 1761 and 1777, as reflected in his accounts. Today these pieces are scattered across the globe. Other artists of cabinet-making include Riesener, Leleu, Carlin, Dubois and Weisweiler, while for seating particular mention should go to Foliot, Boulard, Sené and the peerless Georges Jacob, who is regarded as the inventor of the most original and expensive designs, made in either mahogany or traditional woods. In relation to ormolu mounts, particular distinction goes to Forestier, Gallé, Turpin and Gouthière – who made almost all the ormolu mounts for Riesener's creations – and, later, Gouthière's pupil Thomire.

However rather than dwelling on monotonous

lists of the great masters of the style, of which there were hundreds in the 18th century, we shall instead move on to the two main categories into which Louis XVI pieces can be divided on the basis of their importance. The first category comprises Parisian furniture, which can be divided into classic and fine quality pieces; the second comprises rustic or provincial furniture, which in turn can be classified as ordinary pieces used by the lower social classes and elegant or decorated rustic pieces.

The rules for making Parisian furniture were the same as those we have already discussed, in other words their carcases had to be made entirely in oak. However we shall summarise them briefly.

A piece is termed classic when it is simply veneered and ormolu mounts are kept to the minimum (handles, sabots, escutcheons). It is said to be fine or high quality when its veneers are enhanced with inlays of bucolic scenes, or when it has lacquers and decorative ormolu mounts. Mahogany pieces differ from classic pieces in their more extensive ormolu mounting or in their finely-finished details. Rustic or provincial furniture is generally made in regional wood. It is regarded as being for ordinary use when it reproduces the style in shape only and in solid wood, with any ormolu mounts confined to the purely functional (handles, sabots and escutcheons).

Turning now to elegant rustic furniture, on such pieces the typical elements of the style are carved or engraved into the wood, or the veneers are of less precious regional woods such as walnut, cherry, lemon, pear, etc. (walnut was very often coloured to make it look like mahogany).

Some of the more curious aspects we have already discussed in relation to Louis XV furniture also apply here. In some regions, such as Lorraine, Brittany or Normandy, there was no lack of rustic furniture with a mixture of elements from both the Louis XV and Louis XVI styles.

A closer look at the Louis XVI style.

In discussing the furniture of past centuries we have seen that, in most cases, the main source of inspiration influencing shape and decoration is architecture. Gothic architecture gave rise to gothic furniture, which bears a clear, direct relation to the buildings. The same was true of the Renaissance and baroque periods. The Louis XV style was the first to produce furniture which, in its shapes – and its shapes alone – freed itself from all dependency on architecture, preferring, in its spirit of *galanterie*, to imitate the female form. The Louis XVI style can be said to have brought architecture and furniture back into step in a search for their historical roots.

Yet, while architecture often strayed into too close an imitation of ancient Roman or Greek temples, furniture, although it depicted classical subjects, maintained a greater degree of originality, so that its structures only seldom recall the facades of palaces and churches.

One might expect Louis XVI furniture and that of the Renaissance to be the same, or very similar, given that they drew on the same sources of inspiration. But things are not so simple. For, as the centuries unfold, so techniques and materials increase in number, as do the range of pieces that constitute 18th-century furniture.

It is true that Louis XVI commodes, bureaux and buffets are built in straight lines, but they are smaller than Renaissance pieces. Furthermore, French Renaissance furniture had a hybrid aspect stemming from its free reinterpretation of the designs of the Italian Renaissance, and its style was primarily sculptural: pieces were carved, engraved and shaped from a single substance (oak and walnut), to form columns, caryatids, fabulous beasts and mythological or historical scenes. The walnut furniture of the Italian Renaissance, which provided the model for French furniture, was densely, vigorously carved in the round. Its beauty is generally contained in a single colour, with the exception of painted or gilt pieces.

The beauty of Louis XVI furniture, on the other hand, lies in its straight lines and pictorial or, more exactly, polychrome decoration. It is based on either the contrast between the colour of the veneer, the fine quality of the inlays and the gleam of the finely chased ormolu mounts, or the refined and complex decorative scenes – bucolic images being most to the taste of the time – that enliven and break up the straight structures. The combining of woods of different colours between the ormolu mounts produces a totally different effect, in comparison not only to Renaissance furniture, but to all other styles as well.

Louis XVI pieces can immediately be distinguished from Louis XV furniture, despite using the same techniques and materials, due to their symmetrical shapes and decoration. They may be of a similar colour, but are diametrically opposed in their structures and aesthetic ideals: Louis XV = asymmetry; Louis XVI = symmetry.

Having noted the main features of the style, we shall now consider its most important pieces.

Commodes reached the peak of their development, with such a variety of designs that there are almost too many to choose from. The most common form is rectangular with three drawers; one of these, generally the frieze drawer, is narrower and separated by a light traverse from the other two, which together form a single unit. This is a very old design, already found in Italian Renaissance furniture. However the Louis XVI style had at its disposal centuries of experience in cabinet-making and decoration, enabling it to produce the same piece in endlessly different variations. The piece described above always remained the same and variations of basic shape were limited: canted or rounded angles, pilaster or column legs tapering towards the feet ; three rows of drawers beneath the marble top and across the entire width of the commode. Yet everything changes when the style brings to this straight shape its capacity for interpreting the old decorative elements using modern coverings (veneer, inlays, ormolu mounts). The imaginative quality and

endless variety of the subjects portrayed can now provide us with dozens and dozens of pieces that are, aesthetically speaking, all different.

Thus there are commodes veneered with simple geometrical designs (losenges, rectangular or square panels), pastoral scenes or landscapes from antiquity contained within ormolu medallions or rectangular inlaid or ormolu surrounds. Other pieces have lacquers portraying scenes from oriental life, or else flowers and exotic animals.

But the commode was required to adopt new shapes in order to satisfy the demand from clients continually searching for a 'unique piece'. So we see the emergence of half-moon commodes, the creative innovation of the Louis XVI style (although in fact it had already been vaguely prefigured in the transition style), decorated with the different motifs described above. Around 1790 we find the appearance of the first straight-sided or half-moon commodes in mahogany.

We may ask why output grew to such levels, greater than it had ever been before, apparently driven by motives beyond the purely commercial. The answer is that once commodes had returned to the traditional parallelepiped shape, an effort of the imagination was required to give them some innovative aspect in relation to the same pieces in the Louis XV style – whose originality of shape and decoration had taken innovation more or less as far as it could go. Louis XVI commodes assert their novelty in their half-moon shape and mahogany versions, raising a wood which had hitherto been ignored or relegated to a secondary position to the status of a material worthy of art. Yet at the same time, these commodes bear witness to the exhaustion of the vein of creativity in furniture-making, a phenomenon reflected in the way that creativity was applied more in the diversity of decoration and mounts more than in the carcase itself.

In other words, Louis XVI commodes looked to the past rather than to the future for their development, and the same can be said of all the creations of this style. Unable to invent new shapes and decorations it confined itself to bringing original elements to the reproduction of pieces that had already been seen or vaguely prefigured.

And yet, all things considered, these commodes are admirable. The same cannot be said of the bureaux *à cylindre*. Though perfect from the mechanical point of view, the importance given to human activity in their design makes them far too large and functional and, despite their efforts to please with inlays or lacquers, they never manage to shake off a heaviness which makes them more suited to the office than to the salon or drawing-room. They are perhaps the only pieces entirely lacking the grace and lightness typical of the Louis XVI style.

Such remarks cannot be applied to the secretaires, which were timidly prefigured by the *Régence* style and adopted by the Louis XV style. Light, narrow and balanced, they have a verticality inherited from very distant gothic ancestors, and are given an exclusive elegance by the grace and finesse of their neoclassical decoration. The secretaire ranks with the bonheur-du-jour as one of the finest creations of the Louis XVI style.

Let us now turn to the new inventions, including the *table bouillotte*, whose practicality enables it to be both a games table and a table 'of all work'. For even in the 18th century, and far more in our own time, these tables are put to all kinds of uses. They consist simply of a circle on four legs: a wooden disk about 80 cm in diameter, a marble top, an ormolu gallery and the table is complete. With an indefinable quality that instantly commands attention, and despite their almost total lack of artistry, these creations of the Louis XVI style are among the most pleasing, practical pieces of all.

The existence of the mahogany commode desserte and console dessert, not to mention the mahogany dining-table, which is almost always oval or round, reflects the fact that the days of the trestle table were over and that the modern dining-room had made its appearance in the house.

Here we must insert a brief digression concerning mahogany furniture. The use of this wood came directly from England, where it had been employed for some time in 18th-century furniture-making. It was taken up by the French, who thereby turned away from the rich, exuberant decoration of veneered furniture. The most favoured of all the many varieties of mahogany was the very pale wood from the island of Santo Domingo. This was used to produce commodes, dessertes, secretaires, bureaux *à cylindre* and chairs whose beauty was based on the uniformity of the wood's colour and on a precision of shape and *modenatura* which broke up the monotony of the straight structures. Sober ormolu mounting added the final touch to a type of furniture appreciated precisely for its homogeneity and shape. Of course there is no lack of examples of pieces made by the master cabinet-makers in collaboration with master bronziers, who covered them with a very rich decoration of ormolu mounts that rivals and even overshadows the presence of the wood.

With these designs the Louis XVI style can be said to have created a new aesthetic precept founded on the more or less marked contrast between the colour of the mahogany and the ormolu mounts.

All in all and general rules excepted, the Louis XVI style can be said to have produced its furniture in the light of two criteria. The first was rooted in the techniques of the recent past, using and reworking all the materials of the Louis XV style; in other words, it used the same exuberant ingredients, but applied them in a different manner to shapes whose origins lay in the distant past. The second was the adoption of a new material, mahogany, which also became a symbol by which the style can be recognised: this wood had never before been used to make all the different types of furniture that together form a particular style. Needless to say, given this dual aspect to Louis

XVI furniture, opposing groups of collectors uphold the superiority of each type. And tastes are certainly equally legitimate. Let us now turn to a more detailed examination of the advances and regression made by seating.

It is undoubtedly true that the pleasure of sitting is manifested more strongly in the Louis XV style than in that of Louis XVI: the former had made a detailed study of the human anatomy and its chairs reflect its intention to surround the body as if in an embrace. The alternating curves of its cabriolets and *bergeres* radiate softness, idleness, sensuality and well-being.

In contrast, by drawing on the past, the Louis XVI style was obliged to adopt the rigid and far less comfortable shapes that had characterised 16th and 17th century seating. Its backs are lower, however, and the development of seating throughout the 18th century could only result in the softening of any rigidity of form. Thus, with a few exceptions, Louis XVI designs have not entirely abandoned the curves that are indispensable to the comfort of the human body.

Certainly we find straight legs, but the seats are almost always either horseshoe-shaped with a rounded front rail, or round. The backs of the armchairs and *bergeres* are either straight or cabriolet to give more support to the sitter's torso. And while, generally speaking, the marquises and canapes remain rigid due to the severity of their structures, this lack of a comfortable shape is mitigated by heavy padding.

All types of chairs, armchairs and canapes are covered in tapestries showing bucolic scenes or images taken from La Fontaine's fables, proving yet again that the Louis XVI style evolved in a cultural context that extolled the virtues of a return to nature, the simple life and the old morality.

Seats, like other types of furniture, were produced in two forms: those made in traditional woods (beechwood and walnut) and pieces in mahogany.

Yet, generally speaking, the seats are less graceful than those of the Louis XV style, despite the imaginative creation of a greater number of designs. Attempts were made to overcome the obligatory choice between padding or caned backs by using a series of small columns, arcades or stylised motifs reminiscent of the shape of a hot-air balloon, thereby inadvertently creating the most original and successful of chair designs.

In conclusion, details and particular considerations aside, the Louis XVI style represents a decisive turning-point in the history of furniture. This is not because it took its shapes and decorations from classical sources but above all because it began the process of the continual reworking of all the creations from the styles of the past, which it adapted to the present – as all later styles would continue to do – notably pointing the way forward to the 19th century. This was no longer the free and richly imaginative path taken by the adventurous Louis XV style (which had its bizarre aspects, but was able to produce something that truly singled it out in relation to all that had gone before); instead it was a familiar road leading to the ancient Roman, Greek, Egyptian and Etruscan civilisations. Eventually the 19th century, the eternal prodigal son, would grow tired of so many repetitions and reminescences and would once more turn to the rounded forms that the late 18th century had been the first to reject.

Without doubt the Louis XVI style knew where it was going, in the sense that it did not lack creativity when drawing on the past. If, generally speaking, the 18th century was unable to maintain the same artistic level throughout its length, this should be attributed not to the new manner of designing furniture, but to the costs and demands of a newly industrialised production. These factors suppress skill, imagination and creativity and, in the long term, signified the end of art in furniture-making.

Lastly, we should state that, although the Louis XVI style was already carrying the highly contagious virus of an inevitable future decadence, it was the last great style in the history of furniture.

Fakes and copies

Louis XVI furniture has been reproduced, like that of other periods, and pieces have been transformed and faked by unscrupulous cabinet-makers and dealers.

Contrary to what might be feared, the French revolution destroyed very few pieces in any style. The revolutionaries were aware of their value and either appropriated them or sold them to the dealers who poured into the capital from all corners of Europe looking for bargains. Furthermore Napoleon himself seems to have liked to combine Louis XVI furniture with new Empire pieces.

In addition to this there was no furious cultural reaction against the Louis XVI style as there had been to Louis XV furniture. Thus a few decades later, in the reign of Louis-Philippe (1830–1848), the first timid reproductions of Louis XVI furniture appeared, although gothic, *Régence* and Louis XV designs were more favoured. However as the century advanced, even Louis XVI pieces became fashionable again and were reproduced in great quantity.

In the case of 19th century reproductions that have been modified to be sold as originals, the same processes were used as have been discussed for Louis XV furniture. The same rule applies for all transformations and embellishments. However one of the most frequent transformations is the new, strange and unusual case of the bureau *à cylindre* which is turned into a bureau plat. The large, graceless bureau *à cylindre* is literally beheaded, with all its upper part removed down to the top, including the drum containing the sliding cylinder and a set of large and small drawers. Once the sliding writing surface has been fixed (this is the element that enabled the cylinder to slide when it was pulled forwards), the top is cleared of the attachments for the semi-circular sides in whose grooves the cylinder moved. The holes for the screws that held the upper part in place are filled with solid wood and the entire piece is covered with new veneer. Lastly, if necessary, the top is rebound in leather, completing one of the easiest transformations to perform and the hardest to detect when skilfully carried out.

However, given that even the most carefully performed modifications leave traces, let us see how such a fake can be identified. We should start by noting that Louis XVI bureaux *à cylindre* were generally of a standard size: they were longer than twice their depth by several centimetres (five to twelve), exactly the opposite of the usual dimensions of the rare Louis XV bureaux *à cylindre*. The depth of a bureau plat on the other hand, when it has been made as such, is almost always exactly half of its length, though it may be a maximum of two or three centimetres longer or shorter.

Furthermore, most bureaux plats have a single row of three drawers under the top, the central drawer being larger than those on either side. It is very rare to find two more drawers beneath the top two side drawers. On the contrary bureaux *à cylindre* always have two rows of drawers.

A buyer contemplating a bureau plat with two rows of side drawers should always be very careful since, to our knowledge, there are no standard dimensions to refer to.

Knowledgeable dealers do not of course need to make all these calculations, since the parts that have been faked will not escape their practised eyes. Generally speaking the fakes are betrayed by nuances of colour and patina and traces of cutting in wood that is too fresh to be of the period.

Given that the bureau *à cylindre* was not greatly appreciated at the turn of the 20th century and perhaps even before, the transformation of these pieces into bureaux plats was undertaken at the request of owners as well as dealers. As a result Louis XVI bureaux à cylindre have become increasingly rare.

How to find Louis XVI furniture

High quality Louis XVI furniture of any category is now becoming increasingly rare on all the national and international art markets. This is less true of Paris, where it is still possible to find a certain quantity of commodes, secretaires, small tables, bureaux and seats in the antiques dealers' shops and salesrooms. Quality pieces of all kinds can even be found on sale in some of the other French cities from time to time, but the current trend is to centralise all sales of the art and crafts of the past in the capital.

In London and New York Louis XVI furniture is now becoming very rare, although one can still come across it. It is found in the largest sales and in the shopwindows of Madison Avenue.

It is certainly easier to find pieces termed classic, which were produced in remarkable quantities, on these same markets. Rustic furniture for popular use can be found almost only in France, and the same is true of elegant rustic pieces. Such items appear only occasionally on other antiques markets.

In Italy in particular, all categories of furniture are present in very limited quantities in Turin; they are to all intents and purposes absent from Milan, Rome and Genoa.

The constant rise in prices has clear consequences for imports, even where the most traditional pieces of this style are concerned. Thus the process by which Louis XVI furniture is growing rarer becomes more pronounced with every passing year.

Quality and valuation

In all the vast production of Louis XVI furniture, the finest pieces should be sought among works by the great master cabinet-makers. These people knew how to combine, integrate and amalgamate a remarkable quantity of ormolu and sometimes porcelain with wood, to incontestably refined and sumptuous effect, without lapsing into the monotony and heaviness that can arise from the massive use of such ostentatious mate-

rials. This risk was averted by light, precise and refined chasing of the ormolu mounts.

The bureaux plats, commodes, secretaires and small tables by Martin Carlin, who almost always combined ormolu mounts and wood with decorative plaques of Sèvres porcelain, and the designs stamped by or attributed to Riesener, Weisweiler and a few others, represent the peak of quality and value in Louis XVI furniture. Of the more valuable creations it is always the new forms and functional pieces that best suit the tastes of the clientele; for this reason half-moon commodes, the table bouillotte, small bronze *guéridon* tables, buffets and dining-tables are the most sought-after and often the most expensive.

Where refined seating is concerned, we should draw a distinction between traditional seating in beechwood or walnut and designs in mahogany, made or invented by the celebrated carpenter Georges Jacob. The former, greatly-prized and of high quality, particularly when covered with Aubusson, Beauvais or Gobelins tapestries, are less costly than the latter, which sometimes reach exorbitant prices. But, as we have already said, seating in general is rarer and more expensive than other furniture of a similar quality.

Exceptional pieces from any period and style cannot be given a reasonable valuation, since they tend to be sold at auction, where it is difficult to separate the real value of a piece from the competitive price it reaches. However descending from the Olympus of Louis XVI masterpieces, among the more numerous classic pieces it is possible to find a commode, secretaire, bureau plat or armchair that, though excellently made and representing an elegant addition to any interior, does not require a great financial sacrifice. However we should not forget that prices for classic Louis XVI furniture, though lower than *Régence*, Louis XV or transition period pieces, rise with every passing year.

Louis XVI furniture has been highly-prized in France since the end of the Second World War and has undergone a real reappraisal. Previously collectors were interested in only the rarest and most unusual pieces and preferred only the earlier styles. This is also true of the transition period style.

Today the international value of Louis XVI furniture is universally recognised. Even in Italy there was a process of reappraisal in the post-war period, but a love of the Italian regional tradition noticeably slowed the spread of a taste for antique French furniture in general and the Louis XVI style in particular.

In order to facilitate this spread, the antiques dealers tried to import pieces whose aesthetic affinities closely recalled Italian neoclassical regional furniture. The exception was Turin, where the border is more geographical than stylistic, since all kinds of Louis XVI pieces were imported to that city.

In Milan on the other hand there was a preference for French pieces decorated with inlays, as their artistic similarities with the works of Maggiolini facilitated sales.

In Genoa there was an interest in pieces with precious, exotic wood veneers and sober ormolu decoration, since these had a discreet, refined elegance very similar to that of Genoese furniture.

In Rome, home of the baroque, there was a preference for pieces with twisted shapes, mounted with chased ormolu, or those inlaid with Sèvres porcelain plaques, as the combination of the different materials and the glint of the ormolu were reminiscent of the baroque traditions.

But all these attempts to spread a love of Louis XVI furniture have suffered a brutal and general setback since the French franc rose in value against the Italian lira. Today, with a few rare exceptions, only pieces of lesser value are imported. The very valuable pieces that occasionally appear on the Italian market come from former private collections and were imported thirty or forty years ago. Generally speaking, in Italy Louis XVI furniture is valued at less than its real worth. Clients lack, to some extent at least, the minimum of skill and cultural knowledge necessary to appreciate the full value of this style.

Fine commode with three rows of drawers, two *sans traverse*, and a white marble top. The mahogany veneer is extensively mounted with ormolu, which enhances the shape of the piece. The mahogany veneer *à ramages* has a foliate effect, obtained by cutting the tree trunk at an oblique angle. Sold in Paris in 1972: £ 15,400, $ 27,600. 1984 valuation: £ 19,780, $ 26,200. 1991 valuation: £ 36,000, $ 63,700. Current valuation: £ 35,700, $ 59,150, € 53,380.

Fine commode with three rows of drawers, two *sans traverse*, canted angles and a white marble top. The veneer of tulipwood à fils (literally 'with threads') appears to have a close-grained motif, due to the wood being cut along rather than across the trunk. It is divided into panels by extensive ormolu mounting. 1984 valuation: £ 27,950, $ 37,000. 1991 valuation: £ 50,000, $ 88,500. Current valuation: £ 45,900, $ 76,000, € 68,600.

Below: classic commode with three rows of drawers, two sans traverse, flanked by rounded angles and with a white marble top. The butterfly tulipwood veneer with amaranth profiles has elegant inlaid rosettes and classic, sober ormolu mounting. 1984 valuation: £ 10,750, $ 14,250. 1991 valuation: £ 14,000, $ 24,780. Current valuation: £ 15,300, $ 25,350, € 22,880.

Fine breakfront commode with three rows of drawers, two *sans traverse*, rounded angles and a marble top. The tulipwood and amaranth veneer inlaid with losenges is extensively mounted with ormolu, which emphasises the shape of the piece. The breakfront shape is relatively refined and rare in Louis XVI commodes. Sold in London in 1973: £ 18,600, $ 34,600. 1984 valuation: £ 25,800, $ 34,200. Current valuation: collector's price.

Fine small commode with three rows of drawers, two *sans traverse*, canted angles and a white marble top, bearing the stamp of Landrin. The tulipwood and kingwood veneer is inlaid with flowers and vine leaves, with a central medallion representing a fisherman. A ribbon surrounds the marquetry. Ormolu mounts are kept to the minimum: handles, chutes and sabots. 1984 valuation: £ 10,750, $ 14,250. 1991 valuation: £ 20,000, $ 35,400. Current valuation: £ 18,360, $ 30,400, € 27,450.

Fine commode with three rows of drawers, two *sans traverse*, canted angles and a white marble top. The tulipwood veneer is extensively mounted with ormolu. The commode bears the stamp of Ohneberg. Sold in Paris in 1970: £ 5,300, $ 9,200. 1984 valuation: £ 30,100, $ 39,900. Current valuation: collector's price.

Fine commode with three rows of drawers, two *sans traverse*, tulipwood veneer and rich inlays. The top is of Saint-Anne marble. 1984 valuation: £ 15,050 , $ 19,950. 1991 valuation: £ 14,000, $ 24,780. Current valuation: £ 12,240, $ 20,280, € 18,300.

Classic small commode with three rows of drawers, two *sans traverse* and a veined marble top, veneered in tulipwood and amaranth inlaid with losenges and a floral motif, bearing the stamp of M. Ohneberg. Sold in Paris in 1970: £ 880, $ 1,500. 1984 valuation: £ 6,450, $ 8,550. 1991 valuation: £ 14,000, $ 24,780. Current valuation: £ 12,240, $ 20,280, € 18,300.

Atypical commode with two drawers with traverse, canted angles and a veined white marble top. The coloured green sycamore and olivewood veneer has an exuberant floral inlay that forms a design of medallions. The commode bears the stamp of Avril. 1984 valuation: £ 12,900, $ 17,100. 1991 valuation: £ 30,000, $ 53,100. Current valuation: £ 30,600, $ 50,700, € 45,750.

Fine commode with three rows of drawers, two *sans traverse*, rounded, channelled angles and a grey Saint-Anne marble top. Mahogany veneer *à ramages*. The elegant shape, emphasised by extensive, refined ormolu mounting, is of particular note. The commode bears the stamp of Riesener.
Current valuation: collector's price.

Important commode in solid mahogany with three drawers, two *sans traverse*, canted angles and a white marble top, bearing the stamp of Riesener. The ormolu mounts are confined to handles and escutcheons. Commodes of this type faithfully reproduce the pure, sober lines of the style and are much appreciated in France, less so in Italy. This is one of the few examples where the signature adds value to the piece independently of its standing as a work of art.
Current valuation: collector's price.

Classic half-moon commode with a grey Saint-Anne marble top. Veneered in kingwood and tulipwood, inlaid with losenges, framed by ribbons and filets or fine bands. Sold in Paris in 1970: £ 1,760, $ 3,000. 1984 valuation: £ 10,750, $ 14,250.
1991 valuation: £ 23,000, $ 40,700.
Current valuation: £ 22,440, $ 37,180, € 33,550.

Example of a classic half-moon commode whose simple lines contrast with its elegant decoration of ears of corn.
1984 valuation: £ 8,600, $ 11,400. 1991 valuation: £ 18,500, $ 32,750.
Current valuation: £ 15,300, $ 25,350, € 22,880.

Another example of a classic half-moon commode.
1984 valuation: £ 10,750, $ 14,250. 1991 valuation: £ 19,000, $ 33,600.
Current valuation: £ 15,300, $ 25,350, € 22,880.

Fine half-moon commode with two doors and three drawers. The quality of the chased ormolu mounts, which emphasise the shape of the piece and frame its floral inlays, adds to the commode's value. It bears the stamp of C. Topino.
Current valuation: collector's price.

Classic half-moon commode. The tulipwood and amaranth veneer is inlaid with elegant rosettes on the sides and on the two drawers *sans traverse*. Sober ormolu mounting. It bears the stamp of J.P. Bertrand. 1984 valuation: £ 10,750, $ 14,250. 1991 valuation: £ 23,000, $ 40,700. Current valuation: £ 22,440, $ 37,180, € 33,550.

Classic half-moon commode with two doors, three drawers, two sans traverse, and a grey Saint-Anne marble top. The tulipwood and amaranth veneer is soberly mounted with ormolu. The commode bears the stamp of Schey. Sold in Paris in 1973: £ 2,300, $ 4,300. 1984 valuation: £ 8.600, $ 11.400. 1991 valuation: £ 17,000, $ 30,100. Current valuation: £ 15,300, $ 25,350, € 22,880.

Fine half-moon commode with two doors and three drawers, two *sans traverse*, and a grey Saint-Anne marble top. Losenge inlay with a central medallion showing landscapes. 1984 valuation: £ 12,900, $ 17,100. 1991 valuation: £ 25,000, $ 44,250. Current valuation: £ 23,460, $ 38,870, € 35,000.

Fine small half-moon commode with two doors and three drawers, two sans traverse, and a grey Saint-Anne marble top. The tulipwood veneer is entirely decorated with floral inlays. The commode has a decorative medallion across the two drawers sans traverse and original ormolu mounts. 1984 valuation: £ 12,900, $ 17,100. 1991 valuation: £ 28,000, $ 49,560. Current valuation: £ 23,460, $ 38,870, € 35,000.

Fine small gueridon in mahogany with a central shaft and a top that can be tipped up. Of particular note is the extensive ormolu mounting in the form of asparagus, pearls and leaves. Sold in Paris in 1974: £ 3,770, $ 7,400. 1984 valuation: £ 7,740, $ 10,260.
1991 valuation: £ 14,000, $ 24,780.
Current valuation: £ 12,750, $ 21,100, € 19,000.

Classic bureau plat with two drawers, amaranth veneer, inlaid grecques in pale wood and refined ormolu mounts. It bears the stamp of P.C. Montigny. Sold in Paris in 1971: £ 8,950, $ 15,800.
1984 valuation: £ 10,750, $ 14,250. 1991 valuation: £ 23,000, $ 40,700.
Current valuation: £ 20,400, $ 33,800, € 30,500.

Fine small rectangular bureau. The tulipwood veneer with king-wood bands has a refined decoration of inlaid draperies, garlands and trompe l'oeil objects. The bureau bears the stamp of J.J. Mantzer, known as Manser. Sold in Paris in 1970: £ 7,900, $ 13,500. 1984 valuation: £ 10,750, $ 14,250.
Current valuation: collector's price.

Classic small gueridon with a central shaft in mahogany and a white marble top with ormolu gallery. The top can be raised and lowered by means of a ratchet. It bears the stamp of I. Moreau. Sold in Paris in 1973: £ 930, $ 1,700. 1984 valuation: £ 3,440, $ 4,560.
1991 valuation: £ 6,000, $ 10,600.
Current valuation: £ 45,900, $ 76,000, € 68,600.

Fine mahogany commode with ormolu mounts. Of particular note are the two drawers *sans traverse* and the ormolu frieze around the upper section, with its grey Saint-Anne marble top. Current valuation: £ 61,200, $ 101,400, € 91,500.

Fine half-moon commode with tulipwood veneer, ormolu mounts and a *brèche d'Alep* marble top. The two drawers have no visible traverse and are made to form a single panel by the ormolu mounts, which elegantly enhance the value of the piece.
1984 valuation: £ 25,800, $ 34,200.
Current valuation: £ 61,200, $ 101,400, € 91,500.

Very rare fine commode with doors veneered in tulipwood and inlaid with stylised flowers, bearing the stamp of M. Carlin. The shape is emphasised by extensive ormolu mounting. (Photo: Sotheby Parke Bernet). Provenance: the collection of the Earl of Mansfield. Sold in Monte Carlo in 1979: £ 32,160, $ 75,300. 1984 valuation:£ 172,000, $ 228,000. Current valuation: collector's price.

Fine commode *à l'anglaise* of exceptional quality, with tulipwood veneer and amaranth bands, extensively mounted with chased ormolu, bearing the stamp of C.C. Saunier, master cabinet-maker in Paris in 1752. (Photo: M. Meyer, Paris). Current valuation: collector's price.

Facing page: excellent quality commode in amaranth veneer, bearing the stamp of J.F. Leleu. It is said to have been bought by George III of England at a sale held by the French revolutionaries and given to his personal physician, Mr Coningby. It was bought in 1929 by Mrs Henry Walters and sold by Sotheby Parke Bernet in New York in 1941. (Photo: Sotheby Parke Bernet). Sold in Monte Carlo in 1979: £ 80,400, $ 1,882,350. Current valuation: collector's price.

Fine commode in speckled mahogany, attributed to Riesener, master cabinet-maker in Paris in 1768.
Sold in Cheverny in 1990: £ 363,540, $ 647,000.
Current valuation: collector's price.

Exceptional bureau plat in ebony veneer, bearing the stamp of E.J. Cuvelier. Sold in Paris in 1983: £ 628,500, $ 951,700.
1984 valuation: £ 623,500, $ 826,500.
Current valuation: collector's price.

Fine bureau plat in mahogany veneer with sober, elegant ormolu mounting. The decoration of Sèvres porcelain plaques makes this a rare piece, highly-prized by collectors. It bears the stamp of E. Levasseur. Provenance: Hillinton collection. Sold in Monte Carlo in 1979: £ 43,900, $ 102,800. 1984 valuation: £ 30,960, $ 41,000.
Current valuation: collector's price.

Fine salon table of exceptional quality, in ebony veneer with brass and pewter profiles and a marble mosaic top. Richly mounted with chased ormolu. As we have already seen, the Louis XVI style drew heavily on the Louis XIV style in both designs and materials. This is an example of a table using subjects from furniture by Charles Boulle, celebrated cabinet-maker to the Sun King and known for his creations inlaid with marble, brass, pewter, silver and tortoiseshell. It bears the stamp of Martin Carlin. (Photo: Tajan, Paris). Sold in Paris in 1976: £ 127,000, $ 271,200. Current valuation: collector's price.

Facing page: very rare fine table in solid mahogany and mahogany veneer, richly mounted with ormolu. Of particular note are the original shape and the four lyres in patinated bronze and ormolu which support the table top. It bears the stamp of G Jacob. (Photo: Sotheby Parke Bernet). Current valuation: collector's price.

Very rare fine salon table of exceptional quality attributed to Gouthière, the famous chaser, in blue lacquered iron with chased ormolu mounts. The top is supported by mounts in the form of female busts wearing draperies, with plaited hair and cushions on their heads. Sold in Monte Carlo in 1979: £ 87,900, $ 205,880.
1984 valuation: £ 86,000, $ 114,000.
Current valuation: collector's price.

Fine bureau plat of exceptional quality, in mahogany veneer with bands of ebony, richly mounted with chased ormolu and bearing the stamp of P.C. Montigny, master cabinet-maker in Paris in 1766. (Photo: M. Segoura, Paris). Provenance: Georges Petit gallery sale, 26 May 1913. Current valuation: collector's price.

Fine bureau plat in tulipwood veneer, inlaid with grecques in amaranth, enhanced with elegant chased ormolu mounts and bearing the stamp of P.H. Mewessen, master cabinet-maker in Paris in 1766.

(Photo: M. Segoura, Paris).
Sold in Paris in 1985: £ 173,000, $ 223,150.
Current valuation: collector's price.

Fine tripod gueridon with two surfaces surrounded by elegant chased ormolu galleries, bearing the stamp of M. Carlin, master cabinet-maker in Paris in 1766.

This great master's creations are particularly sought-after. (Photo: M. Meyer, Paris).
Current valuation: collector's price.

Left: rare fine work table in mahogany with a Sèvres porcelain top and extensive ormolu mounting, bearing the stamp of R. Lacroix. Sold in Paris in 1979: £ 22,600, $ 52,900.
1984 valuation: £ 23,650, $ 31,350.
Current valuation: collector's price.

Gueridon in chased ormolu with Spanish brocatello marble top and undertier. The period version is rare, highly-prized and expensive. This model has been faithfully reproduced with some variations throughout the 19th and 20th centuries.
1984 valuation: £ 8,600, $ 11,400.
1991 valuation: £ 11,000, $ 19,470.
Current valuation: £ 15,300, $ 25,350, € 22,880.

Rare fine small salon bureau of exceptional quality in precious, exotic wood veneer, with refined inlay and important chased ormolu mounting.

Current valuation: collector's price.

Rare fine work table of exceptional quality in sycamore veneer inlaid with losenges and extensively mounted with ormolu. Attributed to Weisweiler. This type of table was made in the 18th century by the greatest cabinet-makers such as Carlin, Weisweiler and Riesener. (Photo: Tajan, Paris). Sold in Paris in 1979: £ 19,600, $ 45,880. 1984 valuation: £ 21,500, $ 34,200.
Current valuation: collector's price.

Fine console desserte in mahogany veneer, one of a pair, extensively mounted with chased ormolu and bearing the stamp of J. Cosson, master cabinet-maker in 1765. The double undertier is rare and much sought-after.
Current valuation: £ 76,500, $ 126,750, € 114,400.

Fine small console desserte in tulipwood veneer, richly decorated with floral inlays. Soberly mounted with chased ormolu.
1991 valuation: £ 18,500, $ 32,750.
Current valuation: £ 17,850, $ 29,580, € 26,700.

Fine console desserte in satinwood veneer, one of a pair, extensively mounted with chased ormolu. Of particular note are the console's compactness and the refinement of the ormolu emphasising its half-moon shape. It bears the stamp of G. Dester, master cabinet-maker in Paris in 1774. Current valuation: collector's price.

Small salon table *à toutes faces* in mahogany veneer and solid mahogany, with extensive ormolu mounting enhancing the whole piece.

1991 valuation: £ 30,000, $ 53,100.
Current valuation: £ 40,800, $ 67,600, € 61,000.

Rare fine console in silvered bronze and ormolu with a green marble top. Almost identical consoles were made in 1766 for the royal palace of Warsaw to designs by Victor Louis.

(Photo: Sotheby Parke Bernet). Sold in Monte Carlo in 1979: 437,000 FF. 1984 valuation: £ 23,650, $ 31,350. Current valuation: collector's price.

Pair of giltwood corner consoles. Of particular note are the carved garlands and vases on the stretchers, which are typical elements of the style. Current valuation: £ 13,260, $ 22,000, € 19,800.

Fine console, one of a pair, stamped J.F. Leleu, master cabinet-maker in Paris in 1764. These half-moon pieces are enhanced with elegant ormolu mounts and have grey Saint-Anne marble tops.

The pair was sold by Sotheby's in New York in 1993: £ 88,200, $ 132,500. Current valuation: collector's price.

Fine console in mahogany and *plume d'acajou* or 'feathered mahogany' with ormolu profiles. The unusual, elegant and original shape is of particular note.

Sold in Paris in 1988: £ 14,160, $ 25,180.
Current valuation: collector's price.

Rare fine mahogany console desserte, one of a pair, with a rectangular shape, three frieze drawers and a Spanish brocatello marble top. It has eight legs in the form of channelled columns with ormolu capitals, linked by a mahogany undertier. Attributed to Dester, admitted as master in 1774.

Current valuation: collector's price.

Fine salon table of exceptional quality stamped by P. Roussel, master cabinet-maker in Paris in 1745. The piece is veneered in kingwood and lemonwood, inlaid with losenges on the undertier and four-leafed clover on the top. Noteworthy for the extensive ormolu mounting enhancing the entire structure of the piece.
Sold by Christie's in London in 1991: £ 115,000, $ 131,100.
Current valuation: collector's price.

Fine round table or gueridon in mahogany, stamped A. Weisweiler, master cabinet-maker in Paris in 1778. This design of table was one of the most commonly reproduced, either exactly or with variants, in the second half of the 19th century. Sold by Christie's in New York in 1993: £ 194,000, $ 291,450.
Current valuation: collector's price.

Fine half-moon commode, one of a pair, stamped C. Topino, master cabinet-maker in Paris in 1766. The commodes are veneered in tulipwood with refined inlays in coloured woods, enhanced by elegant ormolu mounts. Sold by Sotheby's in New York in 1993: £ 446,800, $ 671,000. Current valuation: collector's price.

Fine half-moon commode of excellent quality in mahogany and *plume d'acajou* mahogany, with elegant ormolu mounts. Current valuation: £ 40,800, $ 67,600, € 61,000.

Fine suite consisting of a pair of armchairs and three chairs with horseshoe backs covered with antique floral tapestry.

Sold in Paris in 1994: £ 23,560, $ 36,000.
Current valuation: £ 25,500, $ 42,250, € 38,100.(Photo: Tajan, Paris).

Fine commode in mahogany with ormolu profiles, three drawers, two sans traverse, and a brown breccia marble top.

Sold in Paris in 1985: £ 13,000, $ 16,700.
Current valuation: £ 45,900, $ 76,000, € 68,600.

Fine pair of encoignures in mahogany, elegantly mounted with or-molu and attributed to Levasseur. They bear the stamp of the master cabinet-makers and are branded with the letters LPO (Louis-Philippe d'Orléans, under the restoration). These encoignures are part of a set of pieces, almost all signed by Levasseur, which belonged to Louis XVI's aunts, Adelaïde and Victoire, at the Chateau de Bellevue.

Sold by Sotheby's in Monte Carlo in 1995: £ 193,900, $ 299,300. Current valuation: collector's price.

Fine jewel case of exceptional quality, bearing the stamp of Schneider, master cabinet-maker in Paris in 1786. The piece is veneered in amaranth and satinwood and is extensively mounted with polychrome Sèvres porcelain plaques with floral motifs, some dated 1778. Provenance: Rothschild collection.
Current valuation: collector's price.

Pair of fine carved giltwood pieces *à l'athénienne*, made around 1773 to a design by Jean-Henri Eberts. This new type of piece, drawing on classical antiquity, is described by Eberts as being intended for a variety of uses: it can be a console, serviteur, jardinière, perfume burner or pedestal. Madame du Barry was the first to buy the new design.

Current valuation: collector's price.

Fine secretaire of exceptional quality in European lacquer, decorated in the Chinese manner and bearing the stamp of J. Dubois. In fact this piece was made by J. Dubois's son René, master cabinet-maker in Paris in 1755, who signed his pieces with his father's name. Of particular note is the upper section, with its pagoda-like shape. As few pieces of this type are known, we can say that René Dubois's work prefigures the characteristic influence and design of the Sheraton style. Sold by Christie's in London in 1974: £ 23,500, 46,200. Sold by Sotheby's in 1993: £ 517,400, $ 777,200. Current valuation: collector's price.

Fine secretaire bearing the stamp of Garnier, in tulipwood, mahogany and amaranth veneer. Of particular note are the elegant ormolu mounts enhancing the structure and the spirally-fluted feet characteristic of Garnier's work. Provenance: former collection of baron Eric de Rothschild.

Sold by Etude Tajan in Paris in 1996: £ 75,400, $ 117,300. Current valuation: collector's price.

Secretaire of exceptional quality in tulipwood veneer extensively mounted with chased ormolu and bearing the stamp of Balthazar Lieutaud, master cabinet-maker in Paris in 1749. Current valuation: collector's price.

Very important bureau plat in boxwood veneer. Richly mounted with chased ormolu. The Corinthian capitals, channelled legs, acanthus leaves and *entrelacs*, all characteristic of the Louis XVI style, are particularly remarkable. The bureau bears the stamp of Jean-François Leleu, master cabinet-maker in 1764. Provenance: Comtesse de Flahaut and her descendants.
Sold in London in 1981: £ 365,400, $ 735,460.
Current valuation: collector's price.

Giltwood armchair of exceptional quality from a Louis XVI salon suite comprising a pair of armchairs *à la reine* and a canape. The rectangular backs have a carved frieze of laurel leaves framed by pearls and a frieze of acanthus leaves. The scrolled armrests are carved with acanthus and laurel leaves; their supports are carved with friezes of pearls and acanthus leaves. The seats are carved with *entrelacs* and rosettes with acanthus leaves at the joints. The tapered, channelled legs are carved with acanthus leaves and pearls. One armchair bears the stamp CARPENTIER (Louis Charles Carpentier, master in 1787).
Current valuation: £ 286,000, $ 430,000, € 436,200.

Fine commode *à vantaux* ('with doors') of exceptional quality in mahogany with three doors and extensive refined ormolu mounting. Of particular note are the channelled columns to the front angles, synonymous with rarity and creativity.

The piece is stamped A. Weisweiler and Riesener. Pieces bearing the signatures of two different cabinet-makers are not uncommon. Sold by Sotheby's in Monte Carlo in 1992: £ 581,400, $ 1,000,000. Current valuation: collector's price.

Fine bureau *à gradin* of exceptional quality, in mahogany and or-molu, stamped J.H. Riesener, master cabinet-maker in Paris in 1768. The bureau was exhibited at the Musée des Arts Décoratifs in Paris from December 1955 to February 1956.

Sold by Sotheby's in New York in 1993: £ 235,000, $ 353,300. Current valuation: collector's price.

Fine armoire in mahogany with elegant ormolu mounts, bearing the stamp of Riesener, master cabinet-maker in 1768.

Sold by Sotheby's in Monte Carlo in 1996: & 290,000, $ 450,000. Current valuation: collector's price.

Fine suite of salon furniture bearing the stamp of I. Pothier, master carpenter in Paris in 1750 and comprising a canape and four arm-chairs with flat backs in carved giltwood. Provenance: the collection of Lord Michelham.

The canape was sold by Sotheby's in New York in 1993: £ 470,300, $ 706,500. Current valuation: collector's price.

Set of four fine large armchairs with flat gilt backs, a rich carving of
channels and laurel garlands and tapestry covers, bearing the stamp
of Pothier (admitted as master in 1750). The other seats of the set
were sold by Sotheby's in New York on 17 November 1984: £ 36,100,
$ 47,900 and 20 May 1992: £ 87,700, $ 154,000.
Current valuation: collector's price.

Fine marquise in carved giltwood, bearing the stamp of G. Jacob,
master cabinet-maker in Paris in 1765.
Current valuation: £ 25,500, $ 42,250, € 38,100.

Fine armchair, one of a set of four in giltwood with medallion backs, carved with ribbons, acanthus leaves, gadroons and scrolls. Of particular note are the rich carving and the armrests in console form which, like the medallion backs, are typical of the Louis XVI style.

Sold in Paris in 1995: £ 26,600, $ 41,150.

Current valuation: £ 51,000, $ 84,500, € 76,250.

(Documentation: Couturier Nicolay).

Exceptional rectangular secretaire of fine quality, in tulipwood and amaranth veneer with boxwood and kingwood bands, inlaid with cubes inside frames with geometric designs. It has two doors, a leather-bound fall-front which opens to reveal three drawers and a pigeonhole, canted angles and a solid base. Superbly decorated with chased ormolu mounts in the form of baguettes, broad channelling with an asparagus design, laurel leaves and capital chutes with gadroons, bâtonnets, pearls and large flowers. The secretaire bears the stamp of Delorme (Adrien), admitted as master on 22 June 1747. (Photo: Tajan, Paris). Sold in 1994: £ 72,400, $ 110,900. Current valuation: £ 91,800, $ 152,100, € 137,250.

Fine commode with a slight breakfront in ebony veneer. It is decorated with black and gold Chinese lacquered panels showing figures, landscapes and plum trees. It has three frieze drawers and three doors concealing a secret compartment. Extensive chased ormolu mounting.

Red griotte marble top. Attributed to Molitor. (Photo: Tajan, Paris). Sold in Paris in 1997: £ 94,100, $ 176,000.
Current valuation: collector's price.

Fine rectangular commode with doors and a slight breakfront in mahogany, veneered in mahogany *à ramages*. It has one frieze drawer and three doors separated by pilasters which open to reveal drawers. The front is flanked by detached, channelled columns. The commode stands on six tapered legs with twisted channelling. Extensively mounted with chased ormolu including friezes of gadroons and sabots. Red griotte marble top. The piece bears the stamp of A. Weisweiler, cabinet-maker admitted as master in 1778. (Photo: Tajan, Paris). Sold in Paris in 1997: £ 641,000, $ 1 050,000. Current valuation: collector's price.

Fine commode of exceptional quality, with a slight breakfront, attributed to Foullet, master cabinet-maker in 1765. Veneered in amaranth, satinwood and lemonwood, with oulined inlaid panels showing baskets of flowers, knotted ribbons, medallions, figures and foliage. Veined white marble top and important chased ormolu mounts including laurel wreaths, a frieze of entrelacs, tied ribbons, acanthus leaves and rosettes. (Photo: Couturier Nicolay). Sold in Paris in 1995: £ 60,600, $ 93,500. Current valuation: collector's price.

Pair of fine giltwood armchairs, carved with channelling and covered
with Gobelins tapestries showing cartouches on a red background.
Attributed to Delanois, admitted as master in 1761.
Current valuation: collector's price.

Important fine console in mahogany and veneered in mahogany *à ramages*. It has three drawers to the front and stands on eight tapered legs, with brass channelling, joined by a triple stretcher. Tapered toupie feet. Chased and partially regilt ormolu mounts. Bleu turquin marble top.

Traces of the stamp of A. Weisweiler, admitted as master in 1778. Provenance: the Hodgkins collection and the Seligman collection. (Photo: Tajan, Paris). Sold in Paris in 1996: £ 140.,700, $ 219,000. Current valuation: collector's price.

Fine bureau plat with rounded angles, the top surrounded with ormolu. The piece has five frieze drawers with ormolu profiles and bears the stamp of J.H. Riesener.
1984 valuation: £ 1,720, $ 2,280. Current valuation: collector's price.

Large classic gueridon with a central shaft in mahogany and a grey marble top with ormolu gallery. Sold in London in 1978: £ 1,400, $ 3,150. 1984 valuation: £ 2,580, $ 3,400.
1991 valuation: £ 10,000, $ 17,700.
Current valuation: £ 10,200, $ 16,900, € 15,250.

Small fine rectangular bureau plat in mahogany. Its elegant shape is emphasised by extensive chased ormolu mounting.
1984 valuation: £ 15,000, $ 19,950.
Current valuation: collector's price.

Rare fine gueridon in mahogany with five legs and a central ratchet, bearing the stamp of Weisweiler.
Current valuation: collector's price.

Rare fine bureau in tulipwood veneer and black ground lacquer decorated with polychrome and gilt landscapes and flowers.
1984 valuation: £ 17,200, $ 22,800.
Current valuation: collector's price.

Rare fine gueridon in iron and ormolu with a pink breccia marble top. Sold in Paris in 1971: £ 18,450, $32,000.
1984 valuation: £ 21,500, $ 28,500.
Current valuation: collector's price.

Classic games table in mahogany veneer, with folding top and ormolu profiles. Sold in Paris in 1972: £ 1,560, $ 2,800
1984 valuation: £ 2,580, $ 3,400.
1991 valuation: £ 8,000, $ 14,160.
Current valuation: £ 12,750, $ 21,100, € 19,000.

Rare fine gueridon in chased and patinated ormolu with a top and undertier in Greek green marble. Sold in Paris in 1971: £ 6,100, $ 10,700. 1984 valuation: £ 8,600, $ 11,400.
1991 valuation: £ 20,000, $ 35,400.
Current valuation: £ 25,500, $ 42,250, € 38,100.

Unusual rectangular table in mahogany having a round top with folding panels. A large round lid in the centre allows the table to be used as a jardinière. Pieces of this type are highly unusual, rare and sought-after. 1984 valuation: £ 7,740, $ 10,300.
1991 valuation: £ 10,000, $ 17,700.
Current valuation: £ 13,300, $ 22,000, € 19,800.

Rare fine gueridon with a central shaft and bronze gallery in tulip-wood with a *brèche d'Alep* marble top. The strong but harmonious structure bears the stamp of J.G. Canabas, regarded as one of the great master cabinet-makers under Louis XVI. Sold in Paris in 1971: £ 17,900, $ 31,580. Current valuation: collector's price.

Fine small grey painted table, bearing the stamp of François Garnier. Of particular note are the spirally-fluted legs, signifying quality, and the extensive gilt decoration of leaves and rosettes to the frieze. Sold in Paris in 1965: £ 2,100, $ 2,800.
1984 valuation: £ 5,160, $ 6,800. 1991 valuation: £ 10,000, $ 17,700.
Current valuation: £ 13,300, $ 22,000, € 19,800.

Rare fine small table in tulipwood veneer, inlaid with losenges and decorated with four Sèvres porcelain plaques. Sold in Paris in 1971: £ 3,100, $ 5,500. 1984 valuation: £ 7,740, $ 10,300.
1991 valuation: £ 10,000, $ 17700.
Current valuation: £ 20,400, $ 33,800, € 30,500.

Below: rare fine bureau plat in mahogany veneer with exceptional ormolu mounts, stamped in one drawer. In his book *Les Ebénistes du XVIIIe siècle* François de Salverte notes that many creations by David Roentgen are marked R or 4/R: the 4 corresponds to the 4th letter of the alphabet, D is for David, Roentgen's first name. Sold in Paris in May 1984: £ 73,100, $ 69,900.
1984 valuation: the same.
Current valuation: collector's price.

Fine bureau plat in tulipwood and amaranth veneer inlaid with four-leafed clover and soberly mounted with ormolu, bearing the stamp of Pierre Garnier, master cabinet-maker in Paris in 1742.
(Photo: Tajan, Paris). 1984 valuation: £ 49,500, $ 65,600.
Current valuation: collector's price.

Classic games table with tulipwood veneer, mahogany legs and a folding top. The ormolu profiles enhance the value of the piece. 1984 valuation: £ 7,740, $ 10,300. 1991 valuation: £ 14,000, $ 24,800. Current valuation: £ 13,770, $ 22,800, € 20,600.

Below: fine trictrac table in tulipwood and amaranth veneer. It has a removable top with a chessboard in ebony and ivory on one side and is richly mounted with chased ormolu. (Photo: M. Meyer, Paris). Current valuation: collector's price.

Important fine quality oval table in tulipwood and kingwood veneer inlaid with large roses and ribbons, with ormolu sabots and profiles. 1984 valuation: £ 8,600, $ 11,400. 1991 valuation: £ 20,000, $ 35,400. Current valuation: £ 35,700, $ 59,150, € 53,380.

Half-moon commode of exceptional quality with shelves to the sides. The mahogany is enhanced with ormolu mounts, emphasising the originality of the design. Sold in Paris in 1972: £ 6,100, $ 11,000. 1984 valuation: £ 30,100, $ 39,900.
Current valuation: collector's price.

Rare fine bonheur-du-jour. The narrower upper section is decorated with five Wedgwood plaques with a decoration of figures and has two doors. The lower section consists of a drawer with fall-front and an undertier with a white marble top. The piece is richly mounted with ormolu and is attributed to Weisweiler.
Sold in Paris in 1973: £ 21,400, 39,800.
Current valuation: collector's price.

Rare fine bureau *à cylindre* of exceptional quality in lacquer with a black ground decorated with landscapes, birds, flowers and figures in gold. Extensive ormolu mounting enhances the value of this work of high cabinet-making, bearing the stamp of Weisweiler.
Current valuation: collector's price.
Seen from front and back.

Fine small bureau *à cylindre* in mahogany. Extensively mounted with chased ormolu, it bears the stamp of J.H. Riesener, regarded as one of the most prestigious of the French cabinet-makers under Louis XVI. Sold in Paris in 1971: £ 8,950, $ 15,800.
Current valuation: collector's price.

Classic écritoire-bonheur-du-jour in mahogany. The upper section has three fall-fronts, a Saint-Anne marble top and ormolu gallery, the lower section has five drawers. It is attributed to J.F. Leleu. Sold in Paris in 1974: £ 2,850, $ 5,580. 1984 valuation: £ 12,900, $ 17,100. 1991 valuation: £ 23,200, $ 30,800.
Current valuation: £ 22,400, $ 37,200, € 33,550.

Important, unusual bureau *à cylindre* in mahogany, with a *brèche d'Alep* marble top. The simplicity of the style and architecture contribute to the elegance of this piece, regardless of its size.
1984 valuation: £ 12,900, $ 17,100. 1991 valuation: £ 20,000, $ 35,400.
Current valuation: £ 20,400, $ 33,800, € 30,500.

Classic bureau *à cylindre* in mahogany. The upper section has three drawers, with a marble top and ormolu gallery. The lower section has five drawers. Fine quality examples aside, pieces of this type have never been greatly valued or sought-after, due to their large size. Sold in Paris in 1969: £ 1,700, $ 3,000.
1984 valuation: £ 12,900, $ 17,100. 1991 valuation: £ 17,000, $ 28,700.
Current valuation: £ 20,400, $ 33,800, € 30,500.

Classic secretaire-bonheur-du-jour in mahogany. The lower section has a single drawer and undertier, the upper section has a fall-front with writing surface, one drawer and a marble top with ormolu gallery. 1984 valuation: £ 10,750, $ 14,250.
1991 valuation: £ 17,500, $ 31,000.
Current valuation: £ 17,850, $ 29,600, € 26,700.

Fine secretaire in blue lacquer with concave angles and a *brèche d'Alep* marble top. Painted panels depicting amorous games are enhanced by an ormolu surround. Of particular note on the fall-front is the ormolu eagle of queen Marie-Antoinette, to whom this piece belonged. It bears the stamp of J. Dubois. Sold in Paris in 1973: £ 55,800, $ 103,850. Current valuation: collector's price.

Important and very rare fine secretaire with a grey-veined white marble top. Veneered in ebony inlaid with aventurine. The piece is decorated with red and gold lacquered panels depicting vases of flowers and with remarkably rich and suggestive ormolu mounts. This secretaire bears the stamp of M. Carlin. Sold in Paris in 1973: £ 93,100, $ 173,000. 1998 valuation: collector's price.

Small classic écritoire-bonheur-du-jour in natural cherrywood, with amaranth profiles and a marble top with ormolu gallery. This is a provincial piece of high quality. Sold in Paris in 1973: £ 1,400, $ 2,600.
1984 valuation: £ 2,580, $ 3,400.
1991 valuation: £ 4,500, $ 7,960.
1998 valuation: £ 5,100, $ 8,450, € 7,600.

Important and very rare fine secretaire in amaranth and tulipwood veneer inlaid with floral bouquets. The fall-front bears the letters M and A. The overall shape is emphasised by extensive ormolu mounting. This piece, which belonged to the Lalive de Jully family, is attributed to the renowned master cabinet-maker J.F. Oeben and seems to have been made for queen Marie-Antoinette. Sold in Paris in 1973: £ 72,600, $ 135,000. 1998 valuation: collector's price.

Fine secretaire with canted angles and elegant medallions depicting monuments and figures with heads and limbs in ivory.
1984 valuation: £ 193,500, $ 25,650.
1991 valuation: £ 37,500, $ 66,400.
Current valuation: £ 81,600, $ 135,200, € 122,000.

Centre: fine secretaire with canted angles and a marble top. It is decorated with birds, parrots, figures and lilies in semi-precious stones on a tulipwood and amaranth ground. Extensive ormolu mounting completes the whole, which bears the stamp of N. Petit. Sold in Paris in 1972: £ 14,500, $ 25,900. Current valuation: collector's price.

Small classic secretaire with canted angles.
1984 valuation: £ 6,450, $ 8,550. 1991 valuation: £ 10,000, $ 17,700. Current valuation: £ 7,140, $ 11,800, € 10,680.

Small secretaire, partly classic, partly fine, in black Chinese lacquer with canted angles. 1984 valuation: £ 15,000, $ 20,000.
Current valuation: £ 40,800, $ 67,600, € 61,000.

Fine secretaire in mahogany mounted with ormolu. Sold in Paris in 1972: £ 11,300, $ 20,300. 1984 valuation: £ 21,500, $ 28,500. Current valuation: collector's price.

Fine secretaire with small gilt rosettes highlighting the ormolu profiles. 1984 valuation: £ 30,100, $ 40,000. Current valuation: collector's price.

Below centre: fine secretaire in mahogany with elegant ormolu friezes. Sold in Paris in 1970: £ 1,100, $ 1,900. 1984 valuation: £ 15,000, $ 20,000. 1991 valuation: £ 23,000, $ 40,700. Current valuation: $ 30,600, $ 50,700, € 45,750.

Rare fine small secretaire *d'appui* with rounded angles and a marble top with ormolu gallery. The secretaire in in mahogany embellished with Sèvres porcelain plaques decorated with roses. This original type pf decoration is typical of the well-known master cabinet-maker Martin Carlin. Current valuation: collector's price.

Rare fine secretaire with canted angles and a *brèche d'Alep* marble top. It has a polychrome decoration of Chinese houses and figures on a yellow ground with ormolu frames and bears the stamp of F. Rubestuck. Sold in Paris in 1970: £ 7,070, $ 12,250. 1984 valuation: £ 25,800, $ 34,200. Current valuation: collector's price.

Classic secretaire with canted angles, veneered in tulipwood and rosewood with a grey Saint-Anne marble top. Sold in Milan in 1974: £ 3,600, $ 7,050. 1984 valuation: £ 68,800, $ 9,100.
1991 valuation: £ 9,000, $ 15,900.
Current valuation: £ 6,600, $ 11,000, € 9,900.

Unusual large fine secretaire with canted angles and a grey marble top. The delicate ormolu mounts emphasise its purity of shape and style. 1984 valuation: £ 27,950, $ 37,000.
Current valuation: collector's price.

Classic secretaire with canted angles in kingwood and amaranth veneer. It has three drawers with traverses behind the fall-front instead of the more usual panels and bears the stamp of Roussel. Once again this demonstrates the comparative importance of the cabinet-maker's stamp on quality classic pieces, without their attaining the level of rarity or fine cabinet-work. Sold in Rome in 1973: £ 2,800, $ 5,200. 1984 valuation: £ 6,450, $ 8,550. 1991 valuation: £ 7,000, $ 12,400. Current valuation: £ 6,600, $ 11,000, € 9,900.

Classic secretaire with canted angles in tulipwood veneer. This is an example of an unusual, dual purpose piece *à guillotine*, which can also be used as an armoire.
1984 valuation: £ 7,700, $ 10,300. 1991 valuation: £ 10,000, $ 17,700.
Current valuation: £ 10,200, $ 16,900, € 15,250.

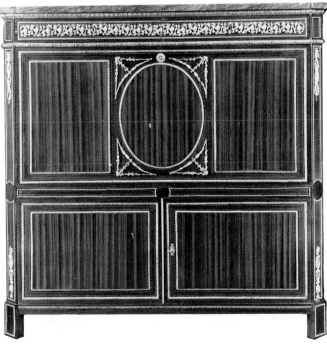

Fine secretaire in mahogany *à ramages* with column angles and a marble top, attributed to Riesener. Mounted with original rare sculpted figures in ormolu, apparently supporting the marble top. Sold in London in 1976: £ 69,980, $ 147,900.
Current valuation: collector's price.

Fine secretaire with canted angles and a *brèche d'Alep* marble top. Impressive for the refinement of its floral inlay on a ground of *bois de fil* tulipwood and for its ormolu mounts. Sold in Genoa in 1975: £ 9,580, $ 19,670. 1984 valuation: £ 17,200, $ 22,800.
1991 valuation: £ 35,000, $ 61,950.
Current valuation: £ 51,000, $ 84,500, € 76,250.

Fine secretaire with canted angles and a grey Saint-Anne marble top, bearing the stamp of P. Roussel. The piece is veneered in tulipwood and amaranth with a refined decoration of four-leafed clover. Of particular note is the interior, which is richly decorated with flowers. Such a detailed finish to the interior is fairly rare in Louis XV and Louis XVI secretaires. 1984 valuation: £ 27,950, $ 37,000.
Current valuation: collector's price.

Fine, refined secretaire in mahogany veneer with a white marble top. The large surface of the fall-front is enhanced with an elegant chased ormolu medallion.
Current valuation: collector's price.

Fine secretaire with canted angles and a white marble top, bearing the stamp of P. Roussel. Decorated overall with landscapes containing figures, this is another illustration of the many possibilities for innovative and original creations open to the Louis XVI style. Sold in Paris in 1970: £ 4,000, $ 6,900. 1984 valuation: £ 17,200, $ 22,800. Current valuation: collector's price.

Below: fine meuble d'entre deux in tulipwood and amaranth veneer, bearing the stamp of Leleu, master cabinet-maker in Paris in 1764. This is an extremely rare item. (Photo: M. Meyer, Paris). Current valuation: collector's price.

Fine secretaire in tulipwood veneer inlaid with four-leafed clover and extensively mounted with ormolu, bearing the stamp RVLC (Roger Vandercruse known as Lacroix), master cabinet-maker in Paris in 1755. (Photo: Tajan, Paris). Sold in Paris in 1984: £ 43,000, $ 57,000. 1984 valuation: the same. Current valuation: collector's price.

Fine secretaire bearing the stamp of Jean Georges Schlichtig, master cabinet-maker in Paris on 2 October 1765. The piece has a veneer of tulipwood and kingwood, richly inlaid with various motifs: landscapes, vases, flowers, figures and musical symbols, enhanced with ivory and mother-of-pearl. It has a Saint-Anne marble top.
Below: The same piece with doors open. Sold in Paris in May 1984: £ 11,200, $ 14,800. 1984 valuation: the same.
Current valuation: collector's price.

Classic small commode in mahogany with three drawers with traverses, canted and channelled angles and a Saint-Anne marble top. The ormolu profiles emphasise the shape. 1984 valuation: £ 7,700, $ 10,300. Current valuation: £ 15,300, $ 25,350, € 22,880.

Fine commode, one of a pair, known as *d'entre deux* ('between two'), as it would be placed between two balconies, doors or other pieces of furniture. These commodes have a veneer of tortoiseshell, brass, pewter and ebony, in the style of pieces by Boulle, and are extensively mounted with ormolu. They are attributed to Levasseur. (Photo: Tajan, Paris). Sold in Paris in 1983: £ 125,700, $ 190,300. 1984 valuation: the same. Current valuation: collector's price.

Fine cabinet in lacquer and ebony veneer, extensively mounted with ormolu. Of particular note are the concave sides, which are synonymous with quality. The piece is attributed to Martin Carlin. (Photo: Tajan, Paris). Sold in Paris in 1983: £ 104,000, $ 157,500. 1984 valuation: the same. Current valuation: collector's price.

Important, rare bibliotheque of fine quality in mahogany, with two doors, bearing the stamp of C.C. Saunier. It has rounded angles and refined ormolu mounts. Sold in Paris in 1972: £ 10,870, $ 19,480. 1984 valuation: £ 21,500, $ 28,500. Current valuation: £ 35,700, $ 59,150, € 53,380.

Classic commode with three rows of drawers with traverses and rounded angles. Tulipwood and amaranth veneer and sober ormolu mounting. Saint-Anne marble top. 1984 valuation: £ 5,200, $ 6,800. Current valuation: £ 81,600, $ 135,200, € 122,000.

Fine secretaire in tulipwood, lemon and sycamore veneer. A touch of colour is added by the fine chased and mercury-gilt ormolu mounts. It bears the stamp of C.C. Saunier, master cabinet-maker in Paris in 1752. (Photo: M. Meyer, Paris). Current valuation: collector's price.

Fine console of exceptional quality in carved giltwood with a red-veined, green marble top. The great finesse of the carvings is of particular note. The French sculptors rarely displayed the great skill and precision that can be seen in the work of their Italian counterparts: 18th century mirrors and consoles are generally heavier and less finely carved in comparison to those made in Italy.

This piece is undoubtedly an exception to the rule. (Photo: Tajan, Paris). A photograph of this console is included in *Le Style Louis XVI* by Seymour de Ricci. Sold in Paris in 1981: £ 15,000, $ 30,300.
1984 valuation: £ 19,350, $ 25,650.
Current valuation: collector's price.

Fine console of excellent quality, one of a pair, in ebony veneer with refined chased and mercury-gilt ormolu mounts. It bears the stamp of R. Dubois, master cabinet-maker in Paris in 1752. (Photo: M. Segoura, Paris). Provenance: the Rueff-Behgin collection.
Sold in Paris in 1986: & 108,000, $ 158,700.
Current valuation: collector's price.

In the vocabulary of architecture the term 'console' originally referred to the rounded, projecting stones supporting a cornice. In the late 17th century the term was used to refer to the giltwood elements attached to walls or table legs, a detail of whose shape they repeated. Around 1765 the term 'console table' or simply 'console' came to be used for an essentially decorative piece of furniture.

Fine console veneered in exotic woods with refined chased and mercury-gilt ormolu mounts. It was made by Jean-Henri Riesener, cabinet-maker to the court of Louis XVI and regarded as one of the greatest cabinet-makers in history. This console was made for Marie-Antoinette's study in Versailles, probably to designs by Jacques Gondoin, and was then placed in the Chateau de Saint-Cloud.

The quality of the chased ormolu mounts is clear from their refinement and creativity. The console bears the inventory number 3099. Sold by Sotheby's in London in 1988: £ 1,510.,500, $ 2,685,700. Current valuation: collector's price.

Rare fine trapezium-shaped console of exceptional quality, in mahogany veneer, extensively mounted with finely chased ormolu. One of the four drawers beneath the white marble top bears the following inscription: 'Ferdinand Schwerdieger M.e Ebeniste à Paris 1788'. (Photo: Tajan, Paris). Sold in Paris in 1976: £ 106,900, $ 225,950. Current valuation: collector's price.

Left: Rare pair of fine encoignures in tulipwood and amaranth veneer, inlaid with landscapes and richly decorated with chased and mercury-gilt ormolu mounts. The top is of *brèche d'Alep* marble. These encoignures bear the stamp of P. Roussel, master cabinet-maker in Paris in 1745, aged only twenty.
Current valuation: collector's price.

Rare fine half-moon commode with a veneer of satinwood cut along the grain and richly decorated with chased and mercury-gilt ormolu mounts. It bears the stamp of C.C. Saunier, master cabinet-maker in Paris in 1752 aged only eighteen. He was not enrolled in the statute of the corporation until 1765, following the death of his father, for whom he had worked until that date.
Current valuation: collector's price.

Very rare secretaire of exceptional quality in Chinese lacquer with tree and flower motifs, attributed to Adam Weisweiler. All the details of the piece are highlighted by very refined chased ormolu mounts. The history of this piece is something of a mystery. It is said to have been lent to the Victoria and Albert Museum in London in 1886 and is later found in the collection of H. Dandy Seymour, about whom very little is known. The piece was said to have been the work of Gouthière, the celebrated bronzier of the second half of the 18th century, and to have belonged to queen Marie-Antoinette. (Photo: Sotheby, Parke Bernet). Sold in London in 1983: £ 1,127,000, $ 1,706,500.

Current valuation: collector's price.

Fine secretaire in tulipwood veneer inlaid with losenges with ivory flecks, bearing the stamp of N. Grevenich, master cabinet-maker in Paris in 1768. The very valuable ornamental detail of its enamel drawer handles decorated with landscapes is of particular note.

Many cabinet-makers, including De Loose, Schlichtig and Grevenich and particularly those of Flemish origins, liked to enhance their creations with details in ivory.

Current valuation: collector's price.

Fine secretaire of exceptional quality in black lacquer, decorated in the Chinese manner and attributed to Weisweiler. Every detail of the shape is emphasised by chased and mercury-gilt ormolu mounts.

Provenance: the collection of the Duc de Talleyrand.
Current valuation: collector's price.

Fine secretaire in tulipwood veneer inlaid with vases of flowers and furniture. Elegant chased and mercury-gilt ormolu mounts.

It bears the stamp of Nicolas Petit.
Current valuation: £ 81,600, $ 135,200, € 122,000.

Fine secretaire of exceptional quality bearing the stamp of A. Weisweiler, made around 1784. The Sèvres porcelain decoration and chased and mercury-gilt ormolu mounts make this piece a masterpiece of cabinet-making. Provenance: Grand Duchess Maria Fedorovna, wife of Tsar Paul I.
Sold by Sotheby's in London in 1988: £ 873,200, $ 1,552,700.
Current valuation: collector's price.

Fine secretaire of exceptional quality, attributed to P. Foullet, in tulip-wood veneer inlaid with architectural and floral motifs. Important chased and mercury-gilt ormolu mounts. Other similar pieces are known, one of which is in the Wallace Collection and bears the stamp 'Foulet'. Sold by Sotheby's in London in 1988: £ 396,500, $ 705,000. Current valuation: collector's price.

Unusual, rare footstool of excellent quality, in carved giltwood and bearing the stamp of J.B. Sené. Francis Watson has written a history of this footstool. It seems to have been one of a pair made by Sené, with other important seats, for Marie-Antoinette. One of these stools, which were originally intended for the Chateau de Saint-Cloud, is now in the chateau de Fontainbleau.

(Photo: Sotheby Parke Bernet).
Sold in Monte Carlo in 1979: £ 16,650, $ 37,880.
1984 valuation: £ 15,900, $ 21,100.
Current valuation: collector's price.

Armchair, one of a set of four of excellent quality, in finely carved gilt-wood and attributed to C. Sené. Eight armchairs similar to those signed by Sené are now in the Musée Camondo in Paris. (Photo: Tajan, Paris). Sold in Paris in 1983: £ 216,700, $ 328,200. 1984 valuation: the same. Current valuation: collector's price.

Below, right: very rare fine x-shaped folding stool, one of a set of four, in finely carved giltwood, made by Foliot but without a stamp. The design is identical to that of four other x-shaped stools preserved in the queen's bedroom in the palace of Versailles and later bought for the Chateau de Compiègne. The prototype of this design was made by Foliot in 1769 for Marie-Antoinette. Of particular note are the vigorous carvings and cross-pieces with twisted channelling, synonymous with quality in the range of Louis XVI furniture. (Photo: Tajan, Paris). Sold in Paris in 1990: £ 361,200, $ 642,700. Current valuation: collector's price.

Fine cabriolet armchair, one of a set of six, in finely carved beech-wood. Some pieces bear the stamp of J.B. Lelarge, a member of the Parisian family of carpenters comprising the founder, his son and grandson, who were active throughout the 18th century. No seating bearing the stamp of the eldest of these carpenters is known; the two others may have used the same stamp, but it was the youngest who became famous for the remarkably pure lines and harmonious proportions of his seating. Current valuation: collector's price.

Fine secretaire in tulipwood veneer with very fine trompe l'oeil inlays, bearing the stamp of J. Kemp.

1984 valuation: £ 25,800, $ 34,200.
Current valuation: collector's price.

Fine secretaire in tulipwood and amaranth veneer with refined decoration in kingwood with a floral motif. It bears the stamp of J. Boudin, master cabinet-maker in 1761, also known as a dealer in fine furniture made by other cabinet-makers. Extensive, elegant chased and mercury-gilt ormolu mounts.
Current valuation: collector's price.

Fine armoire in mahogany and amaranth, extensively mounted with ormolu. The affordable price is due to its large size, which makes it harder to sell. (Photo: Couturier-Nicolay). Sold in Paris in 1982: £ 14,400, $ 25,100.

1984 valuation: the same. 1997 valuation: £ 26,150, $ 42,800. Current valuation: £ 51,000, $ 84,500, € 76,250.

Left: pair of fine encoignures, each with a single door and white marble top. They are decorated in polychrome and gold lacquer with branch, flower and bird motifs on a black lacquer ground. Sold in Paris in 1971: £ 900, $ 1,580. 1984 valuation: £ 21,500, $ 28,500. Current valuation: £ 51,000, $ 84,500, € 76,250.

Fine secretaire in lacquer, decorated with motifs in the Chinese manner and extensively mounted with chased and mercury gilt ormolu highlighting every detail of its shape. It bears the stamp of Benneman, master cabinet-maker in Paris in 1785. (Photo: M. Meyer, Paris). Current valuation: collector's price.

Classic encoignure in mahogany, one of a pair. Each has a bombe front, one drawer and one door, enhanced with extensive ormolu mounting. 1984 valuation: £ 8,600, $ 11,400.
1991 valuation: £ 20,000, $ 35,400.
Current valuation: £ 25,500, $ 42,250, € 38,100.

Fine encoignure, one of a pair, in a veneer of *bois de fil* tulipwood with important chased ormolu mounts and bearing the stamp of Nicolas Petit. Sold in Paris in 1971: £ 6,090, $ 10,700.
Current valuation: collector's price.

Pair of encoignures, partly classic, partly fine, each with a single door and marble top. Noteworthy for the unusual, slightly concave shape either side of the door and the double legs which prolong the angles. More extensive ormolu mounting would be enough to raise this design to the status of fine quality.
Sold in Paris in 1972:   £ 900, $ 1,600.
1984 valuation: about £ 6,450, $ 8,550.
1991 valuation: £ 20,000, $ 35,400.
Current valuation: £ 20,400, $ 33,800, € 30,500.

Classic encoignure, one of a pair, in tulipwood veneer with amaranth profiles decorated with motifs of ruins. 1984 valuation: £ 8.600, $ 11.400. 1991 valuation: £ 21,000, $ 37,200.
Current valuation: £ 20,400, $ 33,800, € 30,500.

Fine buffet in mahogany with two doors and one drawer, rounded and channelled angles, concave sides with a shelf and a grey-white marble top. The very simple lines are enhanced with refined ormolu mounts. The piece bears the prestigious stamp of Oeben.
Current valuation: collector's price.

Exceptional pair of fine encoignures with *brèche d'Alep* marble tops. The exotic wood veneers enhance the remarkably fine marquetry. Each encoignure has a single door: One opens to reveal shelves, the other a small secretaire with two small drawers behind its fall-front.
1984 valuation: £ 17,200, $ 22,800.
Current valuation: collector's price.

Important and rare fine breakfront buffet with concave sides, three drawers and three doors. The unusual, elegant shape, extensive ormolu mounting, Sèvres porcelain medallions and stamp of J.H. Riesener give this piece a very high value. Sold in Paris in 1972: £ 34,400, $ 61,700. Current valuation: collector's price.

Fine encoignure, one of a pair, in mahogany. The piece has one drawer literally covered in ormolu, a rectangular door with an ormolu frame and rounded, channelled angles.
1984 valuation: £ 10,750, $ 14,250. 1991 valuation: £ 30,000, $ 53,100.
Current valuation: £ 30,600, $ 50,700, € 45,750.

Fine console with concave sides, one drawer and a white marble top with an ormolu gallery. It is made in solid mahogany with rare, refined ormolu mounts emphasising every detail of the shape.
1984 valuation: £ 10,750, $ 14,250. 1991 valuation: £ 20,000, $ 35,400. Current valuation: £ 25,500, $ 42,250, € 38,100.

Good quality console with three drawers, a white marble top and rounded angles. It has a sober decoration of floral motifs.
1984 valuation: £ 7,700, $ 10,300. 1991 valuation: £ 16,500, $ 29,200. Current valuation: £ 15,300, $ 25,350, € 22,880.

Fine console of exceptional quality stamped Saunier. (Photo: M. Meyer, Paris). Current valuation: collector's price.

Very fine console in mahogany veneer, decorated with Sèvres porcelain plaques and ormolu mounts, bearing the stamp of M. Carlin. Sold in Monte Carlo in 1979: £ 111,000, $ 252,550.
1984 valuation: the same. Current valuation: collector's price.

Good quality half-moon console. Sold in Paris in 1976: £ 870, $ 1,850.
1984 valuation: £ 2,240, $ 2,960. 1991 valuation: £ 7,000, $ 12,400. Current valuation: £ 10,200, $ 16,900, € 15,250.

Large fine console in lemonwood veneer with ebony and amaranth profiles. Sold in Paris in 1982: £ 12,650, $ 22,000.
1984 valuation: £ 12,900, $ 17,100. 1991 valuation: £ 23,000, $ 40,700.
Current valuation: £ 35.700, $ 59,150. € 53,380.

Rare fine console in mahogany with rounded angles.
Sold in Paris in 1971:£ 7,150, $ 12,600. 1984 valuation: £ 17,200, $ 22,800. Current valuation: collector's price.

Fine console in lemon and sycamore veneer. Sold in Paris in 1983: £ 39,000, $ 59,000. 1984 valuation: the same.
Current valuation: collector's price.

Fine console in mahogany with a white marble top and undertier. The shape is emphasised by extensive and vigorous ormolu mounting. 1984 valuation: £ 12,900, $ 17,100.
Current valuation: collector's price.

Fine small console with concave sides and a single drawer, attributed to Saunier. In mahogany with a grey Saint-Anne marble top and chased ormolu frieze, it has two shelves, also in grey marble, with ormolu galleries. 1984 valuation: £ 8,600, $ 11,400.
1991 valuation: £ 18,000, $ 31,900.
Current valuation: £ 15,300, $ 25,350, € 22,880.

Fine gilt armchair, one of a pair. 1984 valuation: £ 5,160, $ 6,840. 1991 valuation: $ 12,000, $ 21,200. Current valuation: £ 15,300, $ 25,350, € 22,880.

Rare, exceptional armchair, one of a pair, in finely carved giltwood, bearing the stamp of Bauve, master carpenter in Paris in 1754. Of particular note are the carved, spirally-fluted legs, a rare and highly-prized detail in Louis XVI seating. Sold in Paris in May 1984: £ 38,700, $ 51,300. Current valuation: collector's price.

Rare and unusual bidet with foliate carving, bearing the stamp of Canabas. Sold in Paris in 1970: £ 620, $ 1,070. 1984 valuation: £ 3,440, $ 4,560. 1991 valuation: 7,000, $ 12,400. Current valuation: £ 7,650, $ 12,675, € 11,440.

Fine gilt armchair, one of a pair, carved overall with foliage and flowers, bearing the stamp of G. Jacob. The value of these armchairs stems from the finesse of the carving. Sold in Paris in 1971: £ 12,550, $ 22,100. Current valuation: collector's price.

Fine regilt armchair, one of a pair, carved overall with foliage and bearing the stamp of J.B. Delaunay. Sold in Paris in 1971: £ 3,440, $ 4,530. 1984 valuation: £ 3,870, $ 5,100. 1991 valuation: £ 10,000, £ 17,700. Current valuation: £ 15,300, $ 25,350, € 22,880.

Pair of classic armchairs in giltwood and polychrome Aubusson tapestries representing themes from La Fontaine's fables.
1984 valuation: £ 3,870, $ 5,100. 1991 valuation: £ 10,000, £ 17,700.
Current valuation: £ 10,200, $ 16,900, € 15,250.

Pair of fine armchairs in white and gold lacquer and polychrome tapestries with motifs of figures and flowers. Of particular note is the twisted channelling, symbolic of refinement, on the armrest supports. 1984 valuation: £ 4,300, $ 5,700.
1991 valuation: £ 12,000, $ 21,200.
Current valuation: 315,300, $ 25,350, € 22,880.

Pair of classic carved giltwood armchairs with medallion backs and polychrome tapestries with motifs of flowers, figures and animals.
1984 valuation: £ 3,440, $ 4,560. 1991 valuation: £ 12,000, $ 21,200.
Current valuation: 315,300, $ 25,350, € 22,880.

Rare *fauteuil de bureau* with swivel seat and console legs, bearing the stamp of G. Jacob, regarded as one of the most prestigious carpenters in the history of late 18th century French seating.
1984 valuation: £ 2,150, $ 2,850. 1991 valuation: £ 10,000, $ 17,700.
Current valuation: £ 10,200, $ 16,900, € 15,250.

Fine small gilt canape carved with *entrelacs*, knots and foliage. The intense decoration and twisted channelling to the legs highlight the perfection of the workmanship. 1984 valuation: £ 2,580, $ 3,400. 1991 valuation: £ 9,000, $ 15,900.
Current valuation: £ 13,770, $ 22,800, € 20,600.

Classic caned *fauteuil de bureau* with a swivel seat in natural wood and *modenatura*, attributed to G. Jacob. Sold in Paris in 1970: £ 620, $ 1,070. 1984 valuation: £ 1,700, $ 2,300.
1991 valuation: £ 4,000, $ 7,100.
Current valuation: £ 3,570, $ 5,900, € 5,340.

Classic armchair, one of a pair, in natural beechwood with an oval back. Sold in Milan in 1975: £ 2.,870, $ 5,900.
1984 valuation: £ 2,580, $ 3,400. 1991 valuation: £ 5,000, $ 8,850.
Current valuation: £ 4,600, $ 7,600, € 6,850.

Giltwood marquise canape, partly classic, partly fine, carved with foliage and entrelacs. Of particular note is the twisted channelling to the legs, signifying refinement. Sold in Paris in 1971:£ 1,340, $ 2,370.
1984 valuation: £ 1,700, $ 2,300.1991 valuation: £ 5000, $ 8,850.
Current valuation: £ 5,100, $ 8,450, € 7,600.

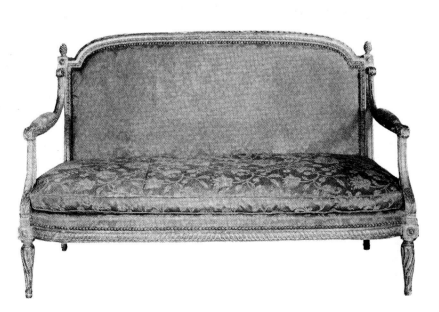

Classic armchair, one of a pair, regilt with medallion backs, carved with pearls and with polychrome tapestries with motifs of flowers and figures. 1984 valuation: about £ 3,000, $ 4,000.
1991 valuation: £ 7,000, $ 12,400.
Current valuation: £ 7,140, $ 11,800, € 10,680.

Centre: rare caned, coloured and gilt armchair, designed to enable the sitter to be carried. This chair is certainly not an item of very great quality, but its value remains high due to the fact that examples of this type are immensely hard to find. 1984 valuation: £ 4,300, $ 5,700. 1991 valuation: £ 7,000, $ 12,400.
Current valuation: £ 7,140, $ 11,800, € 10,680.

Rare fine gondola *bergere*, one of a pair, in regilt wood. Of particular note for the profusion of decorative carvings covering its entire frame. Sold in Paris in 1973: £ 12,100, $ 22,500.
Current valuation: collector's price.

Below: fine gilt canape with polychrome tapestries showing motifs of landscapes, figures, flowers and animals.
1984 valuation: £ 3,440, $ 4,560. 1991 valuation: £ 8,000, $ 14,200.
Current valuation: £ 9,200, $ 15,200, € 13,700.

Classic chair, one of a pair, each with a rectangular back, painted grey. Sold in Paris in 1970: £ 400, $ 700. 1984 valuation: £ 860, $ 1,140. 1991 valuation: £ 2,500, $ 4,400.
Current valuation: £ 2,550, $ 4,200, € 3,800.

Fine chair, one of a set of six, in grey and green painted wood.
1984 valuation: £ 10,300, $ 13,700. 1991 valuation: £ 15,000, $ 26,550.
Current valuation: £ 15,300, $ 25,350 € 22,880.

Centre: classic chair in grey painted wood with polychrome tapestries representing scenes from La Fontaine's fables.
1984 valuation: £ 1,100, $ 1,400. 1991 valuation: the same.
Current valuation: £ 1,530, $ 2,530, € 2,280.

Fine chair, one of a set of six in mahogany. The lyre design is highly-prized by collectors. 1991 valuation: £ 20,000, $ 35,400.
Current valuation: £ 20,400, $ 33,800, € 30,500.

Low nursing chair in grey coloured wood, bearing the stamp of Sené. Chairs of this type are extremely rare and very greatly-prized by collectors. They reach very high prices.
1984 valuation: £ 2,105, $ 2,850. 1991 valuation: £ 3,000, $ 5,300.
Current valuation: £ 2,550, $ 4,200, € 3,800.

Rare ponteuse or voyeuse chair, for sitting astride, in regilt wood with an oval back and bearing the stamp of J.J. Pothier. Sold in Paris in 1974: £ 760, $ 1,500. 1984 valuation: £ 1,500, $ 2,000. 1991 valuation: £ 5,000, $ 8,850. Current valuation: £ 4,100, $ 6,760, € 6,100.

Pair of rare nursing chairs in mahogany with lyre-shaped backs. Sold in Paris in 1970: £ 1,400, $ 2,450. 1984 valuation: £ 2,600, $ 3,400. 1991 valuation: £ 5,000, $ 8,850. Current valuation: £ 4,600, $ 7,600, € 6,850.

Rare fine ponteuse or voyeuse chair, one of a pair, on which the sitter would sit astride to watch a card game, leaning on the toprail, which is padded for that purpose. Lacquered in grey and gold, these chairs have elegant lyre-shaped backs and bear the stamp of C. Chavigny. Sold in Paris in 1974: £ 2,370, $ 4,650. 1984 valuation: £ 4,300, $ 5,700. 1991 valuation: £ 6,500, $ 11,500. Current valuation: £ 7,650, $ 12,700, € 11,440.

Large bed with canopy *à la polonaise*, carved and regilt. Canopy beds are in little demand as they are too large for modern apartments and almost never reach a high price. Sold in Paris in 1974: £ 760, $ 1,500. 1984 valuation: £ 3,400, $ 4,560. 1991 valuation: £ 6,500, $ 11,500. Current valuation: £ 6,600, $ 11,000, € 9,900.

Rectangular footstool in carved, grey painted wood. 1984 valuation: £ 650, $ 850. 1991 valuation: £ 1,300, $ 2,300. Current valuation: £ 1,330, $ 2,200, € 1,980.

Rectangular stool, one of a pair, in mahogany with twisted legs, synonymous with quality. 1984 valuation: £ 3,400, $ 4,560. 1991 valuation: £ 5,000, $ 8,850. Current valuation: £ 5,100, $ 8,450, € 7,600.

Bed designed for an alcove in grey-coloured wood, carved with pearls and foliage. 1984 valuation: £ 3,400, $ 4,560. 1991 valuation: £ 7,000, $ 15,900. Current valuation: £ 7,100, $ 11,800, € 10,680.

Classic *bergere* and armchair, finely carved and lacquered grey. 1984 valuation: the *bergere* £ 2,150, $ 2,850. The armchair £ 645, $ 850. 1991 valuation: the *bergere* £ 4,500, $ 7,950.The armchair £ 1,500, $ 2,650. Current valuation: the *bergere* £ 4,100, $ 6,800, € 6,100. The armchair £ 2,040, $ 3,400, € 3,050.

Classic day-bed in carved giltwood. Sold in Paris in 1973: £ 1,860, $ 3,460. 1984 valuation: £ 3,400, $ 4,560. 1991 valuation: £ 6,000, $ 10,600. Current valuation: £ 6,120, $ 10,100, € 9,150.

Chair, one of a pair, in wood that has been re-coloured grey and gold, with a *montgolfière* back and bearing the stamp of Demay. These chairs seem to have been ordered from the carpenter by the city of Paris, which was to give them to Montgolfier, famous inventor of the hot-air balloon. Sold in Paris in 1973: £ 930, $ 1,730. 1984 valuation: £ 3,000, $ 4,000. 1991 valuation: £ 8,000, $ 14,200. Current valuation: £ 8,200, $ 13,500, € 12,200.

Two fine chairs from a set of six with oval backs, round seats and console legs. They are coloured grey and covered in polychrome tapestries with floral motifs. Attributed to G. Jacob. Sold in Paris in 1970: £ 3,540, $ 6,130. Current valuation: collector's price.

Fine bedside table with an ormolu-galleried marble top. Tulipwood and amaranth veneer and extensive decoration of geometrical designs and ormolu mounts. The table has a writing surface beneath the marble top and a single door. 1984 valuation: £ 7,750, $ 10,300. 1991 valuation: £ 20,000, $ 35,400.
Current valuation: £ 20,400, $ 33,800, € 30,500.

Classic small armoire or double cabinet, inlaid overall on a tulip-wood ground. The upper part has two doors and two drawers, the lower part has a writing surface and two doors.
1984 valuation: £ 10,750, $ 14,250. 1991 valuation: £ 20,000, $ 35,400.
Current valuation: £ 20,400, $ 33,800, € 30,500.

Classic bedside table *d'appui* with three rows of drawers with tra-verses, veneered in kingwood and amaranth and having an ormolu-galleried marble top. Sold in London in 1973: £ 1,860, $ 3,460.
1984 valuation: £ 2,600, $ 3,400. 1991 valuation: £ 4,000, $ 7,100. Current valuation: £ 5,100, $ 8,450, € 7,600.

Classic bibliotheque in tulipwood veneer. The short, cabriole legs of this Louis XVI piece reflect the previous style.
1984 valuation: £ 12,900, $ 17,100. 1991 valuation: £ 2,200, $ 38,950. Current valuation: £ 20,400, $ 33,800, € 30,500.

Classic small commode in butterfly tulipwood veneer with sober or-molu mounting, bearing the stamp of F.I. Papast. Sold in Paris in 1971: £ 3,850, $ 6,800. 1984 valuation: £ 7,750, $ 10,300. 1991 valuation: £ 13,500, $ 23,900.
Current valuation: £ 12,240, $ 20,300, € 18,300.

Classic bibliotheque in mahogany veneer, with channelled angles and two glass doors, bearing the stamp of J.I. Cossen. Sold in Paris in 1971: £ 1,700, 3,000. 1984 valuation: £ 3,900, $ 5,100. 1991 valuation: £ 8,500, $ 15,000.
Current valuation: £ 8,700, $ 14,400, € 12,960.

Classic armoire in mahogany with two doors and canted angles, bearing the stamp of J. Bircklé.
1984 valuation: £ 7,750, $ 10,300. 1991 valuation: £ 1,150, $ 20,350.
Current valuation: £ 11,200, £ 18,600, € 16,775.

Fine small armoire in mahogany and pink breccia marble. Of particular note for its sober, stylised ormolu mounts and small size, highly prized by today's clientele. It bears the stamp of P.C. Montigny.

1984 valuation: £ 10,750, $ 14,250.
1991 valuation: £ 23,000, $ 40,700.
Current valuation: £ 20,400, $ 33,800, € 30,500.

The *Directoire* style

The *Directoire* style takes its name from the government that ruled France from 1795 to 1799, the year in which Napoleon became First Consul. This period saw the emergence in Paris of a new style which, like many others, was to last longer than the brief regime whose name it bears. In practice the *Directoire* style covers the entire period marking the passage from the France of the kings to the France of emperor Napoleon I, comprising three very short-lived regimes: the revolutionary government of 1789–1795, the *Directoire* of 1795–1799 and the Consulate of 1799–1804. The *Directoire* style had a great influence on cabinet-making in a large part of Europe and particularly in Italy. It can be dated from 1789 to 1804, in other words from the end of the Louis XVI style (1789) to the start of the Empire style (1804).

As is well known, not only did a great many people lose their heads in the French Revolution, but the court and aristocracy also lost all their privileges. The aim of the revolutionaries was not simply to rebel against the dominant class, but to destroy everything that belonged to it as well. In their demands for equality and fraternity they could not but condemn the luxurious furniture of the nobility. The costly materials used in sophisticated Louis XVI commodes, secretaires and seating signified a world they were making every effort to destroy.

However the new Tribunes (Robespierre, Marat, Barras) and political figures who replaced the old aristocratic elite had not yet formed any very clear ideas where fashion was concerned. The arts and trades corporations disappeared, swept away by the revolutionary movement, and this led to the removal of the strict controls that had been the best guarantee of product quality. The social upheavals of the Revolution gave rise to a new high society consisting of the privileged, the nouveaux riches and adventurers, all of whom had large financial resources at their disposal, but neither the knowledge nor the necessary ability and rigour to set new standards for refinement and taste. They were in fact incapable of promoting a new style different from what had

gone before, contrary to what had happened during the *Régence*, for example.

Moreover, had any attempt been made to produce truly innovative furniture, it would have gone against the spirit of the times and the post-revolutionary credo. This advocated a greater simplicity of style, always remaining within the classical sphere of influence. For it was classicism that had so excellently expressed the austerity of the ancient Roman heroes whom the politicians of the day had adopted as models.

In addition to this, economic conditions in the country were not sufficiently healthy to allow people to acquire furniture of great value and variety.

This is the context in which we see the emergence of Directoire furniture, whose essence is the result of a synthesis of three main factors: firstly, the use of parallelepiped shapes continued (the structures remained fundamentally the same as those of the Louis XVI style); secondly, the pieces produced appeared more sober in decoration and structure; lastly new decorative elements were adopted, including revolutionary symbols.

Shapes remained straight but, in contrast to the Louis XVI style, with none of the canted or rounded angles that formerly softened the geometrical aspect of pieces, nor the same attention to details of joinery and finishing. *Directoire* commodes, buffets, small vitrines and bonheur-du-jour manifest an increased rigidity of form and none of the details and semicircular mounts used by the Louis XVI style at every point where horizontal and vertical elements of the frame met.

Directoire furniture thus has a more geometrical shape, with sharp, precise angles prefiguring the Empire style. This does not mean that curves completely disappeared: small round tables were still produced, but these are rare and differ from those of the Louis XVI style in their pilaster supports and square elements. The table tops often have more geometrical, hexagonal shapes, closer to the Pompeiian models.

The half-moon forms so typical of the preceding style fell into disuse. Where seating was concerned, curves were still used for chair backs, which leaned slightly outwards (in the Etruscan manner), imitating the shape of backs represented on some ancient vases. The back legs were often splayed outwards *en sabre* ('in a sabre shape'). Front legs were straight, as in the preceding style, but were tapered and occasionally channelled or excessively carved. The extremely rare gondola backs to *bergeres* were retained. At this time France was in a very difficult economic position. Luxury pieces made in precious materials such as mahogany and enhanced with splendid chased ormolu mounts became rare. The *Directoire* did not have many clients for such costly pieces and thus preferred to use more economical materials. Tulipwood and kingwood veneers inlaid with flowers and landscapes completely disappeared.

They were replaced by simple veneers in fruitwood (cherry, lemon, pear, etc.), while ormolu mounts were confined to functional accessories (handles, sabots, escutcheons). We can also find pieces made of solid wood and fashionably coloured (pale grey, sky-blue, yellow, pale green). The use of oak in the carcases of pieces and that of walnut and beechwood in seating, formerly the best guarantee of quality work, lost its significance, since the *Directoire* was unable to uphold the regulations which had justly made cabinet-making one of the highest achievements of the French nation. With its confusion and mixture of woods, the lightening of structures and sparser decoration, including mounts, *Directoire* furniture is a simplified, less sophisticated and slimmed-down version of the Louis XVI style. The most typical decorative elements of the Directoire, in mounts, carving and inlays, are the Greek sphinx (bearing a bowl of fruit on its head and not to be confused with the Egyptian sphinx, which bears nothing and is a characteristic element of the Empire style), the palm leaf, the urn-shaped vase with handles representing curled serpents, winged Victory with a lyre-shaped headdress and arrows.

The decorative elements symbolising the French Revolution are the fasces (symbol of the unity that brings strength), oak branches (symbolic of the civic virtues), the triangle with a cen-tral eye (symbol of reason), joined hands (symbol of fraternity), the poplar (symbol of liberty), the cock (symbol of the French people), the Phrygian cap, pikes, cocades and the tablets of the law. These decorative elements soon lost their importance and were quickly forgotten.

A closer examination of the Directoire style

The *Directoire* style was heir to the Louis XVI style, which it reinterpreted in its own way. The innovation it introduced and popularised was a mirror known as the 'psyche', whose originality lies in the fact that the glass itself is movable and can be orientated in different directions. The glass is fixed to the frame by means of two pivot attachments halfway up its sides, so that it can be tipped. The psyche and the gondola chair seem to have been the only inventions of the *Directoire* style. These two pieces were to become very popular under the Empire.

Directoire furniture is born of the contrast between tradition and the tastes of an ephemeral society desperately seeking its own identity after a period of great turbulence. This society took the civilisations of classical Rome and Sparta as its models, but did not manage to provide a stable image of the new France. We can understand this situation if we consider the objectives of the Revolution, whose main concern had been to oppose and destroy the absolute power of the monarchy rather than to create a new form of art. Its priority was people, not furniture. It was only after the merciless activity of the guillotine had completely obliterated the old feudal privileges and the foundations of the constitution and modern human rights had been laid that the Revolution turned its attention to art in general and furniture in particular, to imprint them with its own ideals.

However, unlike regimes that can be destroyed or abruptly and brutally changed, artistic development needs to be borne along by a cultural movement that first rejects the old precepts then generates innovative artistic currents which breathe new life into art. The revolutionary society found itself culturally unprepared to take on the vast artistic heritage of the past. In its disturbed state it preferred to remain faithful to the principles of simplicity, similarity and austerity, seeking to apply them to Louis XVI furniture.

In the first place it simplified shapes and reduced or even eliminated the original decorations, replacing them with warlike symbols. Then, believing it had thus removed the imprint of monarchy, it provided these same shapes with new decorations, better suited than the revolutionary symbols to expressing the historical meaning of the *Directoire*. The style clearly draws on Roman and Greek classicism.

So we see the emergence of winged Victory with a lyre-shaped headdress, laurel crowns, Greek sphinxes, fauns playing the flute, winged lions, swans, mermaids, griffins, arrows, columns, lion's paws, amphora, urns and, lastly, Hunger and Fortune, which the *Directoire* style endlessly reproduced. The interplay of these classical references produced a nobler, more military language heralding the Empire style.

It is precisely because of its historical position between the Revolution and the Empire that the *Directoire* style proves its sensitivity to the past, creating a succession of shapes that always have a different decoration. It was indisputably drawn to the past, perceiving its historical importance and bringing out its most representative aspects (simplicity of form and materials, sober decoration), to herald a glorious future. These characteristics mean that the *Directoire* style has always been regarded as a transitional style; however we do not entirely agree with such a definition. In our examination of transitional styles we have noted that the passage from one style to the next takes place slowly but noticeably, through works whose hybrid aspects display a mixture of elements from both the old and future styles. Unlike the *Régence* style, the *Directoire* saw no great changes in shape or decoration and did not bring about any radical changes. It confined itself to recycling those shapes and decorations of the past it regarded as best able to express and celebrate the present as it unfolded, putting them together in a

new way. We might then expect the *Directoire* to have some affinity with the style of the Louis XV–Louis XVI transitional style, given that both sought their connotations in the past. This is undoubtedly the case, but with a few differences. For the transitional style had chosen the most human aspects of the classic ancient civilisations, stressing beauty and the pleasures of life: small bouquets of flowers, pastoral scenes, symbols of love, etc. The *Directoire*, on the other hand, chose more historical references which seemed better to express its political ideology.

On the other hand it seems to us that there are real, radical and profound similarities with the Louis XVI style. For even though, in its quest for originality, the *Directoire* sought to modify the structures of the furniture of the preceding style, the simplification it carried out was too limited and the traces of the original style are too visible. In practice it confined itself to making commodes, tables and bureaux plats which display a continuity of shape with those of the Louis XVI style, but a different decorative language. And while, in its decline, the *Directoire*'s artistic language and politicised manifestations heralded the Empire, this is not enough in our view to regard it as a transitional style. Given that the Directoire was one of the briefest artistic expressions in the history of furniture, we can regard it as a style that was both static and gestating, perfectly illustrating the instability and confusion of a society which was only just coming into being. When this society took on weight and substance, the Empire was born.

Typical pieces

We shall now attempt to analyse a few of the most significant pieces in this style.

Commodes

Leaving aside the mahogany masterpieces made by the great master cabinet-makers who survived the Revolution, *Directoire* commodes reflect the poverty of materials used in their production and the exhaustion of the seam of creativity. With the abandonment of mahogany, the coloured versions and those made in solid fruitwood no longer bear comparison with the shape, rich decoration and, to put it bluntly, the arrogant beauty of *Régence*, Louis XV, transition period and Louis XVI commodes.

The *Directoire* commode is one of the more unfortunate of 18th-century pieces, and one which best represents the criteria of austerity so exalted by revolutionary ideas. The fact that the commode lost at least part of its importance as the main piece of furniture and entered a more marked phase of decadence is not at all surprising. It first developed out of the coffer, acquiring drawers before becoming the commode at the dawn of the 18th century. In so doing it displayed all that human beings could express in the course of three centuries.

In the late 18th century architecture was also drawing on the past, creating many small spaces within houses. In the *Directoire* period it seems to have been even more keen than under Louis XVI to relegate the commode to its simple function as a piece of furniture for storing clothes. Perhaps unconsciously this suggested that the commode should be placed in the bedroom, where the extent of its decoration clearly became less important, given that it was no longer to be seen by visitors. It is true that commodes of high quality, specially designed for salons, became rare. They were replaced by fall-front secretaires and mahogany buffets with ormolu mounts which, along with the chairs and tables in mahogany or pale wood, best represent *Directoire* elegance. Nevertheless, because of their immutably rectangular form, marble or wooden tops, three rows of drawers to the front and angles decorated with columns or pilasters without channelling, commodes no longer seem to have attracted the attention of the great master cabinet-makers.

Psyches

The great popularity of the psyche reflects the skill attained by the makers of these large mirrors. They are one of the *Directoire* style's few creations and, although surprisingly mobile, are undeniably beautiful. Yet they seem to have been intended more for a dressmaker's workshop or for discreet use by ladies than to add a touch of elegance to an interior.

Seating

Generally speaking, in its austerity and inferior quality in comparison to the preceding style, *Directoire* furniture reflects a lack of taste and financial means. We can make an exception to this observation in the case of seating and that of the small round or hexagonal tables and work tables in mahogany with sober ormolu mounting, which are the style's most refined creations,.

In a trend that was already apparent in the Louis XVI style, padded backs to all types of chair are found increasingly rarely. This allowed the furniture-makers of the time to express their creativity by designing a wide variety of backs described as *à montants aigus* ('with sharp angles'), *à encadrement* ('framed'), or *en bâton de berger* ('shepherd's crook'), to mention only the most common. One of the last creations of the style was the gondola-backed chair, which had never before been made and should not be confused with the Louis XV or Louis XVI gondola *bergere*. The most elegant armchairs have armrests ending in carved lion's or eagle's heads.

In conclusion we can say that the Directoire was linked to both the neoclassicism dominant at the time and, through its history, to the Louis XVI style, of which it is a different and impoverished version. The *Directoire* style also embarked upon a process of popularisation and indeed generalisation of its pieces throughout the society as a whole. After the brief Empire period, this process became unavoidably bound up with the phenomenon of industrialisation, when the making of furniture by craftsmen on a piece by piece basis gave way to production on a grand scale.

Towards industrial production

The output of *Directoire* style furniture was quite extensive given the period's short duration and the fact that those individuals who could afford to buy it often chose to acquire furniture from earlier styles instead. In Paris there were already antiques dealers and collectors who had little taste for the austerity of the new style.

The most important cabinet-makers in the Directoire period are Georges Jacob, Boulard, Sené, Weisweiler and all those we have already mentioned in relation to the Louis XVI style.

Among the creators of the highest quality chased ormolu, we once more find Thomire, who had been the best pupil of the famous master Gouthière under Louis XVI. It was thanks to these masters that the highly selective production of commodes, bureaux, small tables, chairs, armchairs and méridiennes could continue. They were able to survive despite the fact that, in sweeping away all privilege, including the regulations of the cabinet-makers' corporations, the Revolution had laid the way open for anyone, including great unknowns, to set themselves up as furniture makers or dealers.

As we have seen, before the Revolution the corporation of master cabinet-makers had been subject to very strict regulations. These guaranteed the quality of furniture by imposing restrictions on the materials and woods used (oak for cabinet carcases, walnut or beechwood for seating).

In addition, the corporation was divided into two broad categories which craftsmen could enter only once they had passed their 'master's' examination. The first consisted of carpenters who made only seating. The second, that of cabinet-makers, was for those who made other types of furniture.

In addition to these broad categories, which formed the main body of the corporation, there was a third, smaller category of table-makers, who specialised in making small tables, particularly games tables whose tops were inlaid with chequered boards for playing draughts and chess. Under the *Directoire* many table-makers established real small-scale factories making and selling all types of furniture. Their works are small in size, with minutely detailed and refined decorations through which their author can easily be identified. Even famous cabinet-makers such as Georges Jacob, for example, were quick to extend their activities by creating large businesses employing dozens and dozens of workers to produce a vast range of furniture, from cabinets to chairs, as well as associated elements ranging from ormolu mounts to padding and upholstery fabrics for chairs and canapes.

Yet, even when they made works in the *Directoire* style, the great masters of the Louis XVI style had acquired so much experience over time that their knowledge of tradition and skills enabled them to produce refined, prestigious pieces, even at a semi-industrial level.

The same cannot be said of all those who set up large, modern businesses without skill or knowledge, with the sole aim of attaining commercial success irrespective of any artistic merit.

This explains why today we cannot speak of classic, fine or high quality Parisian furniture in the *Directoire* style, nor of provincial or rustic furniture, as we did in relation to all the preceding styles including Louis XVI. For the Directoire only two types of production can be discussed

The first includes all furniture made in mahogany, the second all pieces in fruitwood, including the mahogany-coloured walnut that had already been used for the most commonly-found Louis XVI designs.

The pieces made in mahogany with mercury-gilt ormolu mounts were of course the most prestigious, sumptuous and costly items in the style, the others being made by the dozen at low prices.

The uniformity of this production prevents us from distinguishing fine and classic Parisian pieces from quality provincial furniture. In addition, in the provinces under the Directoire, Louis XV and Louis XVI style furniture was still being made without too much attention being paid to the new fashions of the capital.

This uniformity can probably be attributed to the beginnings of the industrialisation period, for through the Paris exhibitions, publications and the circulation of products, new designs spread throughout the entire country with a speed and precision hitherto unthinkable. It becomes practically impossible to distinguish a Parisian piece from a piece made in the provinces and even, in some cases, a piece made abroad.

In the case of rustic furniture on the other hand, we can state that pieces of this type were untouched by the *Directoire* style and continued to draw on the Louis XVI style.

This confirms the hypothesis that provincial rustic furniture has always needed more time to adapt to new ideas and that it required a longer period than the *Directoire* style was able to give it.

And so, in an ironic twist of fate, the symbols of a revolution that had been brought about 'for the people' did not have time to manifest themselves in the people's furniture.

Fakes and copies

The *Directoire* style is an exception in relation to other styles when it comes to the modifications sometimes made to pieces to enhance their value or the embellishments that were added to enrich a classic piece or to transform a provincial piece into a Parisian piece. For sober decoration is a badge of the style, so that to create embellished Directoire pieces would be a contradiction in terms.

To enrich them would be to transform them into easily recognisable, hybrid pieces.

Nor was it possible to transform a provincial *Directoire* piece into a Parisian piece, given that the production was the same throughout France and that provincial pieces with their own particular characteristics do not exist.

When earlier styles were reproduced in the 19th century, the *Directoire* style was not considered. It was not until the early 20th century that designers once more began to use Directoire shapes and decorations. But this was a passing fad, soon replaced by the imposing Empire style.

How to find Directoire furniture

Directoire pieces are fairly rare on any of the art markets. This style, one of the shortest-lived in the history of furniture, did not have enough time to produce a sufficiently large number of works to enable it to generate a truly independent market. The few remaining pieces are of course found primarily in Paris and then in the rest of France. They are only rarely found in London, New York or some Italian cities.

Quality and valuation

When speaking of the best *Directoire* pieces we should state once again that in practice this style represents the popularisation and impoverishment of Louis XVI and neoclassical designs, albeit with different decorative elements. Generally speaking, from the artistic point of view there is no comparison between *Directoire* furniture and the creations of the Louis XVI style, or of any other style of the 18th century. Starting out from a lower level therefore, pieces made in mahogany with sober ormolu mounting are regarded as being of quality. However these never reach exorbitant prices and, while remaining in the category of craft production, can bring a certain sober, distinguished elegance to an interior. Without costing too much, they always remain a good investment in the way that any sum, large or small, will appreciate with time.

Moving now from *Directoire* pieces regarded as being of high quality to pieces designed for ordinary use, made in woods other than mahogany (in other words walnut, cherry, pear, lemon or maple), such pieces are not only of inferior quality, but vary in colour. The shapes and decorations do not change however. These pieces are more reasonably priced and, where their practical use and investment status are concerned, the same observations apply as for mahogany pieces.

The pieces most sought-after by collectors are those with new or original shapes. For this reason hexagonal or octagonal tables are very much in demand, as they represent one of the more creative, innovative and elegant of *Directoire* designs.

The psyche is valued when it is part of the coiffeuse, as the element bringing new character to a piece whose Louis XV and Louis XVI versions had a mirror set into a folding panel, which could be raised when required.

Mahogany coiffeuses are rare, very highly-prized and more expensive than those made in other woods.

Buffets and secretaires in mahogany are also fairly rare and very highly-prized for their ormolu mounting which, although less extensive than that found on Louis XVI designs, enhances the dark colours of the wood with its brilliance. Even pieces made in different woods and simply veneered or inlaid with geometrical designs are appreciated by the public and sell at comparatively high prices. Sets of six chairs are much sought-after since, though less robust, their value is increased by their elegant form. Gilt seating and designs lacquered white and gold are also elegant, but are less in demand and thus not as expensive.

It is possible to find commodes, secretaires, tables and armchairs in mahogany, with very rare ormolu mounts, known only to an exclusive group of collectors. When the style of these pieces is close to that of Louis XVI or the Empire, they do not have the sparseness and simplicity of shape and decoration that are so typical of the *Directoire*. These pieces are very highly-prized and may reach and even surpass the valuations given to similar Louis XVI or Empire pieces. *Directoire* furniture is much valued throughout France, not just as an important element in an interior or collection but as a historical and stylistic curiosity. Far from looking out of place in a collection of 18th century pieces, a *Directoire* piece will add a very particular note, even if it is placed among extremely valuable items.

The French do not seem very keen on more commonly-found pieces in this style which have no mahogany. In this we believe they are wrong, as all well-made pieces, including the more modest, continually appreciate in value due to two important factors: today's labour costs, which are equivalent to the price of a piece of antique furniture, and modern production, which does not come with the same guarantees of originality and personality as an antique piece. The industrially-made items of today, churned out in their thousands, are always anonymous, however well they may be put together.

In Italy *Directoire* furniture, like that of the transition period, has no real market. This is because many designs of Italian regional furniture are very similar to French pieces. As a result they are comparatively lowly valued.

We should also remember that the rare examples of Italian Directoire pieces do not display the same impoverishment of shape and decoration; these items have neoclassical subjects and decorative elements similar to those of the Louis XVI style, of which they are, in practice, a variant. *Directoire* pieces are not of sufficient commercial interest in Italy to lead Italian antiques dealers to import them. This explains why, with the possible exception of the Piedmont, this style is among the least known and valued in Italy.

Fine secretaire in flecked mahogany, extensively mounted with ormolu. This example is a real exception in relation to the criteria of the Directoire style. With its rich ormolu mounting, this magnificent, imposing secretaire offers a complete contrast to the style's precepts, which are based on simple lines and sober decoration.

Attributed to Molitor. (Photo: Sotheby Parke Bernet). Sold in Monte Carlo in 1979: £ 75,700, $ 172,200.
1984 valuation: £ 43,000, $ 57,000.
Current valuation: collector's price.

Fine armchair in mahogany, one of a pair, bearing the stamp of G. Jacob. The elegance and originality of its scrolled armrests are of particular note. 1984 valuation: £ 6,450, $ 8,550.
1991 valuation: £ 15,000, $ 26,550.
Current valuation: £ 10,200, $ 16,900, € 15,250.

Rare fine armchair in mahogany, with a curule shape (a reference to the ancient Roman seats that were placed on chariots and used by high-ranking magistrates). In accordance with its principles of austerity and morality, the *Directoire* style drew on the ancient civilisations that symbolised civic values. Sold in Paris in 1972: £ 1,360, $ 2,400.
1984 valuation: £ 2,150, $ 2,850. 1991 valuation: £ 5,000, $ 8,850.
Current valuation: £ 5,100, $ 8,450, € 7,600.

Fine armchair in carved giltwood, with padded seat and pierced back, bearing the stamp of G. Jacob. This is a case of where the stamp plays a major part in establishing the value of the piece. The same chair without the stamp would be valued at less than half the price. Sold in Paris in 1984.
1984 valuation: £ 6,000, $ 8,000. 1991 valuation: £ 13,000, $ 23,000.
Current valuation: £ 10,200, $ 16,900, € 15,250.

Elegant *bergere* in finely carved beech, one of a pair. The outward-curving back and sabre-shaped back legs are typical of the Directoire style. 1991 valuation: £ 7,000, $ 12,400.
Current valuation: £ 8,700, $ 14,400, € 12,960.

Unusual pair of armchairs in patinated bronze and ormolu with the back and seat in brown leather. They are valued very highly due to the fact that armchairs made in metal are extremely rare.

The few armchairs in gold and silver that had belonged to Louis XV were melted down during the French Revolution.
Sold in Paris in 1984: £ 14,600, $ 19,400.
Current valuation: collector's price.

Classic bureau plat veneered in mahogany *à ramages* with solid mahogany legs. The ormolu escutcheons are of particular note. The design is typical of the Directoire style. 1991 valuation: £ 4,000, $ 7,100. Current valuation: £ 5,100, $ 8,450, € 7,600.

Very good quality marquise in finely carved mahogany, one of a pair. 1984 valuation: £ 4,300, $ 2,850. 1991 valuation: £ 18,500, $ 32,750. Current valuation: £ 20,400, $ 33,800, € 30,500.

Very good quality chair in blue and red lacquer, one of a pair. The slightly outward-curving back and sabre-shaped back legs are typical of the *Directoire* style. 1984 valuation: £ 2,150, $ 2,850. 1991 valuation: £ 5,000, $ 8,850. Current valuation: £ 5,100, $ 8,450, € 7,600.

Bergere in finely carved beechwood, one of a pair. The frame of this piece is still Louis XVI in style, but lighter, following the *Directoire* trend. On the other hand the carved rosettes on the front legs and the sabre shape of the back legs are typical of the Directoire style.
1991 valuation: £ 11,500, $ 20,350.
Current valuation: £ 10,200, $ 16,900, € 15,250.

Classic armchair in natural mahogany lacquered wood with gilt armrests. Sold in Paris in 1974: £ 950, $ 1,850.
1984 valuation: £ 860, $ 1,140. 1991 valuation: £ 1,000, $ 1,770.
Current valuation: £ 1,530, $ 2,540, € 2,280.

Fine pair of mahogany armchairs. Of particular note are the fine, elegant carving, spirally-fluted front legs, sabre-shaped back legs and slightly curved backs.
1984 valuation: £ 6,450, $ 8,550. 1991 valuation: £ 13,500, $ 23,900.
Current valuation: £ 12,750, $ 21,100, € 19,000.

Rare fine small table écritoire with undertier, in tulipwood veneer. The sabre-shaped legs reflect the *Directoire* style.
1984 valuation: £ 5,200, $ 6,850. 1991 valuation: £ 11,500, $ 20,350.
Current valuation: £ 10,200, $ 16,900, € 15,250.

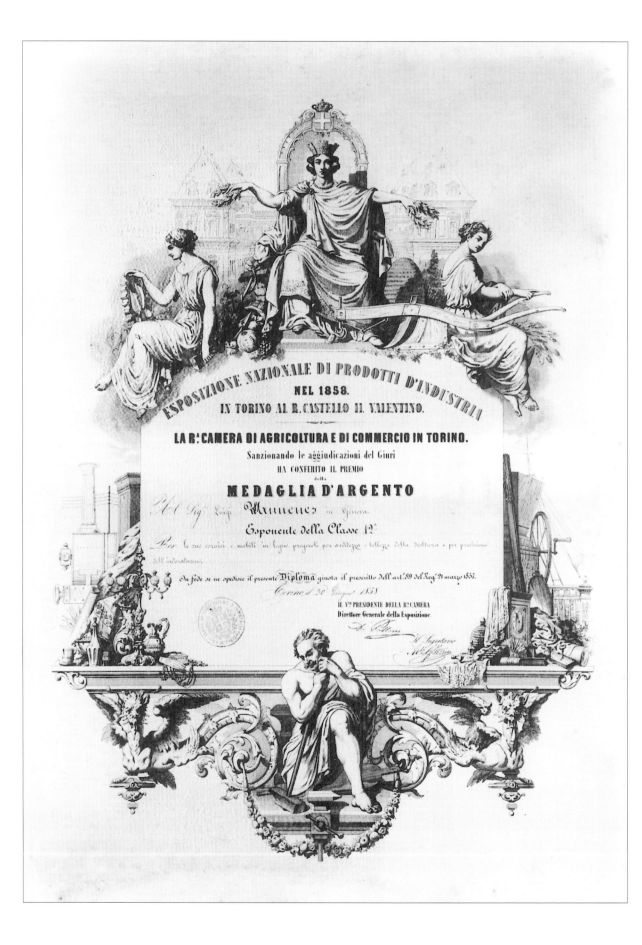

ISBN 0-9700168-0-8

Technical production: studio g.due srl